DAD'S ULTIMATE BOOK: 800 JOKES

THE PERFECT GIFT FOR FATHERS AND GRANDFATHERS: LAUGHTER AND LEARNING...

+ 50 AUTHOR-INSPIRED CROSSWORDS
10 LITERARY TRIVIA QUESTIONS

Includes 50 Unveiled Facts about Father's Day Around the Globe

Bonus of 800 jokes guaranteed to tickle your funny bone!

TABLE OF CONTENTS

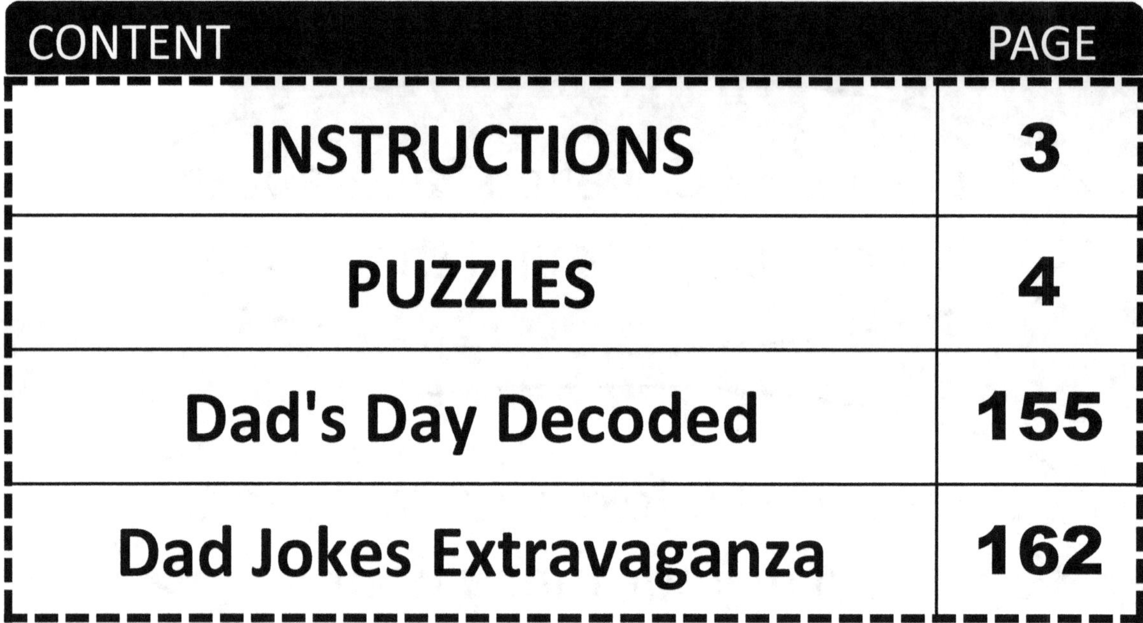

INTRODUCTION

"Are you ready to unlock the ultimate dad experience?"

With "The Ultimate Dad's Playbook", you don't just give a gift, you ignite a journey of joy, wisdom and stimulating fun, tailored exclusively for the amazing dad or grandad in your life!

This powerhouse playbook kicks off with 800 dad jokes, each one a laughter grenade guaranteed to add a sparkle of humor to everyday moments. But the fun doesn't end there. The playbook takes a global leap with fascinating insights on Fatherhood celebrations around the world, offering your dad a chance to appreciate the universal significance of his role.

Now, prepare for the grand finale, our BIG BONUS - a literary adventure like no other! It includes 50 author-themed crossword puzzles that turn your dad's leisure time into a brain-boosting quest. Inspired by literary greats from J.K. Rowling to William Shakespeare, each puzzle is packed with 15 search words and is accompanied by 10 trivia questions and answers that provide a stimulating twist.

"The Ultimate Dad's Playbook" is more than a gift; it's an ongoing celebration of laughter, learning and the thrill of a challenge. So why settle for ordinary when you can make every dad's day extraordinary?

PUZZLES

This section of the book combines word search puzzles and trivia questions, immersing you in the world of beloved authors such as J.K. Rowling, Stephen King, Dan Brown, Nora Roberts, and many more. The game begins with a page dedicated to each author, presenting 20 words for you to find that are related to their life or works.

Following this, a solution page reveals the placements of the words, accompanied by a brief about the author to enrich your understanding. The challenge escalates as you tackle 10 trivia questions associated with each author, testing your knowledge to its limits. The book provides an answer key for these trivia questions, making it a perfect and engaging way to learn more about your favorite authors.

connect with the greatest authors in a unique and engaging way, and let your love for literature soar to new heights.

J.k. Rowling

```
H E R M I O N E Y D Z H A G R I D M W Z
M U U T Y H B X F H U W A N D E J X N Z
M Q C O R H U E E M T M W O E V Z N N V
X W L S T R A W G O H P B Z R W V T W M
A K U F C P B W P Q R X F L B Z R M L D
C Y W R J F Y M U R C C F X E O C D Z S
U R O O S A E I S U G R E P M D E D E I
Q H N E L I D L N Q H E E E D O U O Z
T U O E K D O L A G E N D A E W E R E Z
O Q R H I X O M P P R L E M R D B V E T
Y H M T R K E K E A O Y E G S R N R P K
Q T C B E D F X F V X N F B A T Y A F J
B H T J M C J K L A T Z G F O C T N W W
Q F D E K M L O D O F U E N I R D R L U
B R B B Y S Z M R D S F V W O N S J U B
Y K J W Y Z J B E Z O A R N I R D R Q E
I C N B X F F C B B X R U V N D Y O D I
U U V F O Q S K K Z C S I B O J V F R U
```

Bezoar	Harry	Quidditch
Dementor	Hermione	Ron
Dumbledore	Hogwarts	Snape
Gryffindor	Horcrux	Voldemort
Hagrid	Patronus	Wand

SOLUTION

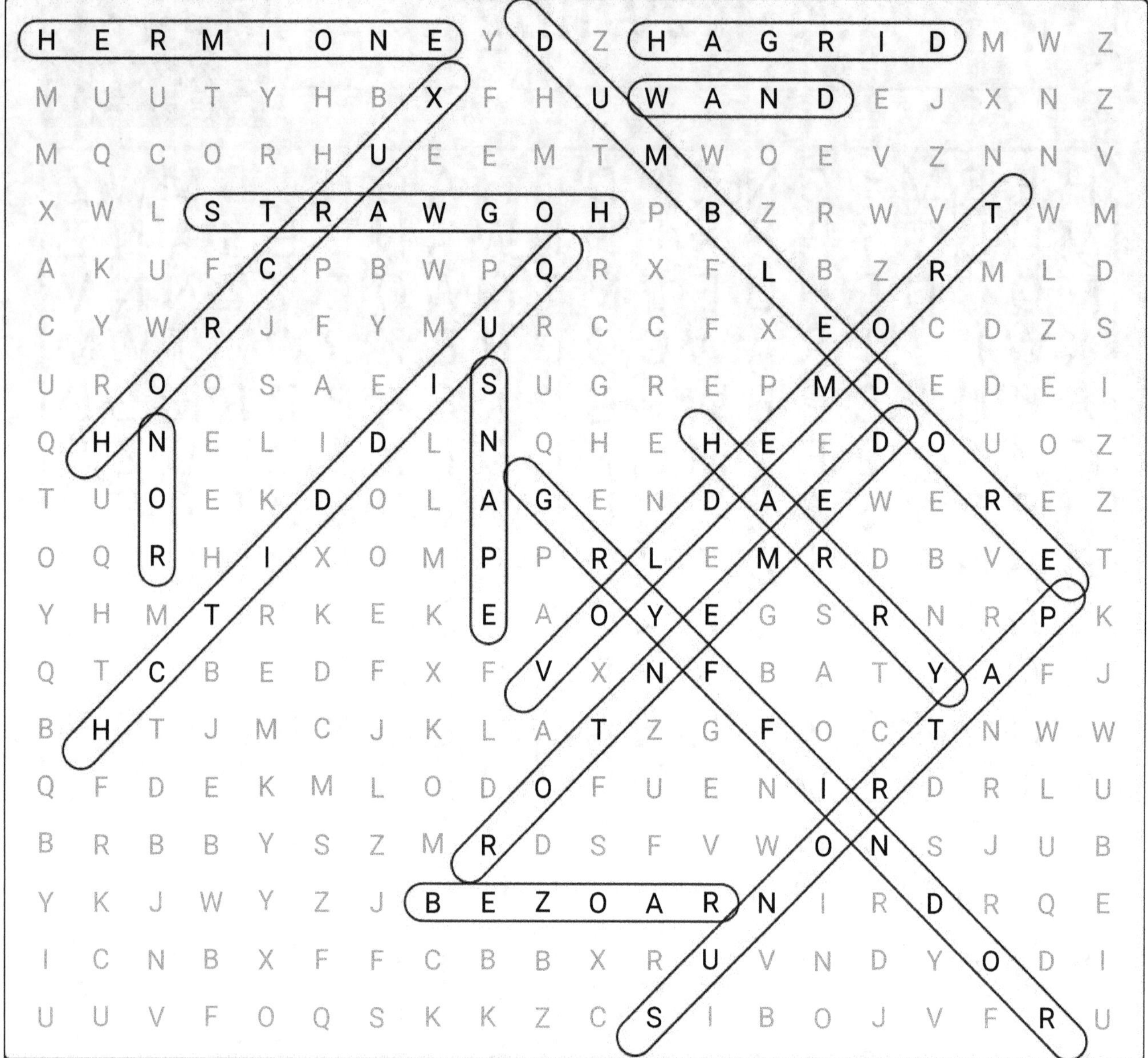

About J.k. Rowling

J.K. Rowling, a renowned British novelist, has achieved international fame for her enchanting Harry Potter series. Her creative and enthralling narratives have garnered her immense success and a dedicated following, impacting the lives of readers across the globe.

Trivia Questions

➢Q1. What is the name of the sport played in the Harry Potter books that is similar to Quidditch, but without the use of broomsticks?

➢Q2. What is the name of the Hogwarts house that Harry Potter is sorted into?

➢Q3. What is the name of the wizarding prison in the Harry Potter series?

➢Q4. Who is the author of the book "Fantastic Beasts and Where to Find Them," which was adapted into a film by J.K. Rowling?

➢Q5. What is the name of the magical object that allows the user to travel through time in the Harry Potter series?

➢Q6. What is the name of J.K. Rowling's pseudonym, under which she published the crime novel "The Cuckoo's Calling"?

➢Q7. In what year was the first Harry Potter book, "Harry Potter and the Philosopher's Stone," published?

➢Q8. Which character in the Harry Potter series has the ability to transform into a rat?

➢Q9. What is the name of the magical creature that Hagrid raises in the Harry Potter series?

➢Q10. What is the name of the final book in the Harry Potter series?

Turn the page upside down to see the answers.

A1. Gobstones. A2. Gryffindor. A3. Azkaban. A4. Newt Scamander. A5. Time-Turner. A6. Robert Galbraith. A7. 1997. A8. Peter Pettigrew (Wormtail). A9. Hippogriff. A10. "Harry Potter and the Deathly Hallows."

Stephen King

```
X C D K C B D J N T N Z X Z W W E I E B
I F R P D Z F G U L O R O N O L A R U X
S E V V Y A O T I T M W J N W B V R S K
C A R R I E C D B Y O C E M E T E R Y V
W L O T I Z B Y H D X Q L R R T W B J C
A X O B A H O R R O R Z S S H S N X O H
W Z T U J Z O X O E U Z D O P K D P J A
G Q H O J W H I V D E U C R A L Q S U B
Z V K V L X X B E L I L M S I U T Q C D
S H I N I N G Z R G J W B X K O Y M E A
F P C K V Q Z D L F M V B H Y R E S I M
D G W U R I N Z O G R E D R U M I W H B
D X H E U A T Q O Q T N D I R W K A D L
X C O I T H D B K C F Q Q L Y D Y B R P
C U O S F H E W O Z G T O N M S A L E M
R R R R D T J S Z T P M N U U I X U X S
O F C S J E R O B K I E F C V N N D Q N
A V P Z Q I L N J U P N Y L A Q X G P I
```

Carrie	It	Redrum
Cemetery	Lot	Salem
Cujo	Misery	Shining
Dark	Overlook	Stand
Horror	Pennywise	Tower

SOLUTION

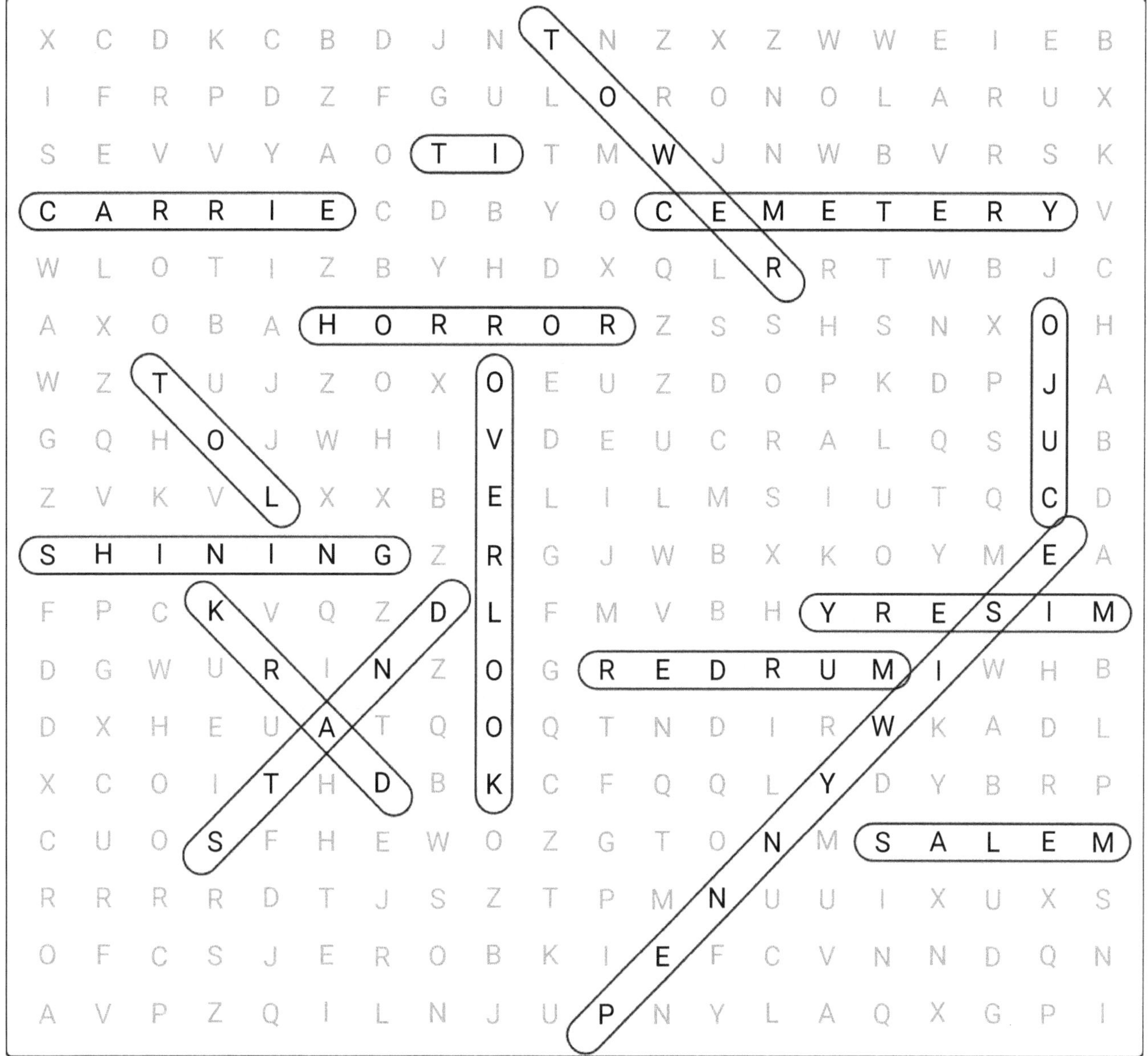

About Stephen King

A master of horror and suspense, Stephen King is an American writer known for his daring and evocative stories. Delving deep into the darkest aspects of the human experience, King has solidified his reputation as a highly influential author with an extensive body of work.

Trivia Questions

➢Q1. In which novel by Stephen King does a clown named Pennywise terrorize a small town?

➢Q2. What is the name of the hotel in Stephen King's novel "The Shining"?

➢Q3. What is the name of the fictional town in Maine that features prominently in many of Stephen King's works?

➢Q4. In which novel by Stephen King do a group of children band together to fight an evil entity that takes the form of a clown?

➢Q5. What is the name of the fictional dog breed that appears in several Stephen King novels?

➢Q6. Which Stephen King novel features a woman who is imprisoned in a house by her abusive husband?

➢Q7. What is the name of the writer who is the main character in Stephen King's novel "Misery"?

➢Q8. What is the name of the creature that serves as the primary antagonist in Stephen King's novel "The Mist"?

➢Q9. Which Stephen King novel features a rabid St. Bernard named Cujo?

➢Q10. In which novel by Stephen King is the town of Derry, Maine, visited by a time-travelling teacher from the future?

Turn the page upside down to see the answers.

A1. "It." A2. The Overlook Hotel. A3. Derry. A4. "It." A5. The "zombie dog" or "Cujo" breed. A6. "Rose Madder." A7. Paul Sheldon. A8. The creatures from the mist are not given a name. A9. "Cujo." A10. "11/22/63."

John Grisham

```
H I K Y A P P E A L R B Y Y R E Y W A L
E M F Z R D V C D W E S Y A T O L M K Y
O E L M O U P Z W T N E M A T S E T I G
M S A M L S B L W O T H Q U T E E R T S
J F A E O Z U K T A R N Z W P U X E P Y
H K Z N X M T F U F A C L I E N T Q B L
J H I Y L A C B C Z P S U J F J U R Y M
E E O D F H B E M X F T K Z I W T J A R
E Z R C A Y R B N Q Q Q M G R Y R T X R
D X G M I S E S R C N N S H M S L B E F
D G B B A N T T Z V Q Z C V S G Z K B O
V E V Y E A H N S G A F V O R W A C O E
R H H M G C R G Y T U E K X Y M Y D I T
D R S S S I E S P S A I I N N O C E N T
D T R M K L N W K O M R G I K X G T M G
B E S D N E T U R B I B A M Y W O N D N
O G B Z R P M V N H R R M X J E F M U K
Q T C F Y R W R U N A W A Y V A Z Y A P
```

Appeal	Firm	Pelican
Brethren	Innocent	Rainmaker
Brief	Jury	Runaway
Chamber	Lawyer	Street
Client	Partner	Testament

SOLUTION

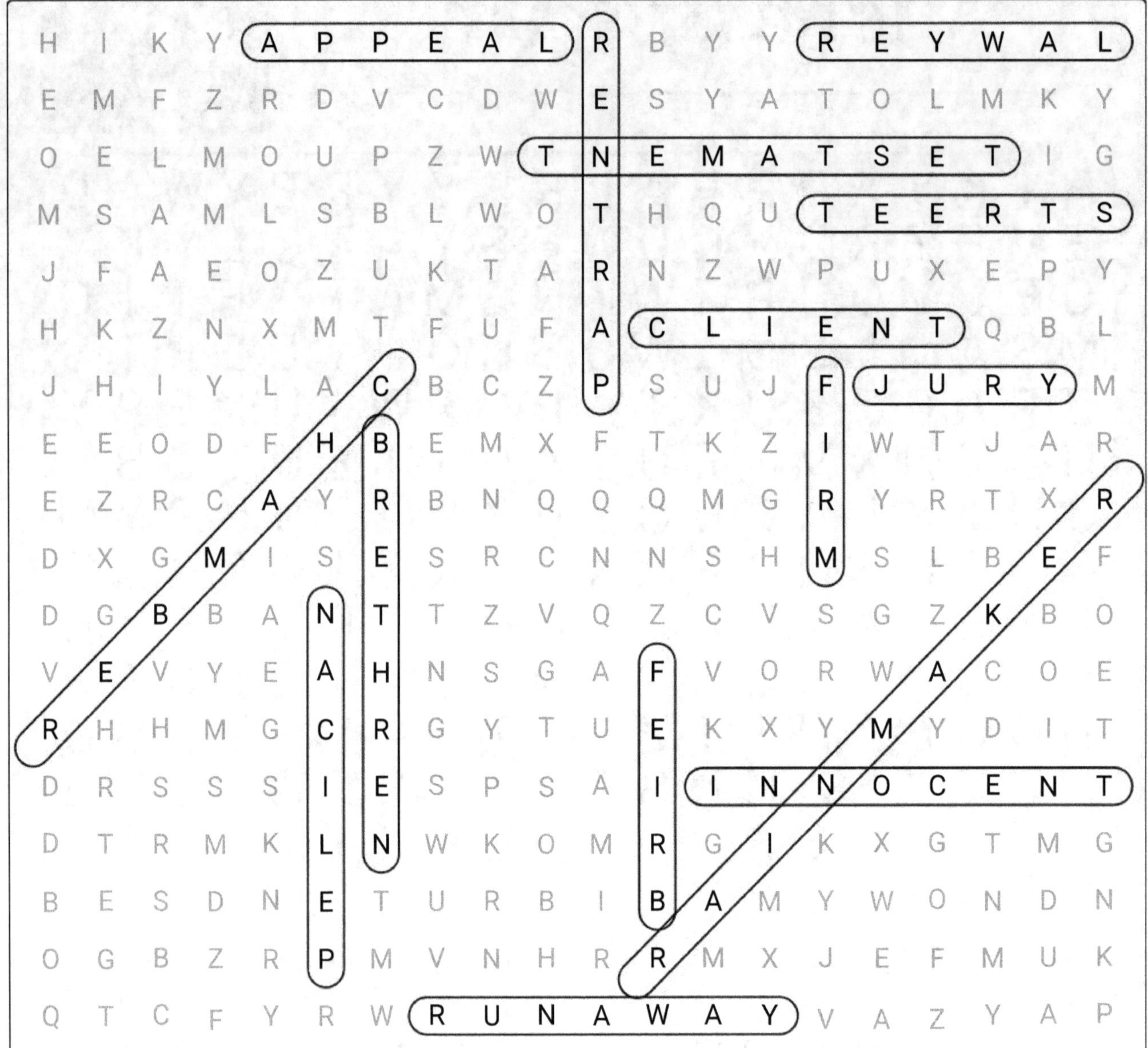

About John Grisham

Specialising in legal thrillers, John Grisham is an American author whose engaging and fast-paced storytelling has captivated readers worldwide. His widespread success and acclaim have made him a prominent figure in modern literature.

Trivia Questions

➢Q1. Which John Grisham novel was adapted into a film featuring Tom Cruise?

➢Q2. In John Grisham's novel "A Time to Kill," what is the name of the central character?

➢Q3. In John Grisham's novel "The Firm," what is the occupation of the main character?

➢Q4. Which John Grisham novel is set in Clanton, Mississippi, and revolves around a high-profile murder trial?

➢Q5. In John Grisham's "The Pelican Brief," what is the name of the law student who plays a central role?

➢Q6. In which John Grisham novel does a juror try to sway the outcome of the verdict?

➢Q7. In John Grisham's "A Painted House," what is the name of the Arkansas town where the story is set?

➢Q8. Which John Grisham novel introduces the character of young attorney Rudy Baylor?

➢Q9. In John Grisham's novel "The Testament," what is the name of the central character?

➢Q10. Which John Grisham novel features a young lawyer who is sent to a maximum-security prison for a crime he didn't commit?

Turn the page upside down to see the answers.

A1. "The Firm." A2. Jake Brigance. A3. Lawyer. A4. "A Time to Kill." A5. Darby Shaw. A6. "The Runaway Jury." A7. Black Oak. A8. "The Rainmaker." A9. Troy Phelan. A10. "The Innocent Man."

J.r.r. Tolkien

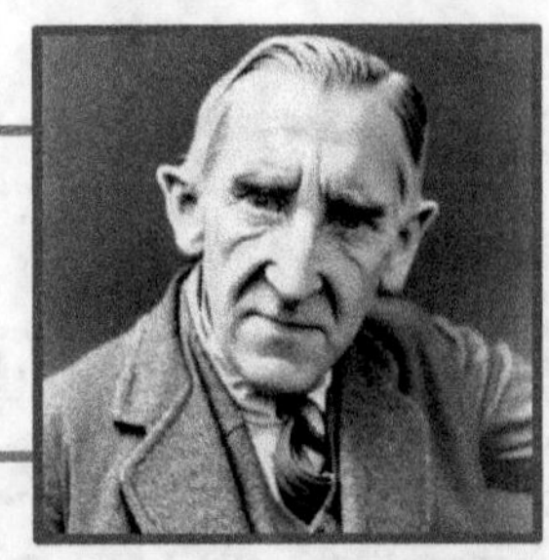

```
V L C K E O S Q J E A R B K S M I U U A
O C H T R A E E L D D I M Y A G G I L L
D T W E Z S H I R E G O S O H L O M A M
A B A L R O G A G U X R D L G Y I J Z X
G L K L V K C R R A F R O O Z W R C I R
E I Z P Z F K B W A N Z N F R D I F N G
E R M S A L O G E L G D W Z Q F N E P F
F B H L D R E D K A E O A W X X G I H J
Z S G O I O Z T J H U X R L D V H A C E
H C H U R P Y D O B R S W N F S M M O C
I G F C W Q F H O B B I T A W S M Z S G
R K G U M R R W N L H C R O S M V Y A Q
A Y D N I I O M I G I A L Z L I T P U G
S K T Q Z A D T Q J Q L S L N Q X U R P
B A H E O R R J J Y E V Q E F V F F O Y
G V E D K R O I R F O I N X J Y K G N B
U O U B V Y M Z S G S T W N Y K E E J W
P G Y R W T E V M R A Y O U K X J Y Y G
```

Aragorn	Gandalf	Mordor
Balrog	Gimli	Orc
Ent	Hobbit	Ring
Fellowship	Legolas	Sauron
Frodo	Middle-earth	Shire

SOLUTION

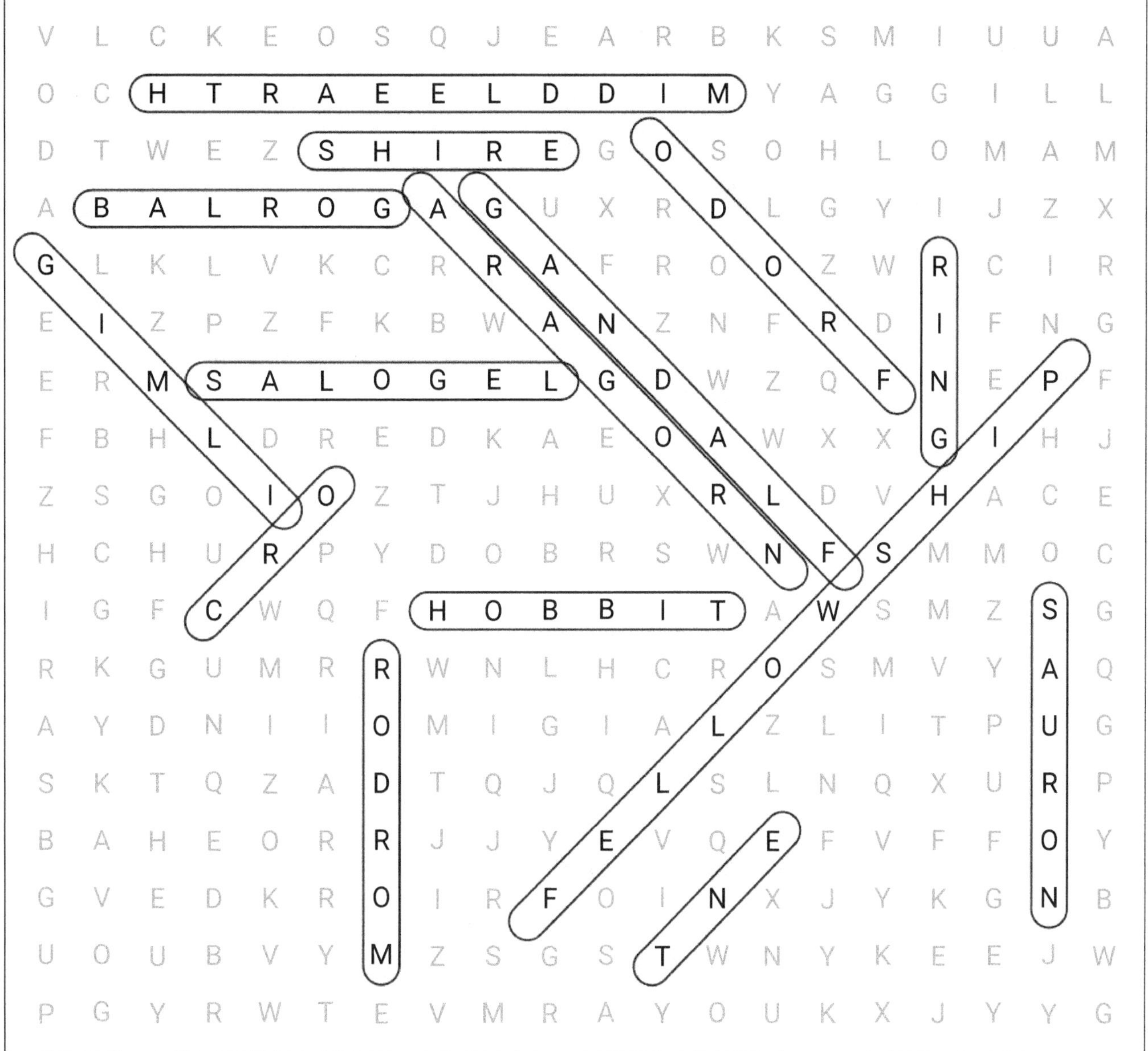

About J.r.r. Tolkien

English author and scholar J.R.R. Tolkien is celebrated for his high fantasy works, such as "The Hobbit" and "The Lord of the Rings." His intricate and immersive world-building has left an indelible mark on readers and authors alike, securing his place as a treasured figure in 20th-century literature.

Trivia Questions

➢Q1. What do the initials in J.R.R. Tolkien's name stand for?

➢Q2. Which British university did J.R.R. Tolkien teach at as a professor of Anglo-Saxon and English Language and Literature?

➢Q3. In addition to writing, J.R.R. Tolkien was a skilled artist. What role did his illustrations play in his published works?

➢Q4. What is the name of the 12-volume series that provides a comprehensive history of Middle-earth and was edited by Tolkien's son, Christopher?

➢Q5. In which year was "The Hobbit" first published?

➢Q6. Which fictional creature, featured in "The Hobbit" and "The Lord of the Rings," was inspired by Tolkien's childhood fear of spiders?

➢Q7. Which friend of J.R.R. Tolkien was also a famous author and a member of their literary group called "The Inklings"?

➢Q8. J.R.R. Tolkien fought in which major historical event before becoming a successful author?

➢Q9. Which unfinished novel by J.R.R. Tolkien, published posthumously in 1977, is set in the First Age of Middle-earth?

➢Q10. In which year did J.R.R. Tolkien pass away?

Turn the page upside down to see the answers.

A1. John Ronald Reuel A2. University of Oxford A3. He created illustrations for some of his own books, including "The Hobbit." A4. "The History of Middle-earth" A5. 1937 A6. Giant Spiders, such as Shelob A7. C.S. Lewis A8. World War I A9. "The Silmarillion" A10. 1973

Dan Brown

```
L D S B E R N I N I V K V D L Q E E L B
J O P F W G A C Q T S V R U S J K I Q I
N A N G E L O P S Y J C H F V N T G T P
L V V H B U C M M P C X R H C K O A X Q
C T L P N E F B X X U P Y Z R H N M R K
O S I Q G K O C V D N S Q B H I C P E C
D O A V R L M R B A U O O H M Q C L H D
E L I E O X Q Y X V Y X D U A S D I N K
H G A L B F R P P I J K L G O R G W Z B
A P Q G E N E T U N G L Y I N I V O O G
Z C U N R Y N E R C I D E I Z A C A U I
Z B A R T J K X F I A N Z T N I L Y R L
P V R C G N S E T C J V S P G F K V G D
M Y R J E A D E K Q D Y M H C G E L P E
Q U D O N K T Y B F I K U A U C A R T W
V T T W L T W O Y S N R K Q X O M J N O
P M N Y S I T B R G K C M C Y Y D W D O
G G S V N P H R E Y S T T Y E S P V T H
```

Angel	Da vinci	Langdon
Bernini	Demons	Lost
Chigi	Harvard	Purgatory
Code	Illuminati	Robert
Cryptex	Inferno	Symbol

SOLUTION

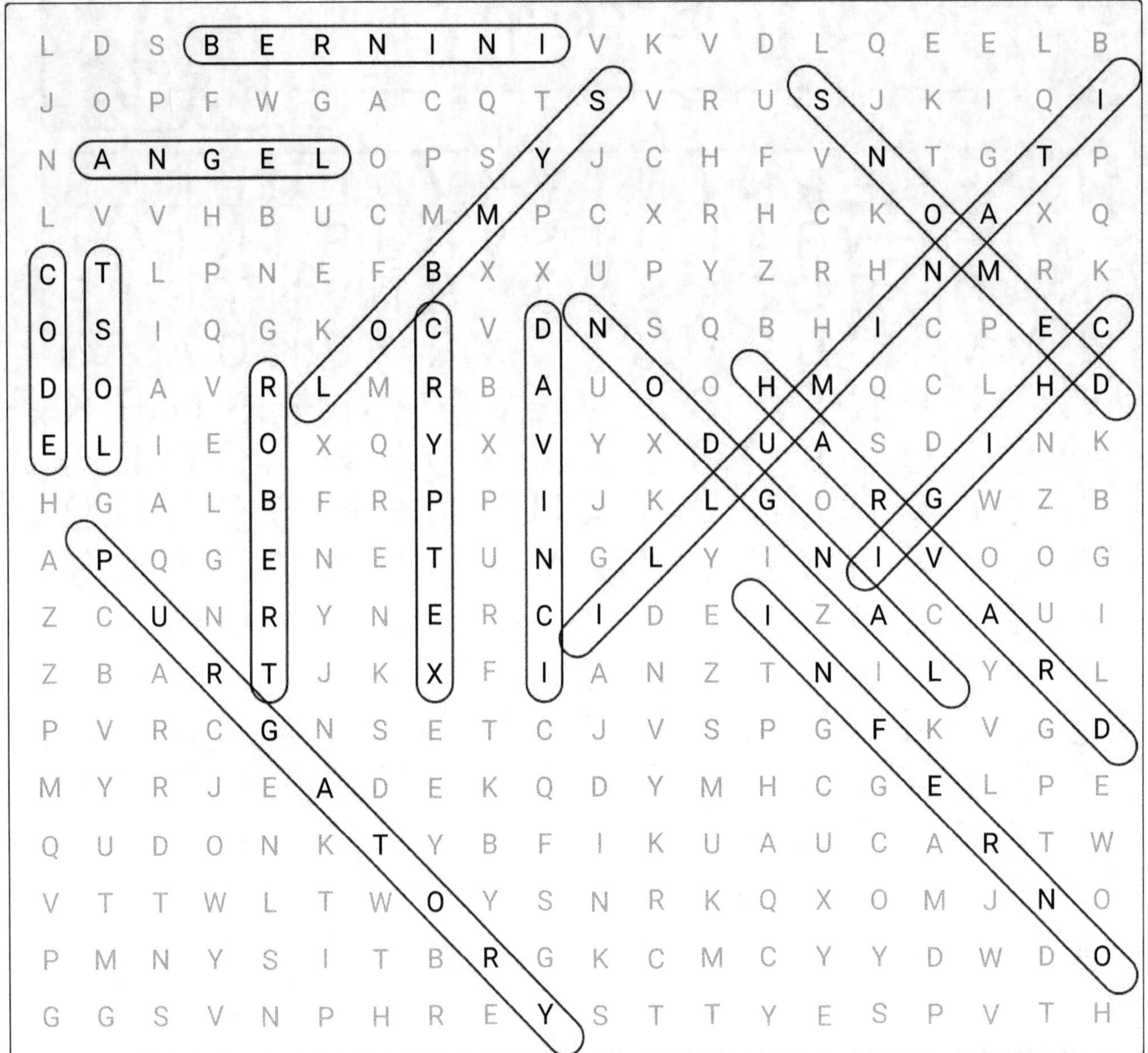

About Dan Brown

American author Dan Brown is recognized for his thought-provoking and riveting thrillers. His novels frequently explore themes of religion, history, and cryptography, encouraging readers to challenge conventional beliefs. Brown's exceptional sales figures rank him among the world's most successful authors.

Trivia Questions

➢Q1. In Dan Brown's novel "The Da Vinci Code," what is the name of the symbologist who plays a central role?

➢Q2. In Dan Brown's novel "Angels & Demons," what is the name of the prominent secret society?

➢Q3. In "Angels & Demons," what device must Robert Langdon locate to avert a disastrous explosion?

➢Q4. In which Dan Brown novel does Harvard symbologist Robert Langdon journey to Spain to probe the death of a colleague?

➢Q5. In "Angels & Demons" and "The Da Vinci Code," what is the name of the clandestine organisation that holds sway over the Catholic Church?

➢Q6. In "The Da Vinci Code," what is the name of the female character who becomes romantically involved with Robert Langdon?

➢Q7. In Dan Brown's novel "Origin," what is the name of the Swiss scientist who develops a powerful new technology?

➢Q8. In Dan Brown's novel "The Lost Symbol," what is the name of the renowned art historian who is abducted?

➢Q9. In which Dan Brown novel does Robert Langdon awaken in a hospital with no recollection of the previous two days and must unravel a mysterious scheme before time runs out?

➢Q10. In Dan Brown's novel "The Da Vinci Code," which ancient religious manuscript plays a pivotal role?

Turn the page upside down to see the answers.

A1. Robert Langdon. A2. The Illuminati. A3. The antimatter. A4. "The Origin." A5. The Priory of Sion. A6. Sophie Neveu. A7. Edmond Kirsch. A8. Peter Solomon. A9. "Inferno." A10. The Holy Grail.

George R.r. Martin

```
A K M N G A T N R N A Z J X U W P W Q H
C Q H D A I O E H X N K U O K L S L H W
E D M X M J T H Q F E O K C Q S X J K V
R I E E E S F D J E G Q I A A O N C C J
S M I H I T E N U F O I W R L X G O C T
E Z S N P W N I U D G R S U Y S I T W H
I B N V H K C V O M A M P M C T I Z L R
E A B N F J U T M F C Z G M F A O E L O
L V P V P D H P U W U A M A I R W L Y N
L M A O Y R X A N S T H G I N K E Z T E
Z T B L A D R N K P E I Z O D F G W A S
K X T K Y Y B S D U P Z V M R B L B R Y
V T I X A R C E Y D J M V E V J K I G J
Q S L Q F A I U V J Z U T S D R C U A Q
T C D B O T W A W N A N W S M C S X R Y
M R F V C M J Y N L I U Y T C N U W Y V
N U S X Z H X M Q W K I Y Z K W F J E A
D G L K H A L E E S I X F Z D E V H N G
```

Arya	Khaleesi	Targaryen
Cersei	Lannister	Thrones
Dothraki	Night's	Tyrion
Game	Snow	Valyrian
Jon	Stark	Winterfell

SOLUTION

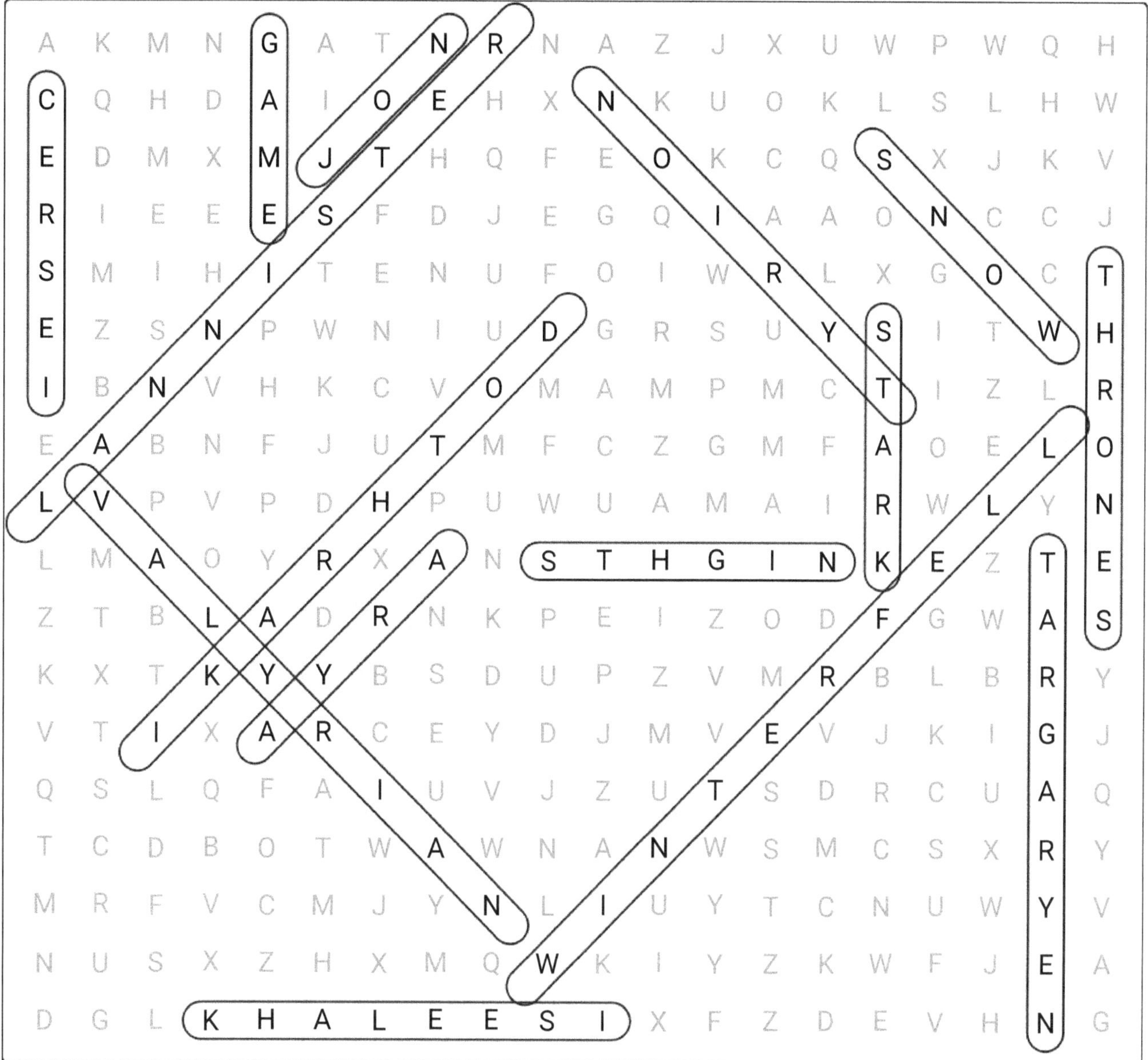

About George R.r. Martin

Famed for his "A Song of Ice and Fire" series, which inspired the HBO hit "Game of Thrones," George R.R. Martin is an American author known for his detailed and visceral storytelling. His loyal fan base and numerous accolades affirm his status as a trailblazing author in the 21st century.

➢Q1. What is the name of the first book in George R.R. Martin's "A Song of Ice and Fire" series?

➢Q2. What is the name of the family that rules over the North in "A Song of Ice and Fire"?

➢Q3. What is the name of the youngest Stark daughter in "A Song of Ice and Fire"?

➢Q4. Which noble house in "A Song of Ice and Fire" features a sigil of a lion?

➢Q5. What is the name of the continent where most of "A Song of Ice and Fire" takes place?

➢Q6. What is the name of the army of undead creatures that threatens Westeros in "A Song of Ice and Fire"?

➢Q7. What is the name of the castle that serves as the seat of House Lannister in "A Song of Ice and Fire"?

➢Q8. What is the name of the dwarf character in "A Song of Ice and Fire" who is played by Peter Dinklage in the television adaptation?

➢Q9. Which character in "A Song of Ice and Fire" is known as the "Mother of Dragons"?

➢Q10. What is the name of the wall that separates the Seven Kingdoms from the lands beyond in "A Song of Ice and Fire"?

Turn the page upside down to see the answers.

A1. "A Game of Thrones." A2. House Stark. A3. Arya Stark. A4. House Lannister. A5. Westeros. A6. The Army of the Dead or White Walkers. A7. Casterly Rock. A8. Tyrion Lannister. A9. Daenerys Targaryen. A10. The Wall.

Agatha Christie

F X A C V A N O R I A F F A J H O U S E
Y N D L K I L C B E Z Y H X A V N K U P
E A C Y M X E J K M R T F R Z S V B H E
N Q K I Y M M N U V I N D I A N S Y J X
G P A C C M B J Z O C Q F G E M X U N A
N E T X H M V Z E V N I H M N Y O E I Z
A L M H Z C T L D Q T C C O N S Q X L C
S E C C C K T Z W L Y E T X A T Q P E R
J D C M X T M V K E L F Q I V E X R Z O
A Z O C I Z C U K P X O T V U R G E P O
K V J L A N R A R U O Y Z H E I G S O K
A D P C Y N A A T D L S Z Z A O A S X E
D K Q G N R M I O K E Q P Z O U R R W D
Y Q R C M B E Q G L A R T O R S Z I M N
O H B W V S P T Y S Z F O G I E V C J M
P G E T H P O T S D T W D M E R Z U E Y
O U K N X N S D Z Y V W L F N H O H P R
G H P F U M R Y G T M K Y S T B W T N G

Affair	Little	Nile
Crooked	Marple	Orient
Express	Murder	Poirot
House	Mysterious	Styles
Indians	Mystery	Ten

SOLUTION

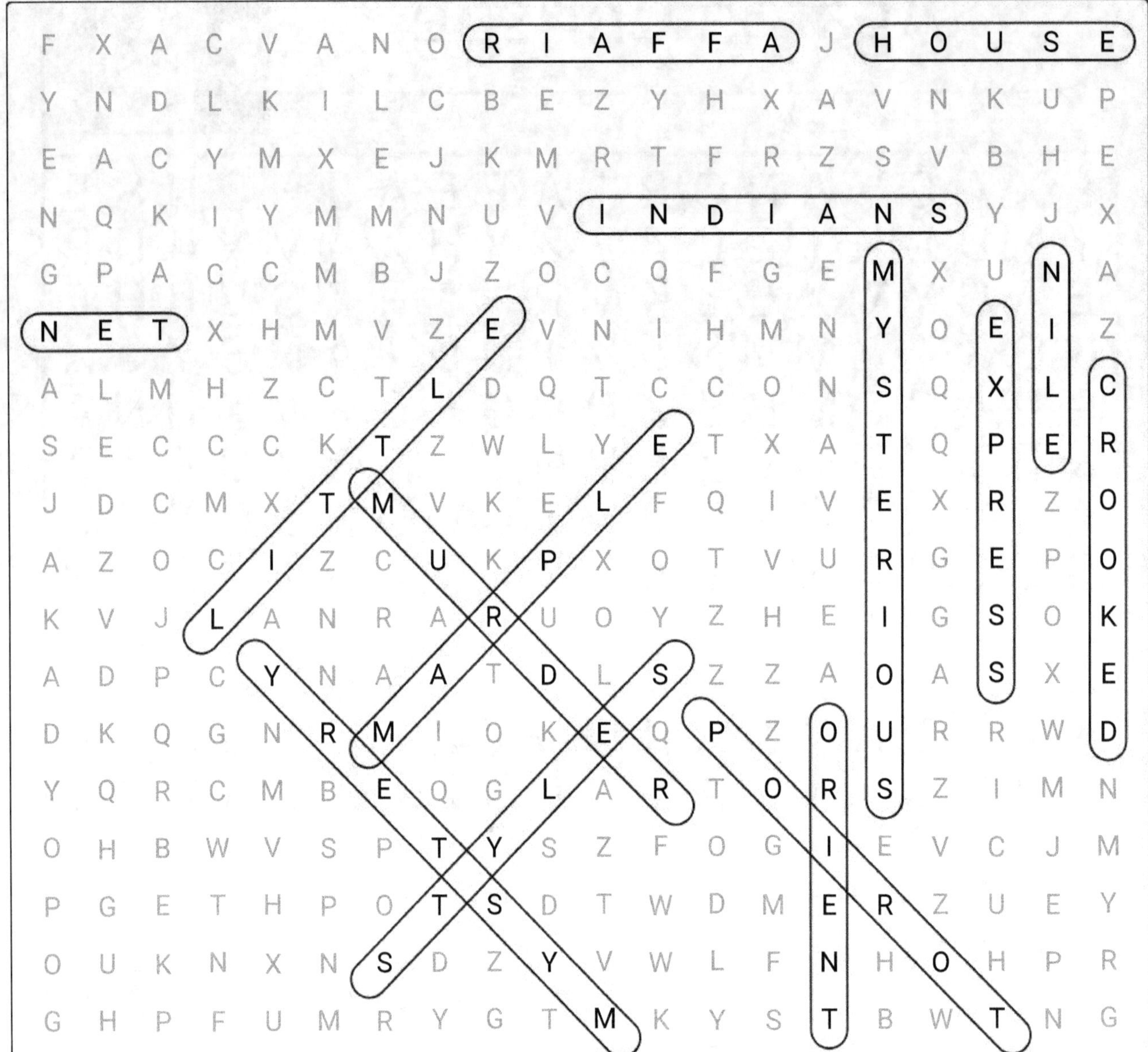

About Agatha Christie

English author and playwright Agatha Christie is celebrated for her detective novels and short stories. Her innovative approach to crime fiction has endeared her to countless fans, solidifying her status as a literary legend. Christie's works have sold over two billion copies worldwide, making her the best-selling author of all time.

Trivia Questions

➢Q1. In which year was Agatha Christie's first novel, "The Mysterious Affair at Styles,"   published?

➢Q2. What was the original title of Agatha Christie's play "The Mousetrap" when it was first performed as a radio play?

➢Q3. Which book did Agatha Christie write under the pseudonym Mary Westmacott in 1930?

➢Q4. In which location was Agatha Christie born on September 15, 1890?

➢Q5. Which of her novels did Agatha Christie consider to be the most difficult to write?

➢Q6. What record-breaking milestone did "The Mousetrap" achieve in London's West End in 2018?

➢Q7. Agatha Christie was a trained expert in which field besides writing?

➢Q8. How many languages have Agatha Christie's books been translated into, approximately?

➢Q9. Which character, featured in many of her novels, was inspired by Agatha Christie's own experiences during World War I?

➢Q10. What is the title of Agatha Christie's only published book of poetry?

Turn the page upside down to see the answers.

A1.1920 A2. "Three Blind Mice" A3. "Giant's Bread" A4. Torquay, Devon, England A5. "The Murder of Roger Ackroyd" A6. The longest-running play in history A7. Pharmacy (or pharmaceuticals) A8. More than 100 languages A9. Tommy Beresford A10. "The Road of Dreams"

Stephenie Meyer

```
V L X Q N E W M O O N H F P D A Z F R U
G S D D W N Z A J E V K O H W S Q I C M
L R F W W M L C E N O I R T D Q B X N Y
A A I A M L F M T Q W K K R C G Q Q Q F
K Z D N E H S B E R L X S A C Y I Z G Z
I U H B Z E W S A F L G M G U V N S T W
H S E Z N S P V U J A C H R L O L K Q G
B U E E J I L W U D F J D L L L R J A J
K R R G L O W Q M O N S L P E T B V O N
K F E C D W Z P Q M T L J O N U R K Q B
N H E A C Z O U H Y G G V V Z R C W O U
J M D G K T H G I L I W T P E I Z C D D
L W T A L I C E O N F W X R H A A C F P
J B D P A M N G O M U V I S Y J A I W Z
I X G S U E G G T M D P U I S H C C G Z
E M S V Z O D U S K M P Z V Y W J A V R
F H D H F K R U V A A S U X W C J A R S
H E D W A R D O V L Z K G S B U X P V P
```

Alice	Eclipse	New moon
Bella	Edward	Renesmee
Breaking	Forks	Twilight
Cullen	Jacob	Vampire
Dawn	La push	Volturi

SOLUTION

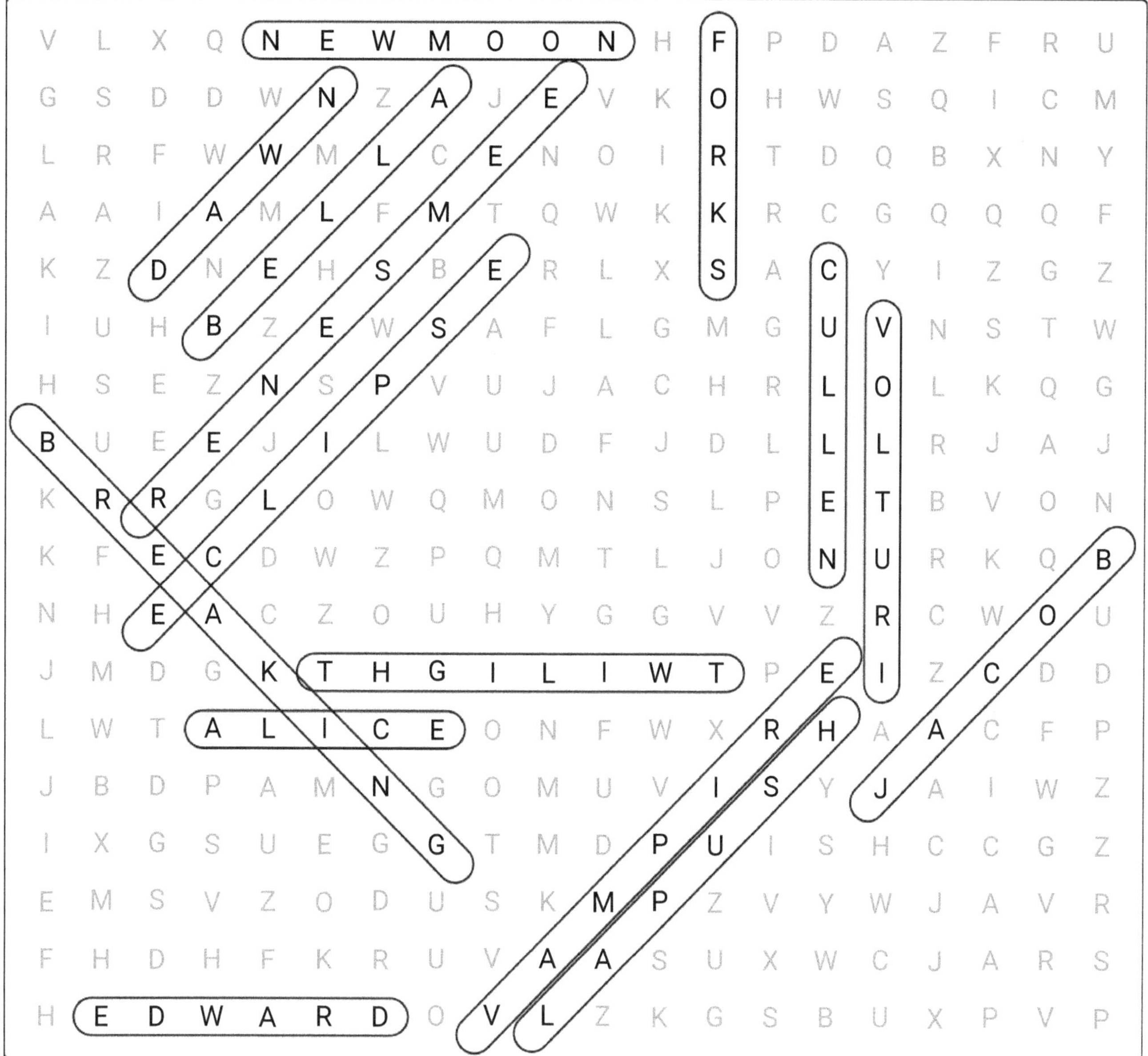

About Stephenie Meyer

Best known for her "Twilight" series, Stephenie Meyer is an American author specialising in young adult paranormal romance. Her emotive and vivid storytelling has resonated with readers globally, securing her place in popular culture and ensuring her success within the genre.

Trivia Questions

➢Q1. Which of Stephenie Meyer's novels is about a young woman who falls in love with a vampire?

➢Q2. What is the name of the fictional town where much of "Twilight" takes place?

➢Q3. What is the name of the high school that Bella attends in "Twilight"?

➢Q4. What is the name of the werewolf who becomes a rival love interest to Edward in "Twilight"?

➢Q5. What is the name of Bella's father in "Twilight"?

➢Q6. In "Twilight," what is the name of the vampire clan that Edward belongs to?

➢Q7. What is the name of the male character in Stephenie Meyer's novel "The Host"?

➢Q8. What is the name of the character played by Robert Pattinson in the "Twilight" movie series?

➢Q9. What is the name of the sequel to "Twilight"?

➢Q10. Which of Stephenie Meyer's novels is set in the future and features a society where people are divided into factions based on their personalities?

Turn the page upside down to see the answers.

A1. "Twilight." A2. Forks, Washington. A3. Forks High School. A4. Jacob Black. A5. Charlie Swan. A6. The Cullens. A7. Jared Howe. A8. Edward Cullen. A9. "New Moon." A10. "Divergent."

James Patterson

```
U G F O J W I T C H H O C F N H S A N K
P C U W Z Z O O Z S P O O R E B M S E B
L U I S F T Z U M E S N E M O W V L R B
Y C X G P A P W W A X I A Q C X G T O L
K V R T Q M Q P R I V A T E I V K V Z D
X C L A E V D Q Q U A P A L Z B R M G H
C E S R C R U L V K V X B X O W T N C P
P W C E G I I L L Q E O P N S D B A A V
K H I K P D R H H L A H O Z V U E Q F C
F E J Z K E R M A P Y M H V L B U S K D
O I C F A L M U S F J H H C I Q S V I N
N V I F G R B R N M X I H I T O O J W C
N T R C J N D D A W F P B U R I L F O Y
H V O I H A T E G J J G D C B Z H Z L Q
S K S O P X C R R A B G B S A U Z H R K
V G U K A Q B K O R Z W W G T R A R U T
H S G M O D A I M A A T R W V U T D A G
E T G F Q G B S O N F F S M U M I X A M
```

Alex	Jack	Ride
Beach	Maximum	Witch
Club	Morgan	Wizard
Cross	Murder	Women's
House	Private	Zoo

SOLUTION

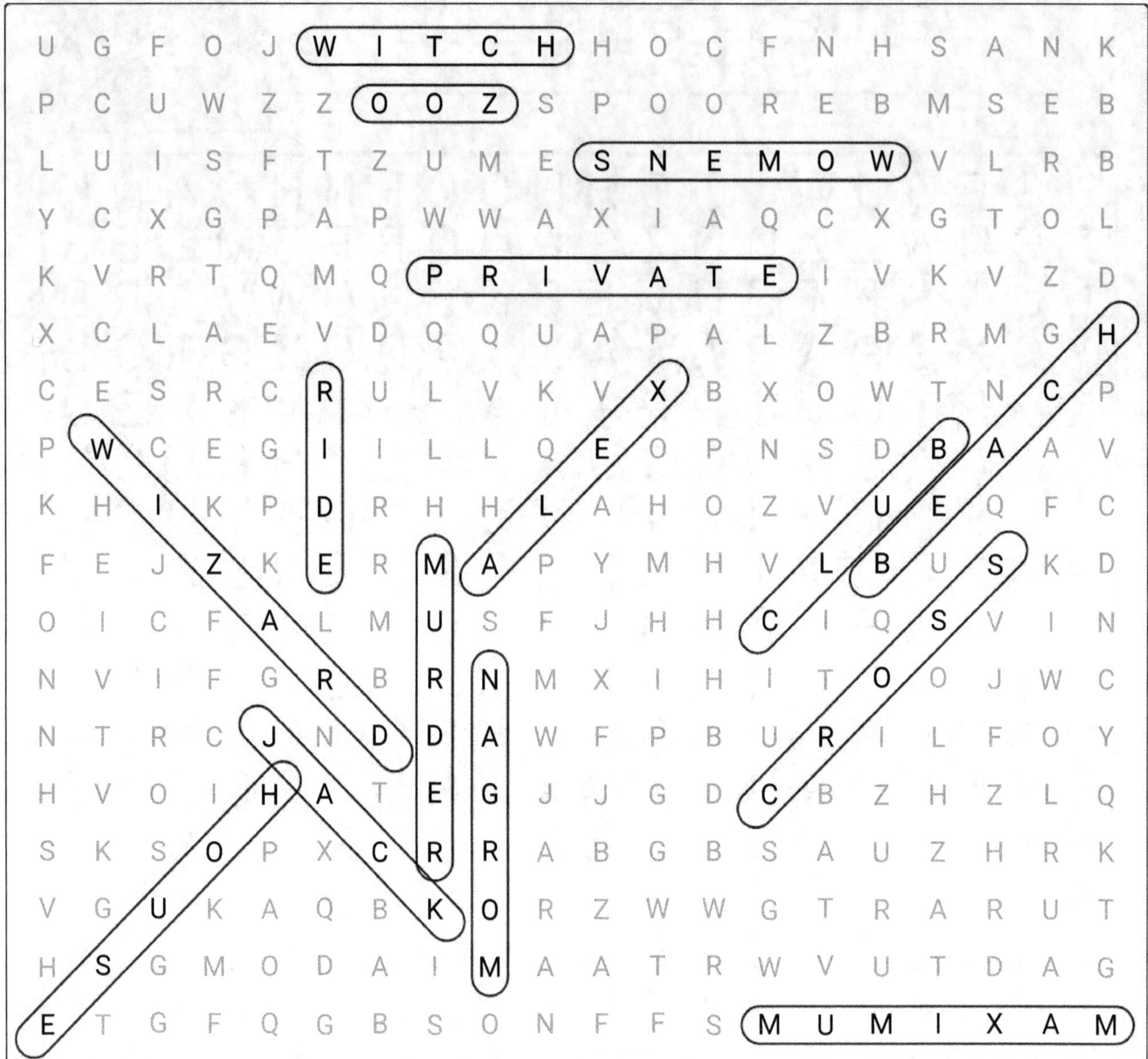

About James Patterson

American author James Patterson has earned recognition for his exhilarating and suspenseful thrillers. With over 300 million books sold, he is considered one of the world's most successful authors. His trademark writing style features brief chapters and dramatic cliffhangers, making his novels an appealing choice for fans of page-turning fiction.

Trivia Questions

➢Q1. In many of James Patterson's novels, which detective frequently takes centre stage?

➢Q2. Which book marks the beginning of James Patterson's "Alex Cross" series?

➢Q3. In which James Patterson novel does Lindsay Boxer, a San Francisco Police Department member, appear?

➢Q4. In a particular James Patterson novel, a group attempts to thwart a serial killer preying on wealthy families' children. What is the title of this novel?

➢Q5. In James Patterson's "Maximum Ride" series, who is the winged main character?

➢Q6. In "Maximum Ride," what is the name of the organisation the characters aim to dismantle?

➢Q7. Which James Patterson novel introduces Michael Bennett, a detective from the New York Police Department?

➢Q8. In which James Patterson novel does Lindsay Boxer investigate a series of connected murders and fires?

➢Q9. In James Patterson's novels, what is the name of the nefarious organisation that repeatedly challenges Alex Cross?

➢Q10. In which James Patterson novel does Dr. Dylan Reinhart, a psychology professor and ex-CIA operative, feature?

Turn the page upside down to see the answers.

A1. Alex Cross. A2. "Along Came a Spider." A3. "1st to Die." A4. "The Women's Murder Club" series. A5. Max (Maxine) Ride. A6. The School. A7. "Step on a Crack." A8. "The 9th Judgement." A9. The Wolf. A10. "Instinct."

Nora Roberts

```
H J W Z U O K O J J X D V Z V Q J M W D
Y D U E W W F B Y D N D J E H A N O Z S
R O T C E L L O C S G P S M B M K N P S
Y J R O M A N C E I S W Z I R P X T I E
S U M L E O E A H Y W Q S Y I E B A B N
Q U A R T E T G G O I R J Q D R W N F T
A O R B D O V A O K O N R T E W N A W I
P L U P P J Q R N T H R E E R M L C Q W
G Y X F I T O D I D B O Q K O I W I N I
R D T A P B J E R E K C B N M U L C F K
C V W I S S D N R Z H P R S U J Q O L D
R V O N B K I R Z F P T Z K E B I R G D
E L O L D D K S T V P P I D Z S O B S Y
L O E E H R K C T T D E T J B J S B E L
B D T K I K N E D E C T R C P N E I L A
A J Y N A L V T Y F R F E W X K C I O K
K C P S B H O X U Z E S W A G T H M K N
W D L C H E S A P E A K E Z W E R L S P
```

Boonsboro	Inn	Romance
Bride	Key	Sisters
Chesapeake	Montana	Three
Collector	Obsession	Trilogy
Garden	Quartet	Witness

SOLUTION

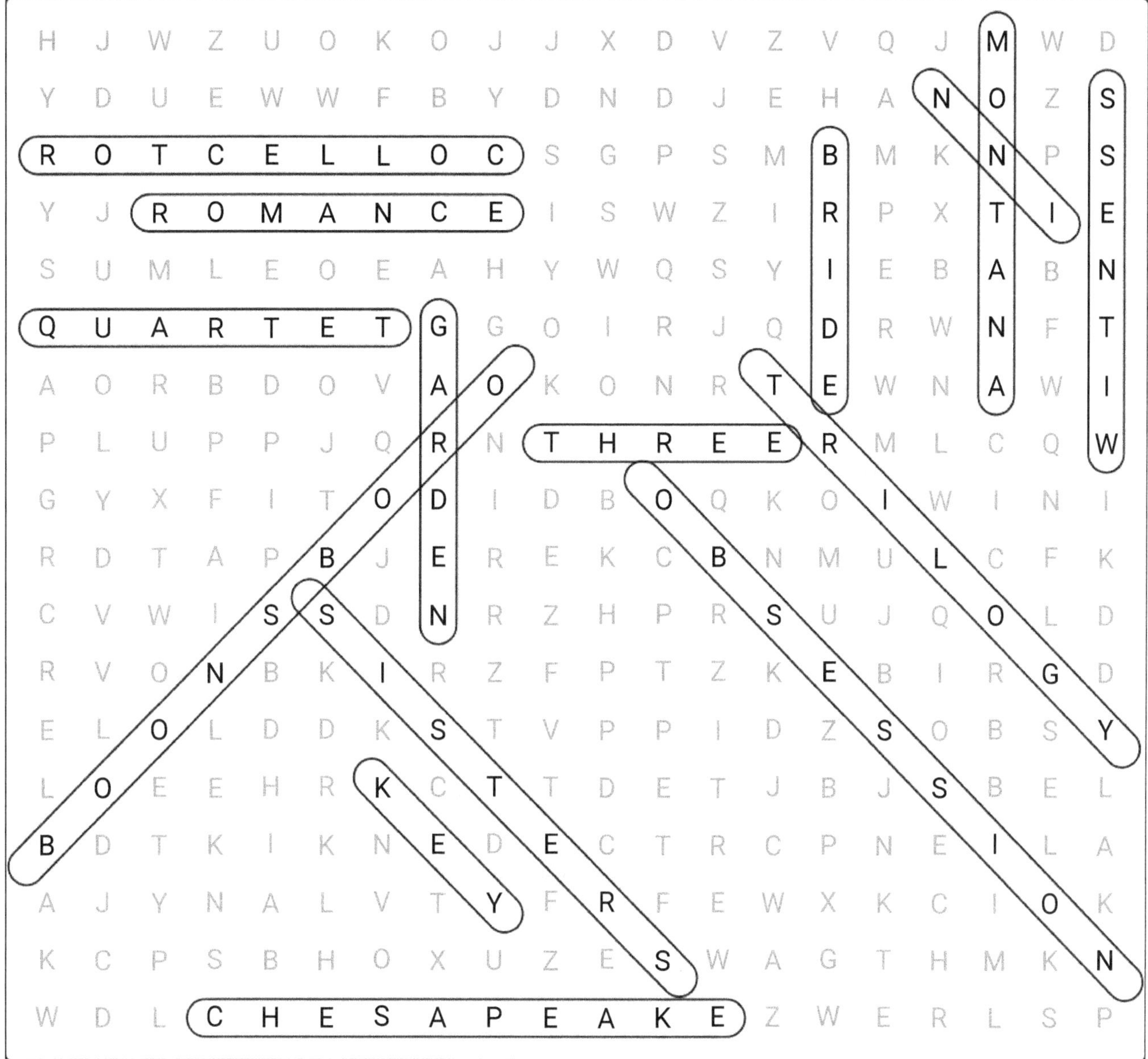

About Nora Roberts

Nora Roberts, an American author, is celebrated for her romance novels showcasing strong heroines, complex relationships, and compelling storylines. Her emotionally rich narratives, vivid world-building, and attention to detail have captivated readers worldwide. With over 500 million copies of her books sold, Roberts is a prolific and influential figure in the romance genre.

Trivia Questions

➢Q1. In Nora Roberts' novel "The Witness," what is the name of the main character?

➢Q2. In which Nora Roberts' novel does homicide detective Eve Dallas from the New York Police Department appear?

➢Q3. In many of Nora Roberts' novels, what is the name of the fictional Maryland town where the stories take place?

➢Q4. In one of Nora Roberts' novels, who is the single father and mechanic named MacKade?

➢Q5. In "The Search," who is the canine search-and-rescue trainer featured as the central character?

➢Q6. In Nora Roberts' novel "The Obsession," who is the photographer and primary character?

➢Q7. In which Nora Roberts' novel does Ripley Todd, a witch, play a significant role?

➢Q8. In Nora Roberts' novel "The Villa," who is the interior designer and central figure?

➢Q9. Which Nora Roberts' novel features event planner Parker Brown as a key character?

➢Q10. In Nora Roberts' novel "The Liar," what is the name of the main character who works as a bartender?

Turn the page upside down to see the answers.

A1. Elizabeth Fitch. A2. "In Death" series. A3. Boonsboro. A4. "The MacKade Brothers" series. A5. Fiona Bristow. A6. Naomi Carson. A7. "Dance Upon the Air." A8. Sophia Giambelli. A9. "Vision in White." A10. Shelby Foxworth.

Suzanne Collins

```
D H A Y O K M S S F Q B C Y G G X A E S
G H M N T Z P E K O F V B B B B H T L V A
K U F F E P M T L K A T N I S S N V E A
W M N Y T A W E P L C L C M I U V A R H
P Z D H G P I D V A A V X U Y A A F D M
Y P S N O W R F P Z D R D I E B G M E P
C S R A H E K I I Y K D K A A T J Y E R
L Y R I Z C T X G N E N I S F E L E N V
P M F X M O T B L D N R J S E O T P U T
R O M Z L C N I S Z E I P G T A W V M L
R C F F M L M D M G R U C E I R F W F C
D K V G P U C V N Y N U Y K L G I Q X N
S I W L E T R U I V A I E B E A C C P G
Y N T O M M H T F W K H V K M Q G L T L
U G T S Q U W Z H J S W W B M S L L T S
V J Y U U G D J O H B S I T Z A M C X O
U A V V L Q D J T U X D W A M O B I M N
P Y Z S V G F O K T V B C V K K K S Z C
```

Capitol	Games	Mockingjay
Districts	Haymitch	Peeta
Everdeen	Hunger	Prim
Finnick	Katniss	Rue
Gale	Mellark	Snow

SOLUTION

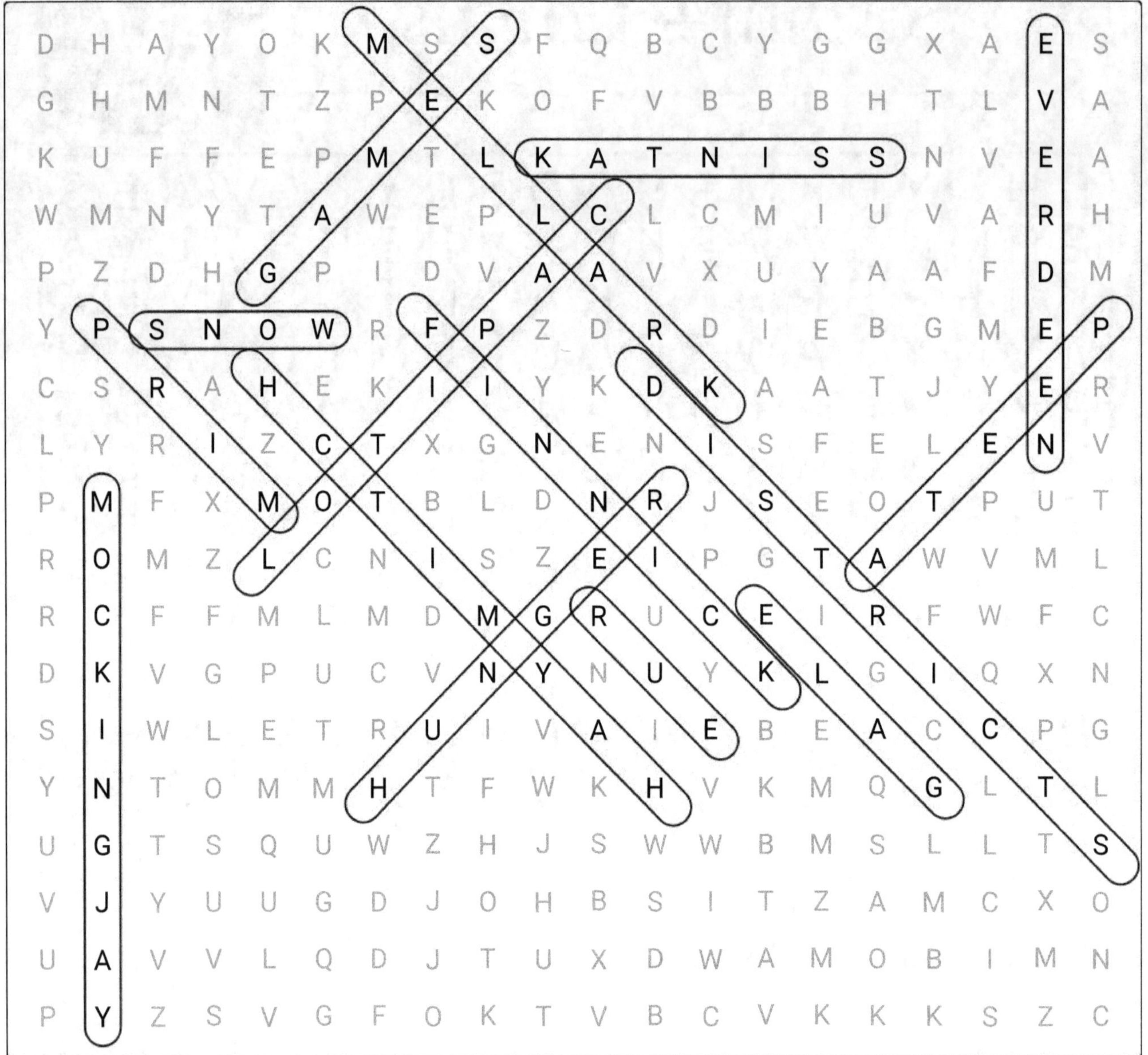

About Suzanne Collins

Suzanne Collins, an American novelist, is acclaimed for her enthralling "Hunger Games" trilogy. Her captivating storytelling and thought-provoking themes have resonated with readers worldwide, establishing her as a prominent figure in the realm of young adult dystopian fiction.

Trivia Questions

➢Q1. In Suzanne Collins' "The Hunger Games" series, what is the name of the main character?

➢Q2. In "The Hunger Games," which district does Katniss Everdeen call home?

➢Q3. Who is the boy from Katniss' district chosen to participate alongside her in the first Hunger Games?

➢Q4. Who is the Capitol stylist that forms an alliance with Katniss in "The Hunger Games"?

➢Q5. In "Catching Fire," the second book of the series, what is the name of the Hunger Games arena?

➢Q6. In the later books of the series, which rebel group does Katniss join?

➢Q7. Throughout "The Hunger Games" series, who serves as the president of the Capitol?

➢Q8. In which Suzanne Collins' novel does Melinda, a girl with the ability to enter and manipulate dreams, appear?

➢Q9. In which Suzanne Collins' novel does a boy named Gregor discover an underground world?

➢Q10. In "The Hunger Games" series, what is the name of the dystopian society?

Turn the page upside down to see the answers.

A1. Katniss Everdeen. A2. District 12. A3. Peeta Mellark. A4. Cinna. A5. The Quarter Quell. A6. The Mockingjay rebellion. A7. President Coriolanus Snow. A8. "The Underland Chronicles" series. A9. "Gregor the Overlander." A10. Panem.

E.I. James

```
G C C S W T J I U N G R C B N T A J Q G
L O W A T A Y L O R B E K W X S J F P J
F N F J N B F R E E D X C D U C B K C X
W T I A F X F G P S M A V B D W A D C G
U R F T W T F N U B L Y M O D M T X G M
H A T T M N E E S I H I J S H A D E S Z
H C Y L Z F H D E F S T M N F D L U Q D
Z T Z I D P E L W S N V A X D Y Q X K A
H R U V Y L L W I A J I B V N U B F O R
K A O E E E M V N E T V M Q Z T Q T W K
Y H R E G O E I O S P E R P P J J Z X E
J G T D O Z M M I Y Y U O G E P N D V R
E S W R H O E R Q Q F M X B X V S B Q X
O P D I D K H A Y M D Z R D F C L X W J
H E I S S C Z R A E X B L S U P H H C Y
R M K N J M R U A F K I G M A J Q P I W
K C R J H I Z P F D Q Z G N P W W Q F Q
K K E B K C N A D I A I S A T S A N A L
```

Anastasia	Dominant	Red room
Bdsm	Fifty	Shades
Christian	Freed	Steele
Contract	Grey	Submissive
Darker	Leila	Taylor

SOLUTION

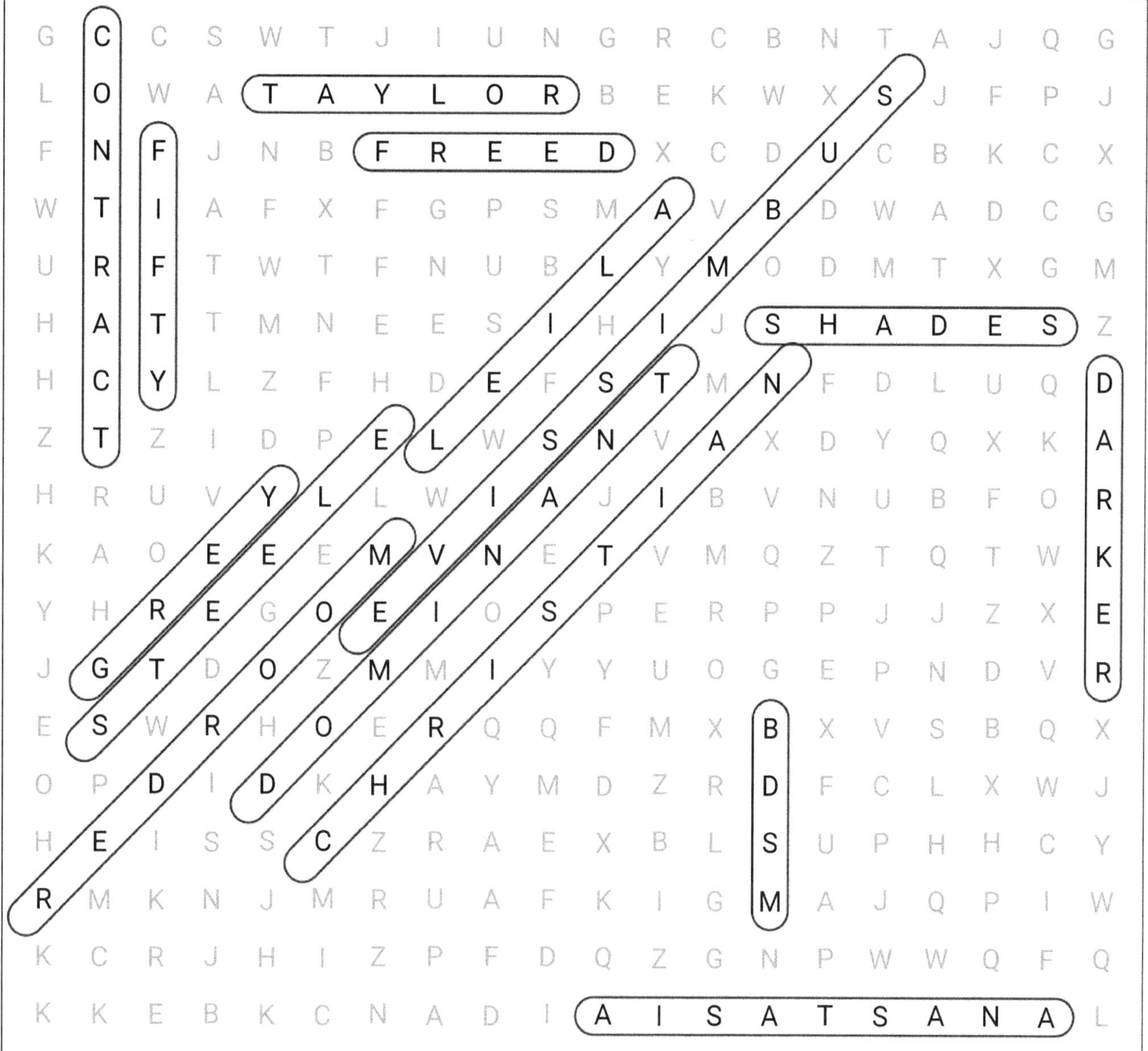

About E.l. James

British author E.L. James gained notoriety for her "Fifty Shades" series, which explores the world of erotic romance. Her bold storytelling and vivid characters have captivated a global audience, making her one of the most successful authors in her genre.

Trivia Questions

➤Q1. In E.L. James' "Fifty Shades" series, what is the name of the main character?

➤Q2. In "Fifty Shades of Grey," who is the affluent businessman and love interest of the central female character?

➤Q3. Who is the best friend of the main character in "Fifty Shades of Grey"?

➤Q4. In "Fifty Shades of Grey," what is the title of the BDSM agreement that the central character signs with Christian?

➤Q5. In "Fifty Shades of Grey," what is the name of the central female character's stepfather?

➤Q6. In "Fifty Shades of Grey," who is Christian's adoptive mother?

➤Q7. Which E.L. James' novel retells "Fifty Shades of Grey" from Christian's point of view?

➤Q8. In E.L. James' novel "The Mister," what is the name of the central character?

➤Q9. In "The Mister," what job does the male lead, Maxim Trevelyan, hold?

➤Q10. In which E.L. James novel does a character named Dr. Simon Stein become romantically involved with the female lead, Kate?

Turn the page upside down to see the answers.

A1. Anastasia Steele. A2. Christian Grey. A3. Kate Kavanaugh. A4. The Dominant/Submissive contract. A5. Ray Steele. A6. Grace Trevelyan-Grey, A7. "Grey," A8. Maxim Trevelyan. A9. Aristocrat. A10. "The Mister."

John Steinbeck

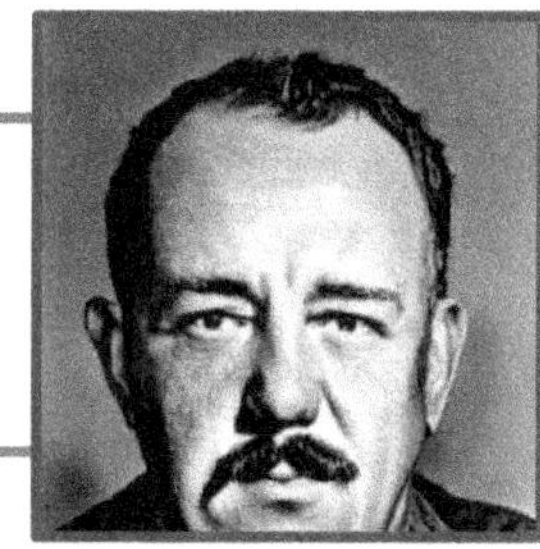

```
C N C L D A A S I B V C A N N E R Y F G
F X R P T Y U I T V J P E W K S Y F E S
A K E A S T A M B U H Z E U D Y W X X S
S K J T Y T O M H L L Y Q C X T J J I A
R W L E T A V M E E Y A E P Y J J Z K L
I D L D F S J S W B N S A R L E O R A Z I
J Z B E L C F C G U F V Z E L Q T Q C N
K Y P N M X O C R W M W O R C A W M T A
W G N B I N W D M R R O S N N I V E M S
G C R H C K R T G S Y E N V B C T I Y U
J Q F G E G A W C E Q P R T E W J O J V
S R Y T H N T W L Z R O V B E D Q N H M
V C V H S C H R S E N I U R W R E E U Z
Y S I S I M A S E E H V M H L G E L S X
Q F V P O H L C P I G M R S G S R Y U J
T K L E C W G M A B A Y S H L K X V Y P
Q T S C U Y O Z R Y U L C W B C P C M V
K W T A J L B F G R V Q M N C G O S V A
```

Bay	Grapes	Salinas
Cannery	Men	Tom
Charley	Mice	Tularecito
East	Monterey	Valley
Eden	Row	Wrath

SOLUTION

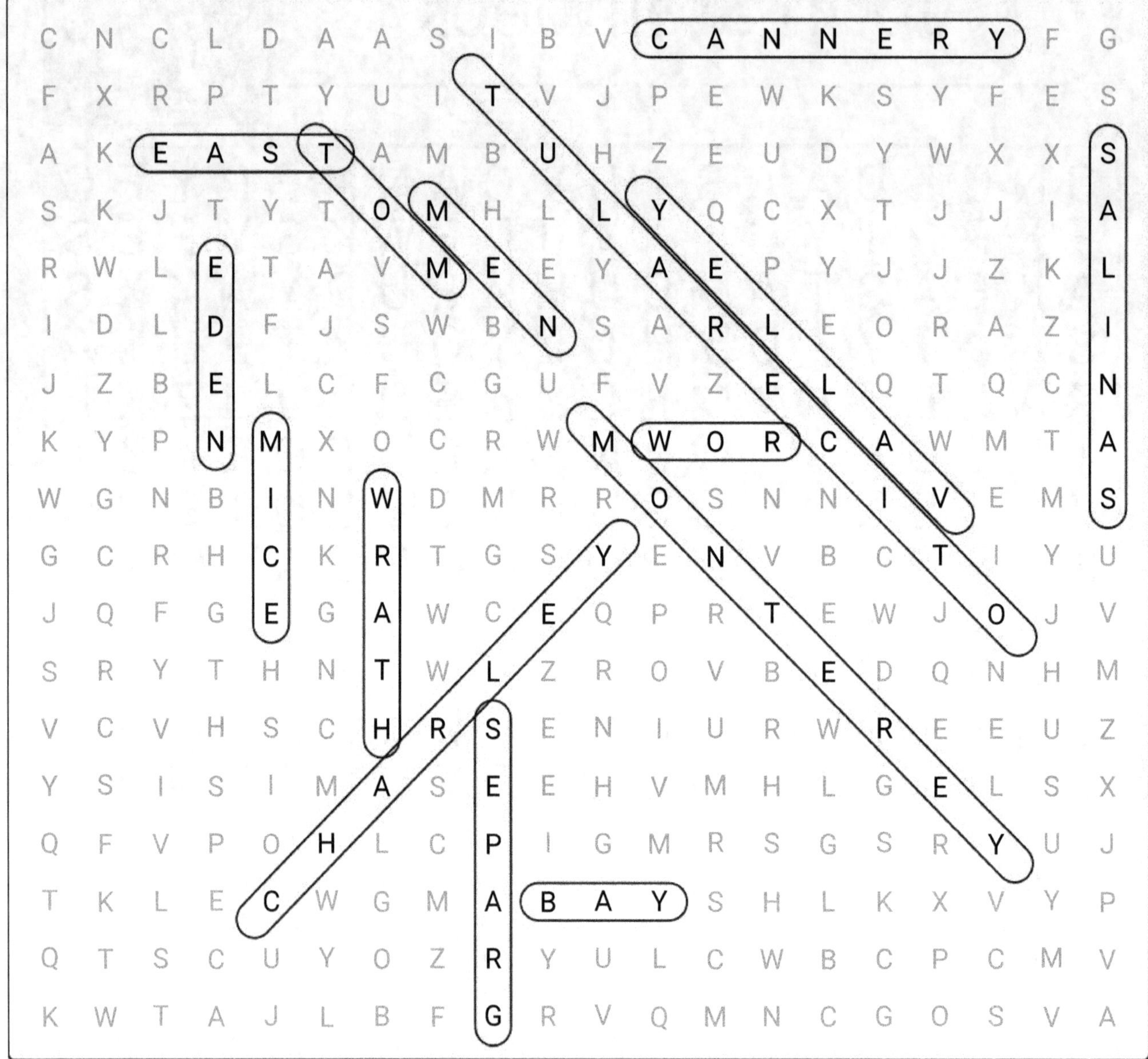

About John Steinbeck

John Steinbeck, an American writer, is renowned for his poignant works that depict the struggles of ordinary people. His masterful storytelling and richly drawn characters have secured his place as a leading figure in 20th-century American literature.

Trivia Questions

➢Q1. Which of John Steinbeck's novels is about a migrant farming family during the Great Depression?

➢Q2. What is the name of the character who dreams of owning a farm with his friend George in "Of Mice and Men"?

➢Q3. Which of John Steinbeck's novels is about a poor fisherman named Santiago who catches a giant marlin?

➢Q4. What is the name of the character in "East of Eden" who struggles with his good and evil nature?

➢Q5. Which of John Steinbeck's novels is about a group of characters who work on the "Cannery Row" in Monterey, California?

➢Q6. Which of John Steinbeck's novels is about the conflicts between a wealthy landowner and a group of striking apple pickers?

➢Q7. What is the name of the Joad family's oldest son in "The Grapes of Wrath"?

➢Q8. Which of John Steinbeck's novels is about a young boy named Jody who raises a red pony?

➢Q9. Which of John Steinbeck's novels is a retelling of the Arthurian legend set in the American West?

➢Q10. Which of John Steinbeck's novels is about a group of characters who work on a ranch in California during the 1930s?

Turn the page upside down to see the answers.

A1. "The Grapes of Wrath." A2. Lennie Small. A3. "The Old Man and the Sea." A4. Cal Trask. A5. "Cannery Row." A6. "In Dubious Battle." A7. Tom Joad. A8. "The Red Pony." A9. "The Acts of King Arthur and His Noble Knights." A10. "Of Mice and Men."

Dean Koontz

```
E O K V A J M D S Y H X L M R B V U F T
T H O M A S R V C M M Q A M G E K F U P
F D T O A U H G K I J A G S J D N U P T
B K N O L A F L T R N W L I L B G U M S
V O H N D I E X E E B T N L P T D W R Y
X O H L R W G I F Y M O E B E V Y E I R
D N J I C Y I H U L S O T N I B H O V Q
Z I C G K D D H T O X S V F S C L L B T
H E S H D Q G A P N I I B D T I A I A C
X T J T D W Z Y G R I H F A M G T Z Y Q
T S E W T Q F L N V L N W L I L J Y Q W
B N R Z U P Y V S Y Y T G D H K R E J Y
H E V E L O C I T Y K J O A B N K S D Z
V K L C O W H U G E R J R O S O T G X
F N F R I F R D D P D R S G Q O O Y F
V A V G D Y D Z Z M L L A Q T K V Z M K
B R A E A O E P R P H A N T O M S T H U
I F J G Q Q R O V I V R U S E L O S Q E
```

Ashley	Lightning	Sole survivor
Bay	Moonlight	Son
Bellamy	Odd	Thomas
Frankenstein	Phantoms	Velocity
Intensity	Prodigal	Watchers

SOLUTION

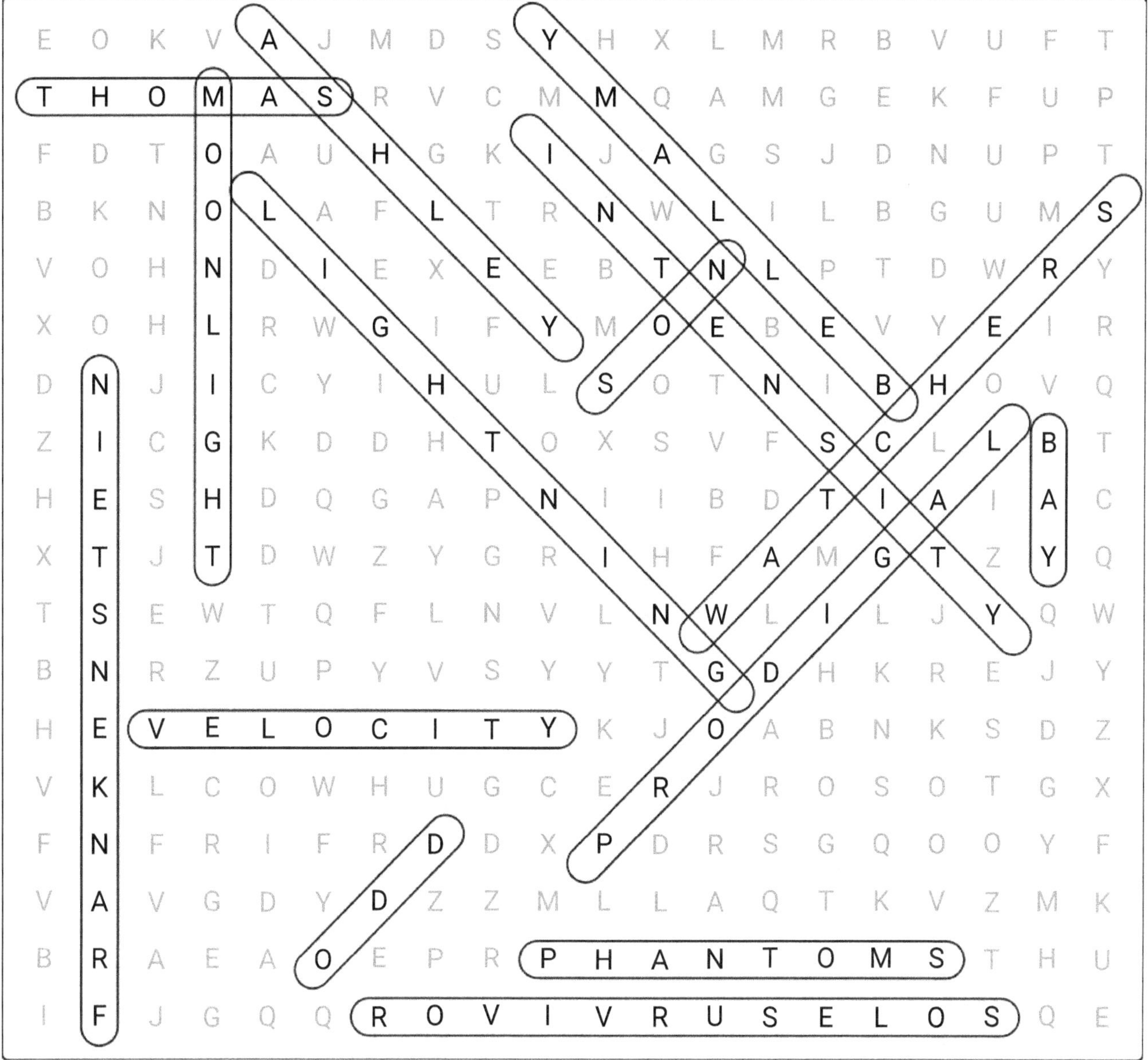

About Dean Koontz

American author Dean Koontz is recognized for his spine-chilling suspense novels and gripping thrillers. His vivid imagination and flair for creating intense, page-turning stories have earned him a dedicated readership and commercial success.

Trivia Questions

➢Q1. Which of Dean Koontz's novels is about a man named Odd Thomas who can see and communicate with ghosts?

➢Q2. Which of Dean Koontz's novels is about a family who is trapped in their own home by a group of violent intruders?

➢Q3. What is the name of the artificial intelligence system that becomes self-aware and starts killing people in Dean Koontz's novel "Demon Seed"?

➢Q4. Which of Dean Koontz's novels features a dog named Einstein who has been genetically enhanced?

➢Q5. What is the name of the small town where many of Dean Koontz's novels are set?

➢Q6. What is the name of the villainous organization that appears in many of Dean Koontz's novels?

➢Q7. Which of Dean Koontz's novels features a character named Christopher Snow who has a rare genetic disorder that makes him sensitive to light?

➢Q8. What is the name of the character in Dean Koontz's novel "Intensity" who is pursued by a serial killer?

➢Q9. Which of Dean Koontz's novels is about a group of people who are trapped in a high-rise building during a terrorist attack?

➢Q10. What is the name of the character who is on the run from the government in Dean Koontz's novel "The Taking"?

Turn the page upside down to see the answers.

A1. "Odd Thomas." A2. "Intensity." A3. Proteus IV. A4. "Watchers." A5. Moonlight Bay. A6. The Company. A7. "Fear Nothing." A8. Chyna Shepard. A9. "The Taking." A10. Molly Sloan.

Margaret Atwood

```
D G T A L E F D O V I Q L J A E A P S L
S T B W X P L A F E L N A S S A S S I N
Z U X P C F M I T Y D E M E S S F D T C
F K P U F S R P Z L Z I N U W E H G M Q
U X G L Y B O O Q U S N B I C A X H W W
A L D W Y Q L L W R N G R L N F Z D O F
T Q E D R Q K E F K V A A D E A B J F P
U J E H L J Z N N I V S M N L K N C X P
W E A Q U S J E N N K A K I D N I L B I
L Y T X W M P P D A I I A K U R Z P Z Q
R O B B E R N A L D P S G P A M G B Y G
G J Y I Y P E D S E T I E A D X R U H R
O L W V T J A E U G J J D W Y I K R G A
L S O K Z C K E P H R R P R D P E L R C
D P M V U A Y S V B K X O E L Z T L K E
E U A E R W C G P O B M A D D A D D A M
E E N C T C C A B F Y E O E P C M L R C
A X Y J A I A H M V C N G N R V C C X Q
```

Alias	Edible	Oryx
Assassin	Grace	Penelopiad
Blind	Hag-seed	Robber
Bride	Handmaid's	Tale
Crake	Maddaddam	Woman

SOLUTION

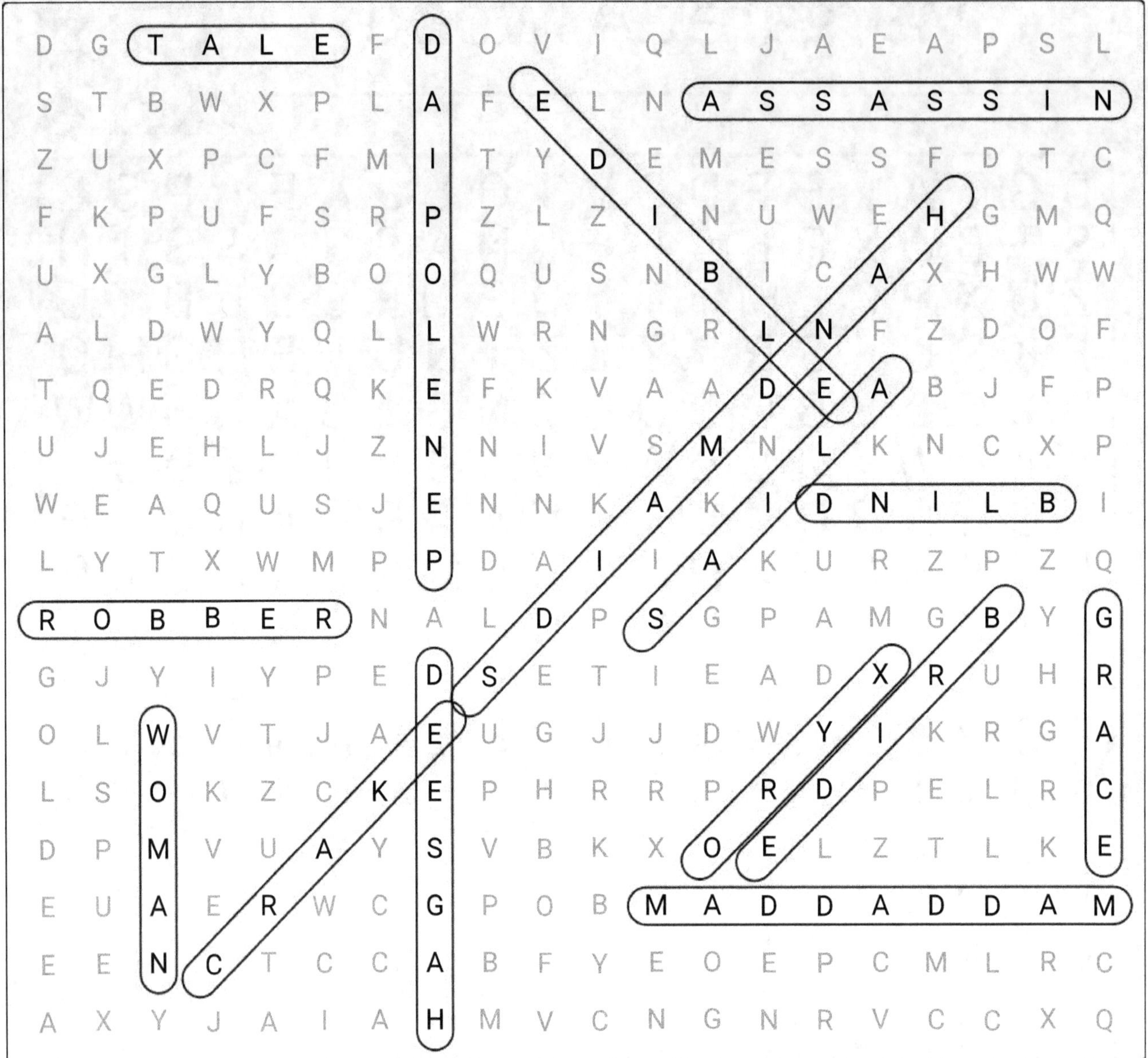

About Margaret Atwood

Canadian writer Margaret Atwood is celebrated for her literary works, which often examine themes of feminism, politics, and environmentalism. Her powerful narratives and thought-provoking prose have established her as a leading voice in contemporary literature.

Trivia Questions

➢Q1. In which of Margaret Atwood's novels is the setting a dystopian society named Gilead?

➢Q2. What is the name of the main character in "The Handmaid's Tale"?

➢Q3. Which of Margaret Atwood's novels is a retelling of "The Tempest" from the perspective of Caliban?

➢Q4. Who is the person convicted of murder in Margaret Atwood's novel "Alias Grace"?

➢Q5. Which of Margaret Atwood's novels features a character named Elaine who is troubled by her past?

➢Q6. Which of Margaret Atwood's novels is about a woman named Marian who joins a group of eco-terrorists?

➢Q7. Who is the main character in Margaret Atwood's novel "The Robber Bride," who is a successful businesswoman?

➢Q8. Which of Margaret Atwood's novels features a character named Offred who becomes a surrogate mother for a wealthy couple?

➢Q9. Which of Margaret Atwood's novels is about a group of individuals stranded on an uninhabited island?

➢Q10. What is the name of the central figure in Margaret Atwood's novel "Cat's Eye," who is an accomplished painter?

Turn the page upside down to see the answers.

A1. "The Handmaid's Tale." A2. Offred. A3. "Hag-Seed." A4. Grace Marks. A5. "Cat's Eye." A6. "The Year of the Flood." A7. Zenia. A8. "The Handmaid's Tale." A9. "The Tempest." A10. Elaine Risley.

Paulo Coelho

```
L L N M Y Z Y M S C S A Q O N Y P F M I
O C X F E X H C K U B X G C T G L U J F
G Q Q K M B E X W H P W L A O P V S H J
W K F X R Q H H Q V A D I Z W E E A H A
K M K H F S B U T K A M T G R Z L U O Q
K A C V P M E X I B Q S S C F G Z H H H
I K S W Z C V N O Y I R E V I R T Z O Y
T H G I L K O T M M E O V A C U Z L W D
E Q L N F R M T E C N P F C M N J R P P
Z A L Q E Y E H C D B W G D P E E K E L
D M K V K R C Z X V E O O R O I R R A W
G I Y F Q L T D Q Y G C G D S Q E E J F
F T A V A J B Y B Z Z V I A H N Q D N R
G A W T R X I T S G Y G T D I K F L R L
H F N W L C Y O G T X K G W E T L D J A
K H W S G X B L W N C N G M W S N R I X
O U B N D Y L T R E E X J K G H A V A Q C
J X B X C I E G A M I R G L I P D K S C
```

Alchemist	Go	River
Coelho	Light	Santiago
Decides	Maktub	Sat
Down	Piedra	Veronika
Fatima	Pilgrimage	Warrior

SOLUTION

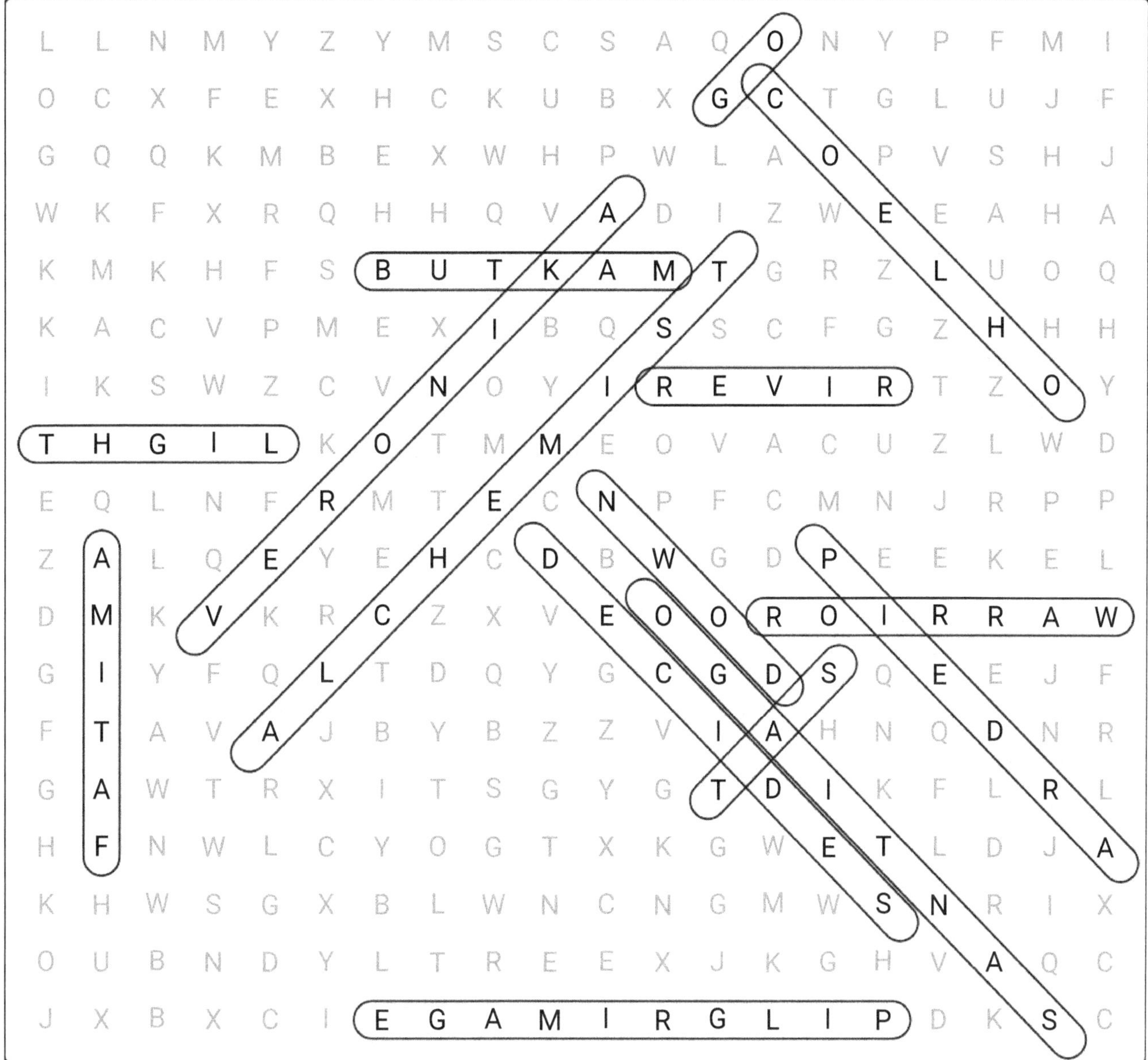

About Paulo Coelho

Brazilian author Paulo Coelho is known for his spiritually infused novels, such as "The Alchemist." His deeply introspective storytelling and exploration of human experiences have resonated with readers worldwide, making him a cherished figure in modern literature.

Trivia Questions

➢Q1. Which Paulo Coelho novel narrates the journey of a young shepherd named Santiago, striving to achieve his dreams?

➢Q2. What is the name of the main character in Paulo Coelho's "Brida," who yearns to become a witch?

➢Q3. Which Paulo Coelho work follows the story of a woman named Veronika, who attempts to end her life?

➢Q4. Who is the character in Paulo Coelho's novel "The Alchemist"?

➢Q5. In which Paulo Coelho book does a woman named Athena go on a journey to discover her destiny?

➢Q6. Which Paulo Coelho story portrays a group of people seeking spiritual enlightenment on a trip to the Mojave Desert?

➢Q7. What is the name of the lead character in Paulo Coelho's "By the River Piedra I Sat Down and Wept," trying to reconnect with a former childhood love?

➢Q8. Which Paulo Coelho novel features a man named Chris, who embarks on a quest to find his true self?

➢Q9. Which book by Paulo Coelho tells the story of a woman named Linda, going on a journey to search for her missing husband?

➢Q10. Who is the central figure in Paulo Coelho's "Veronika Decides to Die"?

Turn the page upside down to see the answers.

A1. "The Alchemist." A2. Brida O'Fern. A3. "Veronika Decides to Die." A4. Santiago. A5. "The Witch of Portobello." A6. "The Valkyries." A7. Pilar. A8. "The Pilgrimage." A9. "The Zahir." A10. Veronika.

Michael Crichton

```
B L H X Z L N L O C P Y C Q H O J D F P
R L R T P D A R V A A N D R O M E D A W
M T P M Z N T R R N B B Q D L T H E Y N
G N E F I R Z K A E Y L D D E C X G C K
C T R M S C K Q F J F W U N B Q A N L F
B J R T I M E L I N E J F S W R V I Q V
C E X Q X T K D K P P N M F S T R A I N
T J Q Y S Q L S Q F I Q M W R B A Q T D
T U I O X C Z X R E I M J Y D S M G L S
Y R L F X Z D G K A E H J P E A C J M H
E A B U O N S W W R T F F Q N R D Q V V
E S L B Z D N T A O C R M B I G P J M J
G S X I L L G W A K S B N C E D L R Y A
T I N R F A Q I Y T J O A C O T O G C Q
F C O T S P H E R E E G C O Y C T B P V
F W B R P U C U T L L H B N G H G R Q X
M U M C E N V Z H Y W X P G M A N Z O N
E S T S T W R A D I S C L O S U R E W Q
```

Andromeda	Lost	State
Congo	Man	Strain
Disclosure	Park	Terminal
Fear	Prey	Timeline
Jurassic	Sphere	World

SOLUTION

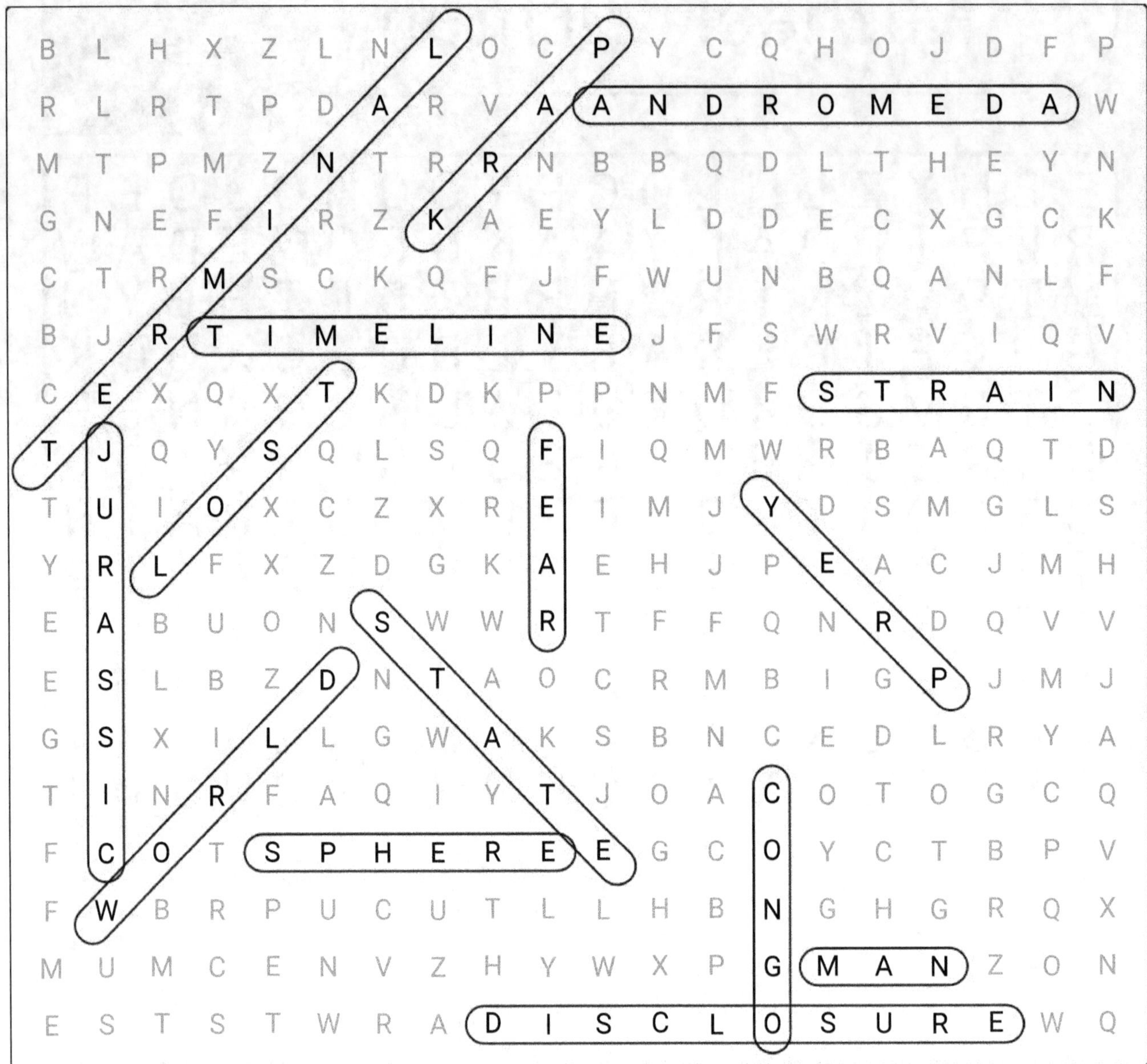

About Michael Crichton

Michael Crichton, an American writer, is best known for his science fiction and techno-thriller novels. His ability to blend cutting-edge science with riveting plots has earned him widespread acclaim and commercial success.

➤Q1. Which of Michael Crichton's novels is about a theme park with genetically engineered dinosaurs?

➤Q2. What is the name of the character who is the mathematician and chaos theorist in "Jurassic Park"?

➤Q3. Which of Michael Crichton's novels is about a team of scientists who travel back in time to the medieval era?

➤Q4. What is the name of the character in Michael Crichton's novel "The Andromeda Strain"?

➤Q5. Which of Michael Crichton's novels is about a virus that threatens to wipe out humanity?

➤Q6. Which of Michael Crichton's novels is about a billionaire who creates a simulated world for people to live in?

➤Q7. What is the name of the character in Michael Crichton's novel "Timeline," who travels back in time to rescue his father?

➤Q8. Which of Michael Crichton's novels is about a group of people who are shrunk down to the size of insects?

➤Q9. What is the name of the character in Michael Crichton's novel "Sphere," who is a psychologist?

➤Q10. Which of Michael Crichton's novels is about a group of scientists who discover a way to travel through time?

Turn the page upside down to see the answers.

A1. "Jurassic Park." A2. Ian Malcolm. A3. "Timeline." A4. Jeremy Stone. A5. "The Andromeda Strain." A6. "Westworld." A7. Chris Johnston. A8. "Micro." A9. Norman Johnson. A10. "Timeline."

Danielle Steel

```
B B K K Z F K N G X S W Y R R R A H P C
B Y D R X F K M Q L Y T N E L I S R Q Z
E P E G A S U S J Z V C L A I D O E F E
L M I Y O F O Y C E W P J V H M C V G A
E X O C H A N G E S Q F E H I K C C Z Z
G R E U E H E A R J Z I N S K R T N L J
A N F Z T V X K F Z K A E G E K C S D N
C Z A U N M L O R S M S R E N N I W K R
Y O S S Y D X O O A F Q R Q P K P O X E
K G T I D J M B Z L Y R M L B Y C W T H
D Y D D J L A V I E C Y G J I T J Q G N T
C G B E N F N A J T Q Y O G W Z N B E U
B R X C Z G D Z C P R Y Q H I A K H M O
Y A E K Z V Z T N R L A I T A J O V U S
M C S R S I N L S J Y R Y S H N Z K F V
W E R N A D A W I K C M G A O B I M Y Q
F L X D U V Q K P Z Q N W R L I M P O M
O L L C X Q I H L Q H A R B O U R G Q P
```

Amazing	Honor	Romance
Betrayal	Legacy	Safe
Changes	Lights	Silent
Grace	Pegasus	Southern
Harbour	Promise	Winners

SOLUTION

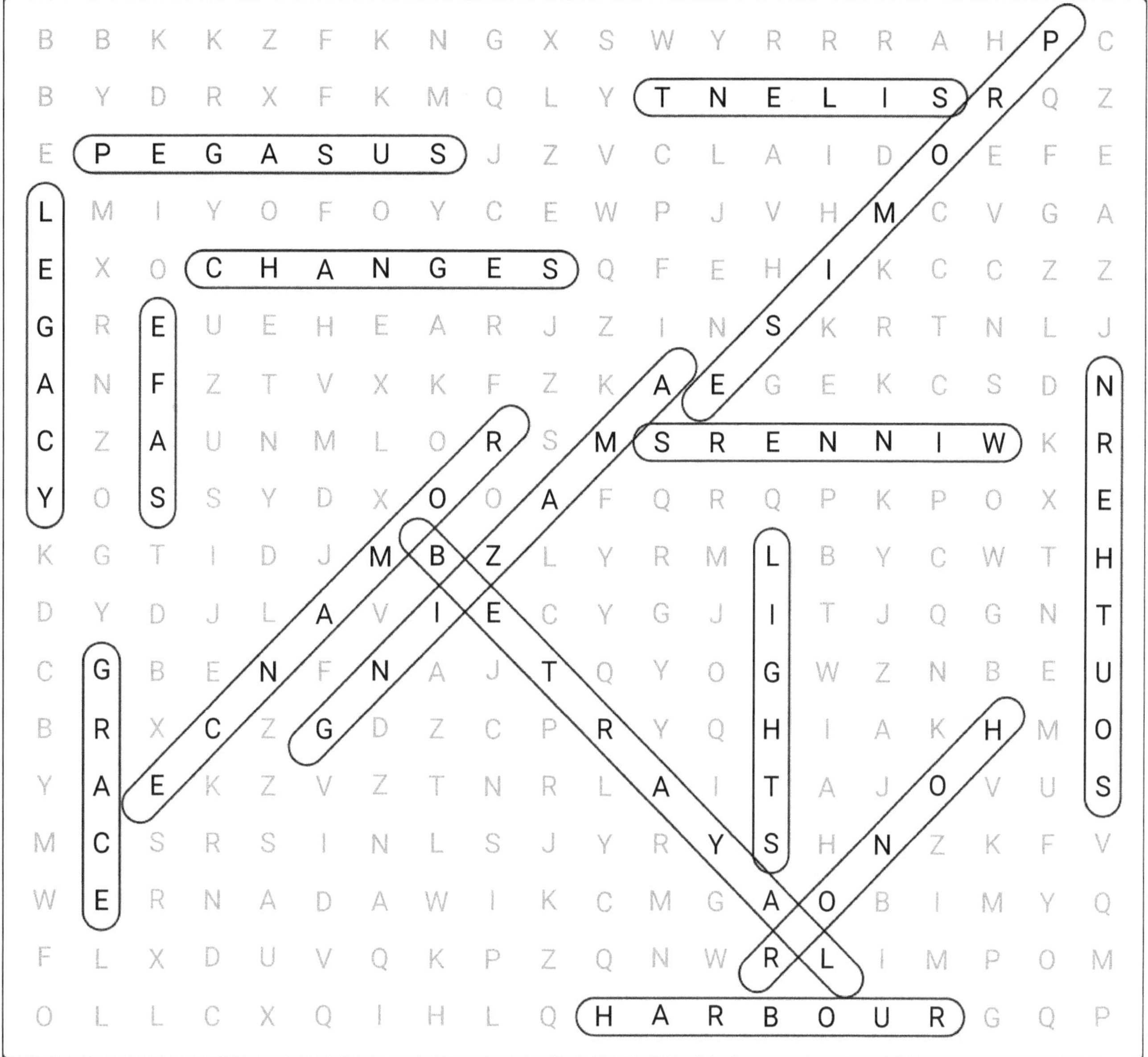

About Danielle Steel

American novelist Danielle Steel has made a name for herself with her emotionally charged romance novels. Her captivating storytelling, relatable characters, and heartfelt themes have endeared her to readers around the world, making her one of the most successful authors in her genre.

Trivia Questions

➢Q1. Which Danielle Steel novel tells the story of a woman named Fiona, who embarks on a new life in San Francisco?

➢Q2. In Danielle Steel's "The Promise," who is the accomplished photographer at the centre of the story?

➢Q3. Which Danielle Steel work features a woman named Maribeth, who is forced to reevaluate her life after a heart attack?

➢Q4. Who is the main character in Danielle Steel's "Going Home," who returns to her hometown following a personal tragedy?

➢Q5. Which Danielle Steel novel portrays the tale of Meredith, who begins a fresh start in New York City?

➢Q6. In which Danielle Steel book does Paige, who has suffered a tragic accident, have to reconstruct her life?

➢Q7. In Danielle Steel's "The Duchess," who is the former model serving as the lead character?

➢Q8. Which Danielle Steel novel follows the journey of Zoe, who is searching for her birth mother?

➢Q9. Which Danielle Steel work features Maxine, who becomes a Hollywood producer?

➢Q10. Who is the successful TV anchor at the heart of Danielle Steel's "A Perfect Life"?

Turn the page upside down to see the answers.

A1. "The Good Fight." A2. Stephanie Adams. A3. Maribeth Klein. A4. Joanna Brennan. A5. "Heartbeat." A6. Paige Watts. A7. Angélique Latham. A8. "Lone Eagle." A9. "Matters of the Heart." A10. Blaise McCarthy.

Stieg Larsson

```
K N L S B Z Y F M N D H V W L E E L V J
G V Y R L M L K G U K R S G L D W G V Y
P X Z W O B L I Z T I A A R E Y U L D Q
V H E C M X R H K N C J L G N C Z W N Q
R S T O K L H Y V V K M B J O J A E W N
Z M U T V N E Y B C E C B C P N M L O T
V N B B I B K P H R D M M N L Q O C M T
F V P I S T I S O L U G K G I O G S E R
S I O H T L T W P I A G Y L T Y E Z N B
I C R L J E T F P S Y M J T Y J L Z N A
N I R E N R U L N B R G A C W T O R B O
O Z D R I T D Y Z E M T W R G X E A J Q
N T O L H N M S Q T A W M M S D Z D S U
Y H O P A Y N W E H R K T I N Z W Z F G
O G E F I N E H T Y W X J A K S O P A I
Y V B U U H S H A D E Q L X T A N E W Z
C N B Q L Z T X H N Y A A K P G E E Z F
Q O V I C S D S W P S I T W I E J L S Q
```

Blomkvist	Hornet's	Nest
Dragon	Kicked	Salander
Fire	Lisbeth	Tattoo
Girl	Men	Trilogy
Hate	Mikael	Women

SOLUTION

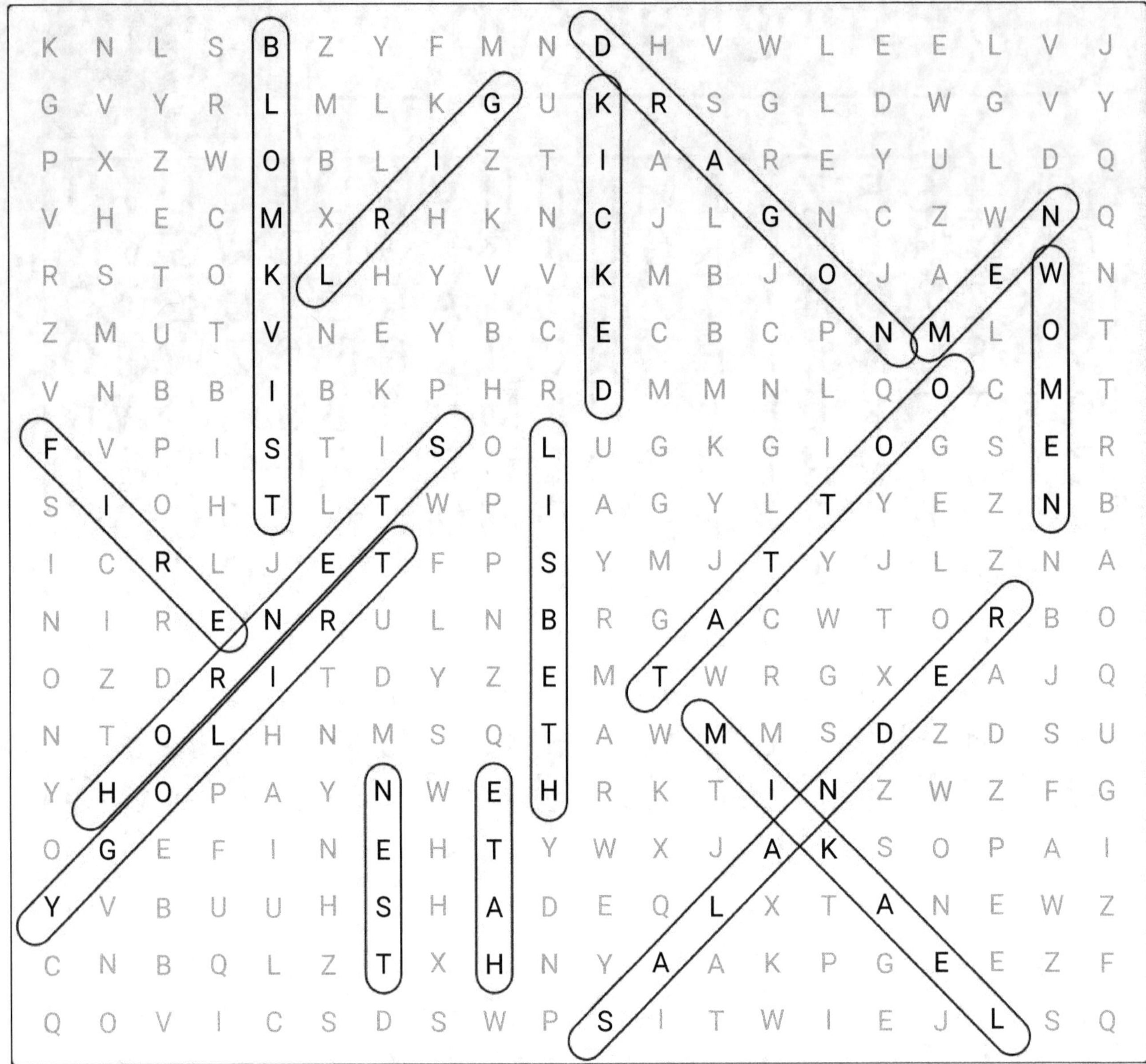

About Stieg Larsson

Swedish author Stieg Larsson is famed for his "Millennium" trilogy, which delves into the world of crime and investigative journalism. His compelling storytelling and complex characters have captivated readers globally, securing his place as an influential figure in contemporary crime fiction.

Trivia Questions

➢Q1. Which of Stieg Larsson's novels is about a journalist named Mikael Blomkvist and a hacker named Lisbeth Salander?

➢Q2. What is the name of the villainous organization that appears in Stieg Larsson's Millennium trilogy?

➢Q3. Which of Stieg Larsson's novels is about a young woman named Zalachenko who is the subject of a government cover-up?

➢Q4. What is the name of the character in Stieg Larsson's novel "The Girl Who Played with Fire"?

➢Q5. Which of Stieg Larsson's novels is about the murder of three people who are about to publish an exposé on sex trafficking?

➢Q6. What is the name of the magazine that Mikael Blomkvist works for in Stieg Larsson's Millennium trilogy?

➢Q7. Which of Stieg Larsson's novels is about a group of people who are investigating the assassination of Swedish Prime Minister Olof Palme?

➢Q8. What is the name of the character in Stieg Larsson's novel "The Girl Who Kicked the Hornet's Nest"?

➢Q9. Which of Stieg Larsson's novels is about a journalist named Mikael Blomkvist who is investigating a series of murders?

➢Q10. What is the name of the hacker who helps Mikael Blomkvist in Stieg Larsson's Millennium trilogy?

Turn the page upside down to see the answers.

A1. Karl Stig-Erland Larsson A2. Sweden A3. "Män som hatar kvinnor" (Men Who Hate Women) A4. Three A5. Journalist A6. 2004 A7. The manuscripts were discovered after his death A8. David Lagercrantz A9. Expo Foundation A10. Violence against women

Ken Follett

```
X L B P E F G S B B X O Z C Q C T O A B
J R T J L S M M V P T Z E X B W R K H G
V S M M G K X E W L S N Z Q F L I I S L
V H T R Q Z Y G D O T O P X I W L N I P
A H W L J E D L A U S J L A L Z O G T N
I T K S M T R S R A L L I P S Z G S E G
P M O H Y O C Y M V P O U K L D Y B A L
Y E L G W V Z D A W P R M H X Z F R R C
A L G E H Y W B Z O W I J L H W U I T Q
B D A C Z K A D T E N R O H Y F C D H D
C E M S Z N P R V A W T E P E R P G W R
G E Q F P M E X P F R T O V D G F E F M
O N K L L T F T S X X Y B C P S K X P S
H H I U T I Z M I H J A U W B J P X N W
R I X D O E G Q M H H L L A F U P J M X
A L N R D P K H U I W W I N T E R N S P
Q J N M L E J H T S T N A I G O U M C H
A U W I Y E W C V E Q J L H R F A L U G
```

Century	Giants	Trilogy
Earth	Hornet	Wedding
Eye	Kingsbridge	White
Fall	Needle	Winter
Flight	Pillars	World

SOLUTION

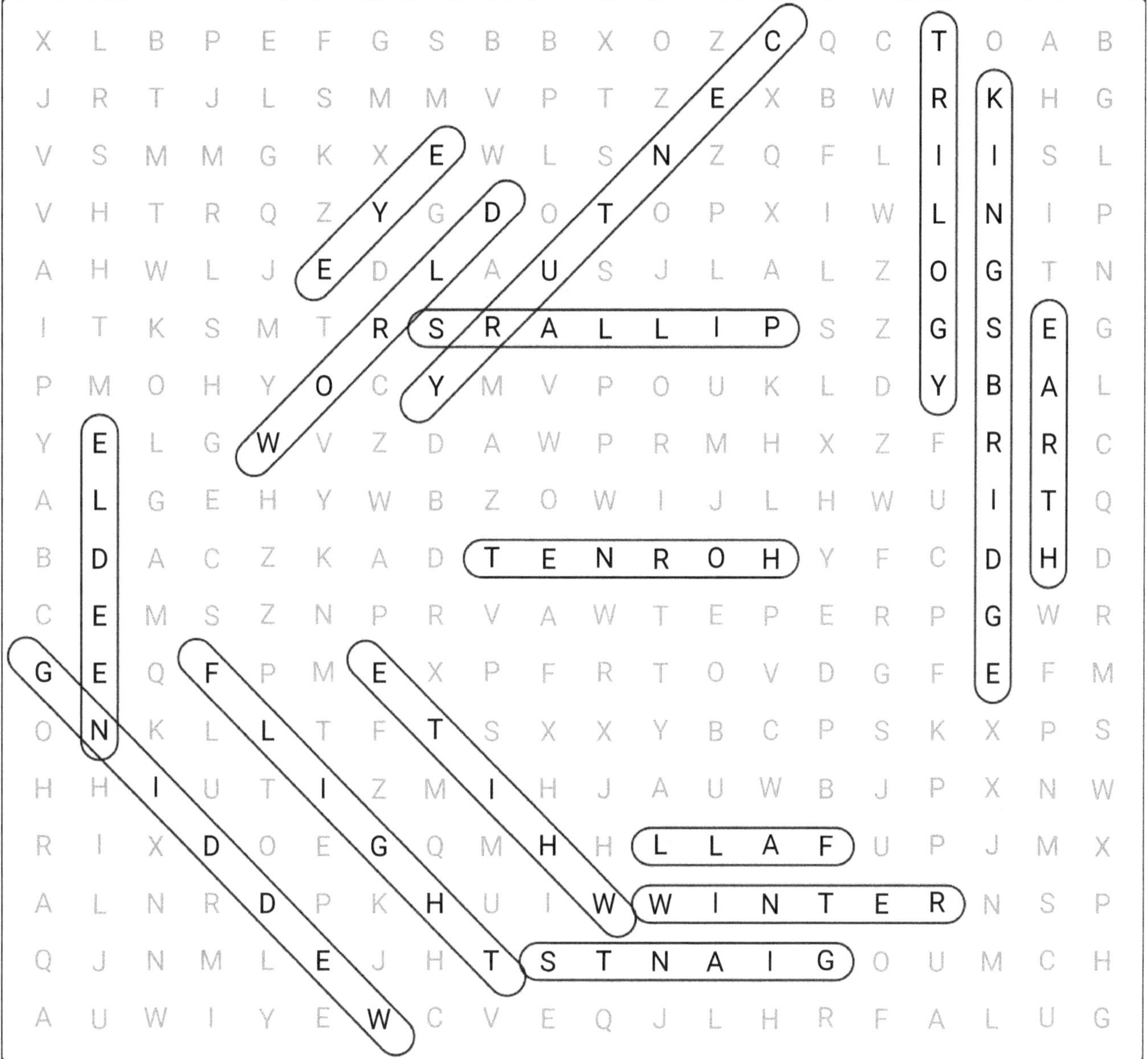

About Ken Follett

British author Ken Follett is recognized for his historical fiction and espionage novels. His intricate plots, meticulous research, and engaging narratives have made him one of the most respected and successful authors in his field.

Trivia Questions

➢Q1. Which of Ken Follett's novels is about the building of a cathedral in 12th century England?

➢Q2. What is the name of the character in Ken Follett's novel "Eye of the Needle," who is a German spy?

➢Q3. Which of Ken Follett's novels is about a group of international spies who are trying to prevent the outbreak of World War II?

➢Q4. What is the name of the character in Ken Follett's novel "The Pillars of the Earth"?

➢Q5. Which of Ken Follett's novels is about a group of people who are trying to save Europe from a terrorist attack?

➢Q6. What is the name of the character in Ken Follett's novel "The Key to Rebecca," who is a German spy in Cairo during World War II?

➢Q7. Which of Ken Follett's novels is about a group of people who are trying to escape from Nazi-occupied France?

➢Q8. What is the name of the character in Ken Follett's novel "Fall of Giants," who is a Welsh coal miner?

➢Q9. Which of Ken Follett's novels is about a group of people who are involved in the Civil Rights Movement in the United States?

➢Q10. What is the name of the character in Ken Follett's novel "A Dangerous Fortune," who is a banker in 19th century London?

Turn the page upside down to see the answers.

A1. "The Pillars of the Earth." A2. Henry Faber. A3. "The Key to Rebecca." A4. Tom Builder. A5. "The Third Twin." A6. Alex Wolff. A7. "Jackdaws." A8. Billy Williams. A9. "Edge of Eternity." A10. Hugh Pilaster.

Ian Fleming

```
C R S O F J C A S I N O O R S D O A V Q
O M U X F R W L O A O Q V D E I M J T R
S U B S O K O W C N I R V X U A L X Y L
P K N Y S E U M Q S I F L V Q M O O M J
E L C K U I E E X C Z O T Z A O I F V Y
C L C H J S A I C B B V I H V N N K M E
T A U N L L A B R E D N U H T D T S J U
R F A R O Y A L E E R J B P D S C L Y F
E Y H H L G V J G Y B H U I J A M E S T
T K J C R A H P R E I Z O Q U A N T U M
I S L K D O M E Z N L Q C E U R B M Q N
C H T Z T G V L H E Y A J R X F Z O M X
F X X Y X E Y M I D H Z F L Q N K Z N A
V R G X R P I V A L Z I U N P F U S Y D
R L V O B D D M B O J F I Z F E U J X A
K E F S Z H N P F G Z N U X H U N H E D
S M O N E Y P E N N Y R K I N F F K Y W
Z A L V M K S N C A G Y A G P Z I P O X
```

Bond	Goldeneye	Royale
Casino	James	Russia
Diamonds	Love	Skyfall
Forever	Moneypenny	Spectre
From	Quantum	Thunderball

SOLUTION

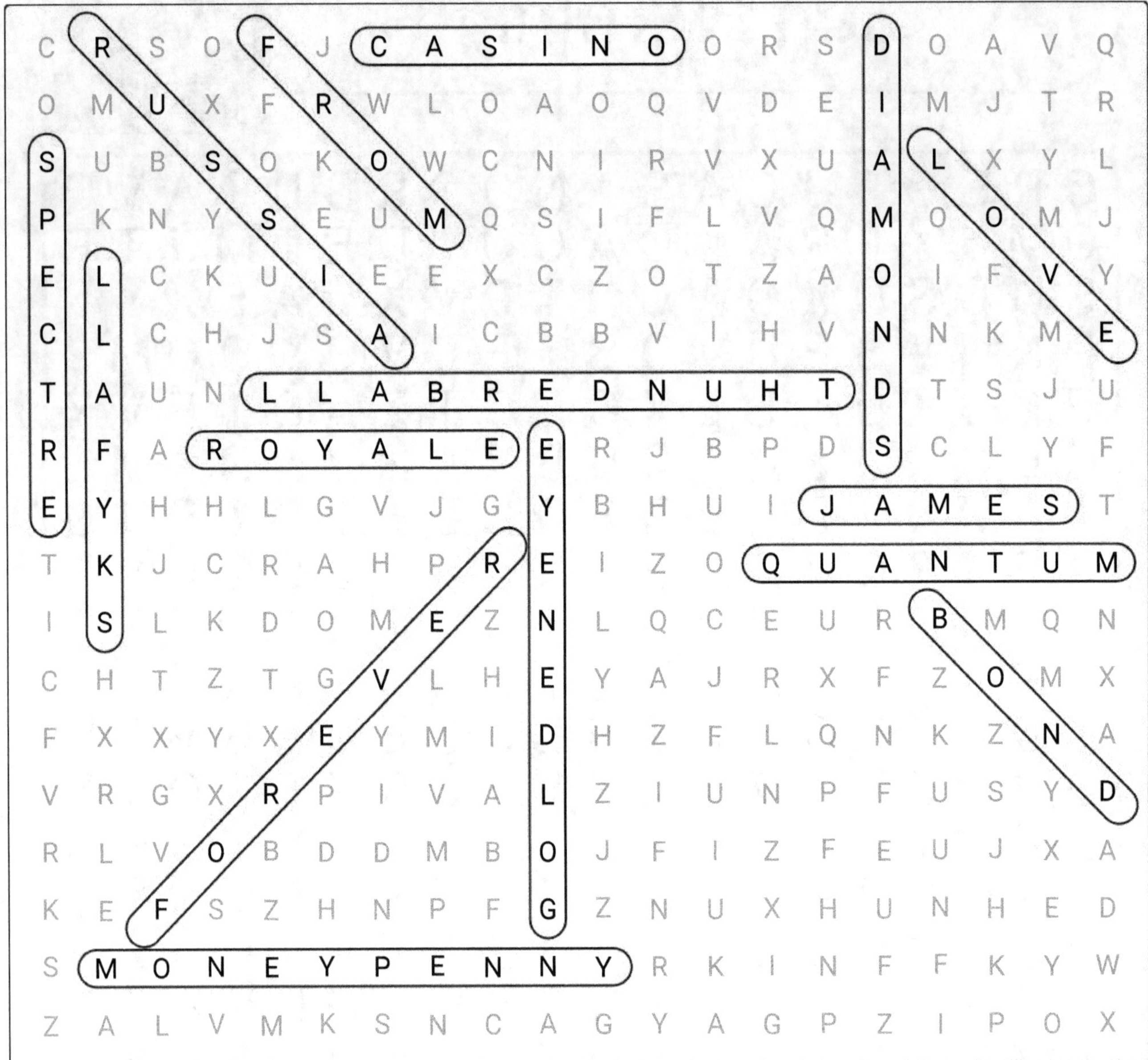

About Ian Fleming

British writer Ian Fleming is renowned for his creation of the iconic spy character, James Bond. His thrilling espionage adventures and engaging narratives have earned him worldwide fame, making him a defining figure in the spy fiction genre.

Trivia Questions

➢Q1. Which famous fictional spy did Ian Fleming create?

➢Q2. What was the title of Ian Fleming's first James Bond novel?

➢Q3. Before becoming a novelist, what profession did Ian Fleming have during World War II?

➢Q4. In which Jamaican estate did Fleming write all of his Bond novels?

➢Q5. Which James Bond novel was inspired by a real-life failed assassination attempt on Ian Fleming?

➢Q6. How many James Bond novels did Ian Fleming write in total?

➢Q7. What was the title of the children's book written by Ian Fleming in 1964?

➢Q8. Which Ian Fleming novel was the basis for the 1967 film "Casino Royale"?

➢Q9. What was the name of the operation that Ian Fleming devised to maintain the security of Gibraltar during World War II?

➢Q10. Which character from the James Bond series was inspired by Ian Fleming's experiences as a British naval intelligence officer?

Turn the page upside down to see the answers.

A1. James Bond A2. "Casino Royale" A3. Naval intelligence officer A4. Goldeneye A5. "From Russia with Love" A6. Fourteen A7. "Chitty-Chitty-Bang-Bang: The Magical Car" A8. "Casino Royale" A9. Operation Goldeneye A10. M (the head of the Secret Intelligence Service, also known as MI6)

Haruki Murakami

```
G P J W T F L L L P O Y S H T T C R F U Y
V N E V S W E E T H E A R T M G S S Z N
E X C E K C T N S P U T N I K S P V L O
M B F R H C V A Q K D Q C D U C E L W R
U Z X I V S F L Z L T S S M Y O R B H W
L U O C H J O N K A H X F F Q L S W T E
B Z T D O T A R S I K U Q H N O Z M C G
I C K L S V V T X N G I J R V R P D C I
T N F Y H W X D N R Y L N L Y L E W L A
T M L X O V K O S M S Z D G I E X R B N
T Y J A R M M T F A P I A U J S B I R D
R J D H E V M I S G D V N V T S W H F Q
Q M X G C M G T J U Z W C B I I I W F K
G X F G P S W X T Z K R E J P X Z O O H
A K F A K A W W I N D U P V V G D O V A
R G A E F R L V B T P M R B F U M D F G
A S M R M S G S U M X G A U P Y R U Y W
K Q O T Q Q F M N C H R O N I C L E M U
```

Bird	Norwegian	Sweetheart
Chronicle	Rat	Tazaki
Colorless	Sheep	Tsukuru
Dance	Shore	Wind-up
Kafka	Sputnik	Wood

SOLUTION

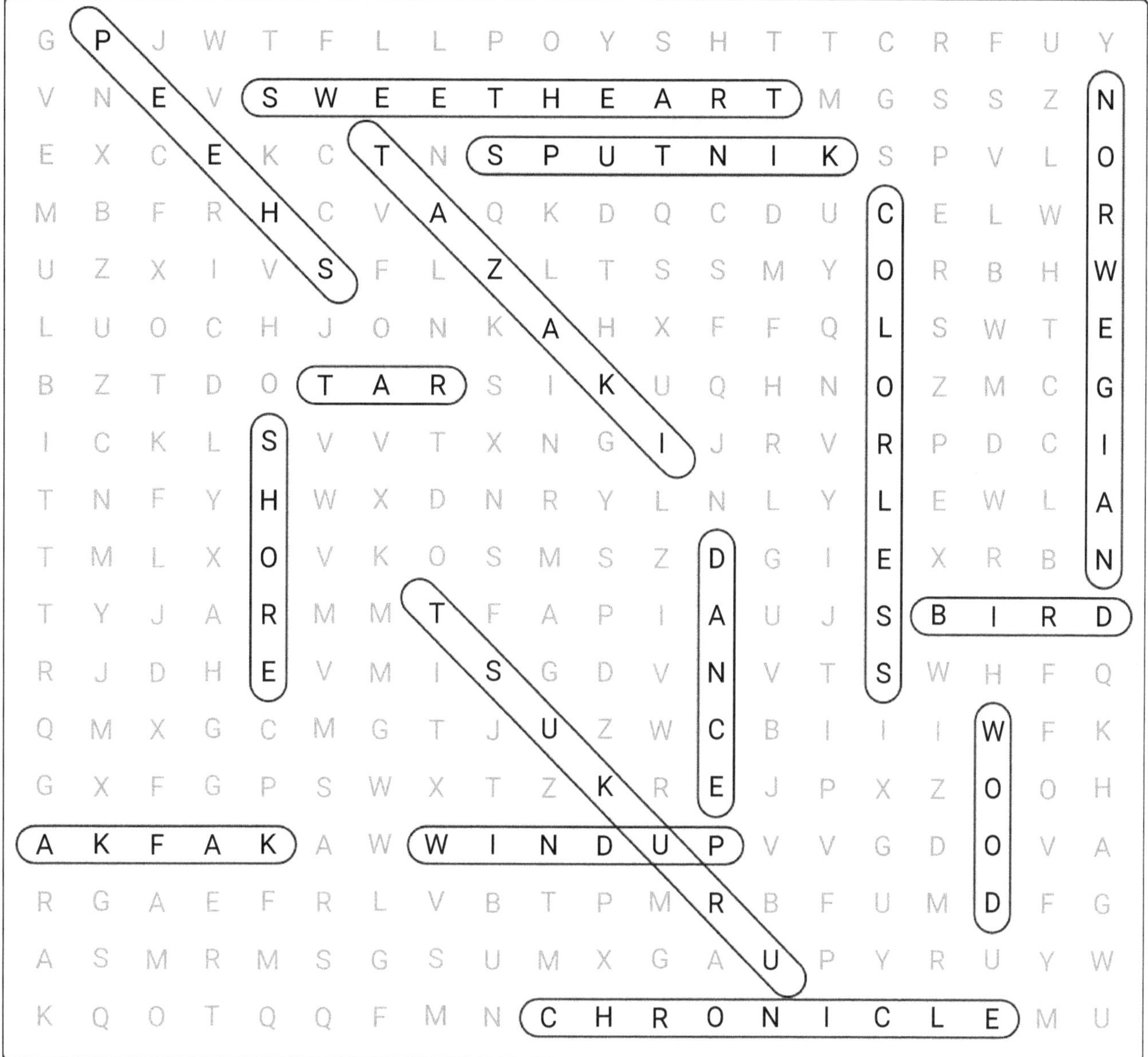

About Haruki Murakami

Haruki Murakami, a Japanese author, is celebrated for his surreal, metaphysical novels that explore themes of loneliness, love, and the human condition. His unique storytelling and poetic prose have garnered him a dedicated international following and critical acclaim.

Trivia Questions

➤Q1. Which of Haruki Murakami's novels is about a young woman named Mari who spends a night wandering around Tokyo?

➤Q2. What is the name of the character in Haruki Murakami's novel "The Wind-Up Bird Chronicle"?

➤Q3. Which of Haruki Murakami's novels is about a man named Toru who is searching for a woman named Naoko?

➤Q4. What is the name of the character in Haruki Murakami's novel "Kafka on the Shore"?

➤Q5. Which of Haruki Murakami's novels is about a man named Tsukuru who is trying to understand why his friends abandoned him?

➤Q6. Which of Haruki Murakami's novels is about a man named Hajime who reconnects with a childhood love?

➤Q7. What is the name of the character in Haruki Murakami's novel "Norwegian Wood"?

➤Q8. Which of Haruki Murakami's novels is about a man named Watashi who is searching for a sheep?

➤Q9. Which of Haruki Murakami's novels is about a group of people who are trapped in a town that is cut off from the rest of the world?

➤Q10. What is the name of the character in Haruki Murakami's novel "Colorless Tsukuru Tazaki and His Years of Pilgrimage"?

Turn the page upside down to see the answers.

A1. "After Dark." A2. Toru Okada. A3. "Norwegian Wood." A4. Kafka Tamura. A5. "Colorless Tsukuru Tazaki and His Years of Pilgrimage." A6. "South of the Border, West of the Sun." A7. Toru Watanabe. A8. "A Wild Sheep Chase." A9. "1Q84." A10. Tsukuru Tazaki.

Jackie Collins

```
Y K Z E R M C P L R A T S I R U A A N V
O B O X D I K G S H O L L Y W O O D V V
P Y E R D B P N N B G Q L M K F R U N M
P W R P V E C O N F E S S I O N S R M R
Y V K R T K T R C W C M Z S X O I O Z W
T Q E R D C H V H Q H M W K J T L B S M
T O I N K M I Z A I I V N I S X L X P K
U G L S D S J Y N S L W N A M C W L X V
E K P V J E V O C F D X N K R Q S R Z B
L F R R D V T B E U D T C U X J S J I V
U M L M O I U T S M A O L T X P B K Y Y
J M C N B W S C A N R Z Q M J O D O D L
L L C Y X Z N I G D P U F N U L S F A B
U L O V E R S E N X C K R S I D Z G L O
C Z E W D L L Z J N K F Y W Y A E K O T
K I X Q X O G Y Y H E S H B J I B O S S
Y H A N S R S T Z X C R R B W M F V K J
E E V B V R O M G G O E S T O S E K K I
```

Boss	Lady	Sinners
Chances	Lovers	Star
Child	Lucky	Vendetta
Confessions	Rock	Wild
Hollywood	Santangelos	Wives

SOLUTION

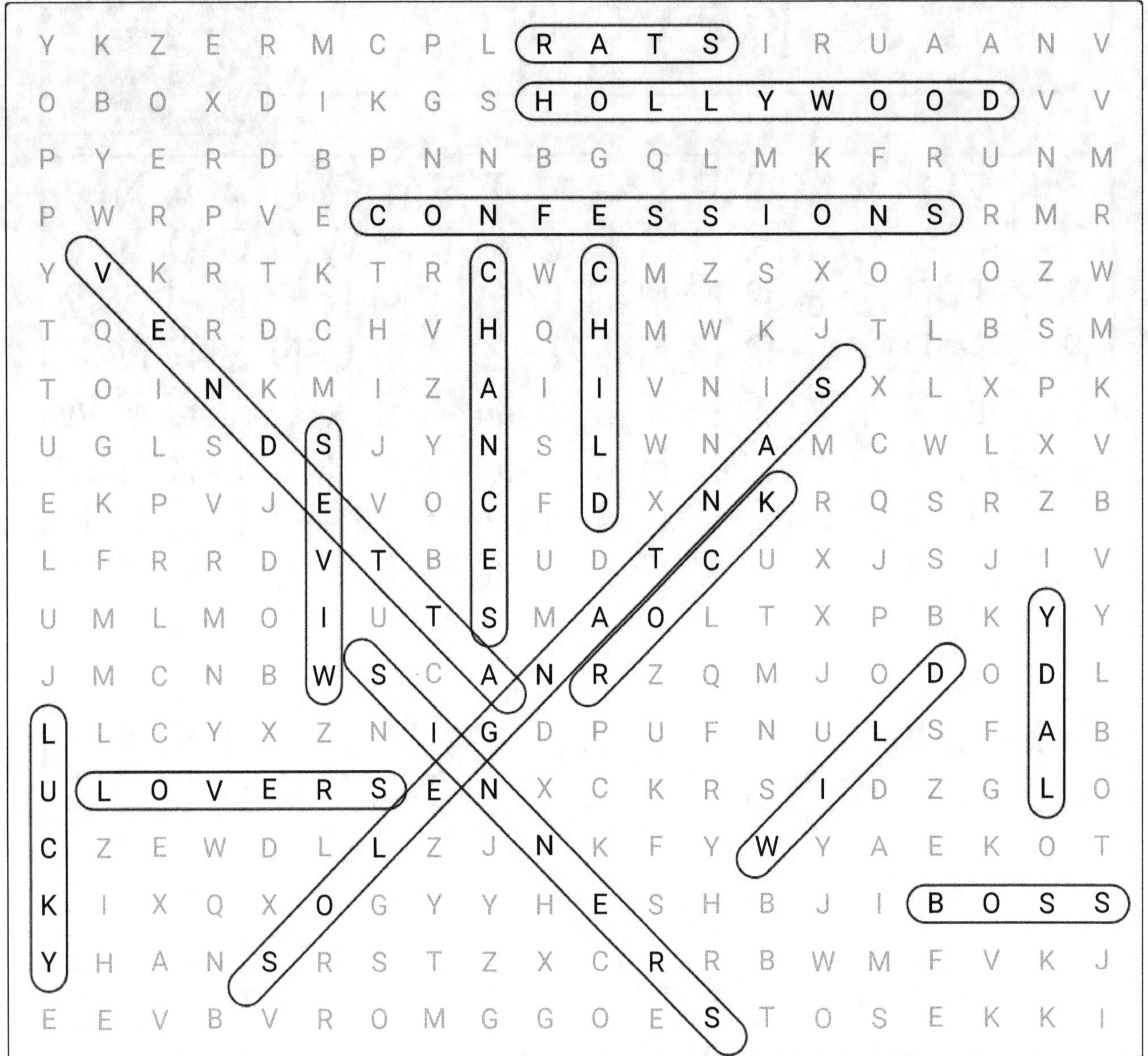

About Jackie Collins

British novelist Jackie Collins captivated readers with her steamy and scandalous tales of Hollywood glamour and intrigue. Her gripping storytelling and larger-than-life characters made her a best-selling author and a beloved figure in the world of popular fiction.

Trivia Questions

➢Q1. Which of Jackie Collins' novels is about a woman named Lucky Santangelo who becomes a successful businesswoman?

➢Q2. What is the name of the character in Jackie Collins' novel "Hollywood Wives"?

➢Q3. Which of Jackie Collins' novels is about a woman named Madison Castelli who is trying to make it in Hollywood?

➢Q4. What is the name of the character in Jackie Collins' novel "The Stud"?

➢Q5. Which of Jackie Collins' novels is about a woman named Fontaine Khaled who is trying to save her husband's business empire?

➢Q6. Which of Jackie Collins' novels is about a woman named Tracy who is trying to find her missing sister?

➢Q7. What is the name of the character in Jackie Collins' novel "Lethal Seduction"?

➢Q8. Which of Jackie Collins' novels is about a woman named Gino Santangelo who becomes a powerful crime boss?

➢Q9. Which of Jackie Collins' novels is about a woman named Denver Jones who is trying to solve a mystery surrounding her family's past?

➢Q10. What is the name of the character in Jackie Collins' novel "Chances" who rises from poverty to become a successful businesswoman?

Turn the page upside down to see the answers.

A1. "Chances." A2. Neil Gray, A3. "Hollywood Kids." A4. Tony Blake. A5. "Lucky." A6. "Thrill!" A7. Madison Castelli. A8. "Lady Boss." A9. "Drop Dead Beautiful." A10. Lucky Santangelo.

Ernest Hemingway

```
B G T Y F J P V G P R I E C T L Y W U S
S H M P T Y A T H L U Z N S V Z M R S M
K R S B C C C N S W N U O X M M C E T Z
X N J N W H Z R S N S N T N L A J H Q Z
U W M O O K T Q E P Z B G E I Q D C R K
B C P T Y W K F B K G A Q O G C A A P M
U D W T G X S W P U C B R M X W K Q I Q
F W U G H M Q U V R V T I Y O U J H X G
A V M E T O L L S A W P S Q J H C R L E
R M G A S A S L B Y T C E Y M C W D Y P
E U Q U N S E M E I X A S Z W A X P I M
W D Z A U Z D D L B A V L Y R U G L G M
E D O D R T E K L L X A S E O P L K K
L K O S H M B T R N O G T I O U Z D J Y
L N A E S G S C U R R O H G H I L G P F
Z F F R A O H C V E O Y P E E O H D H K
T M J O P F V O Z B F E G E H O Y Z V T
O E I S U S L L F D I Z U W X G G I F H
```

Adams	For	Sea
Also	Man	Snows
Arms	Nick	Sun
Bell	Old	Tolls
Farewell	Rises	Whom

SOLUTION

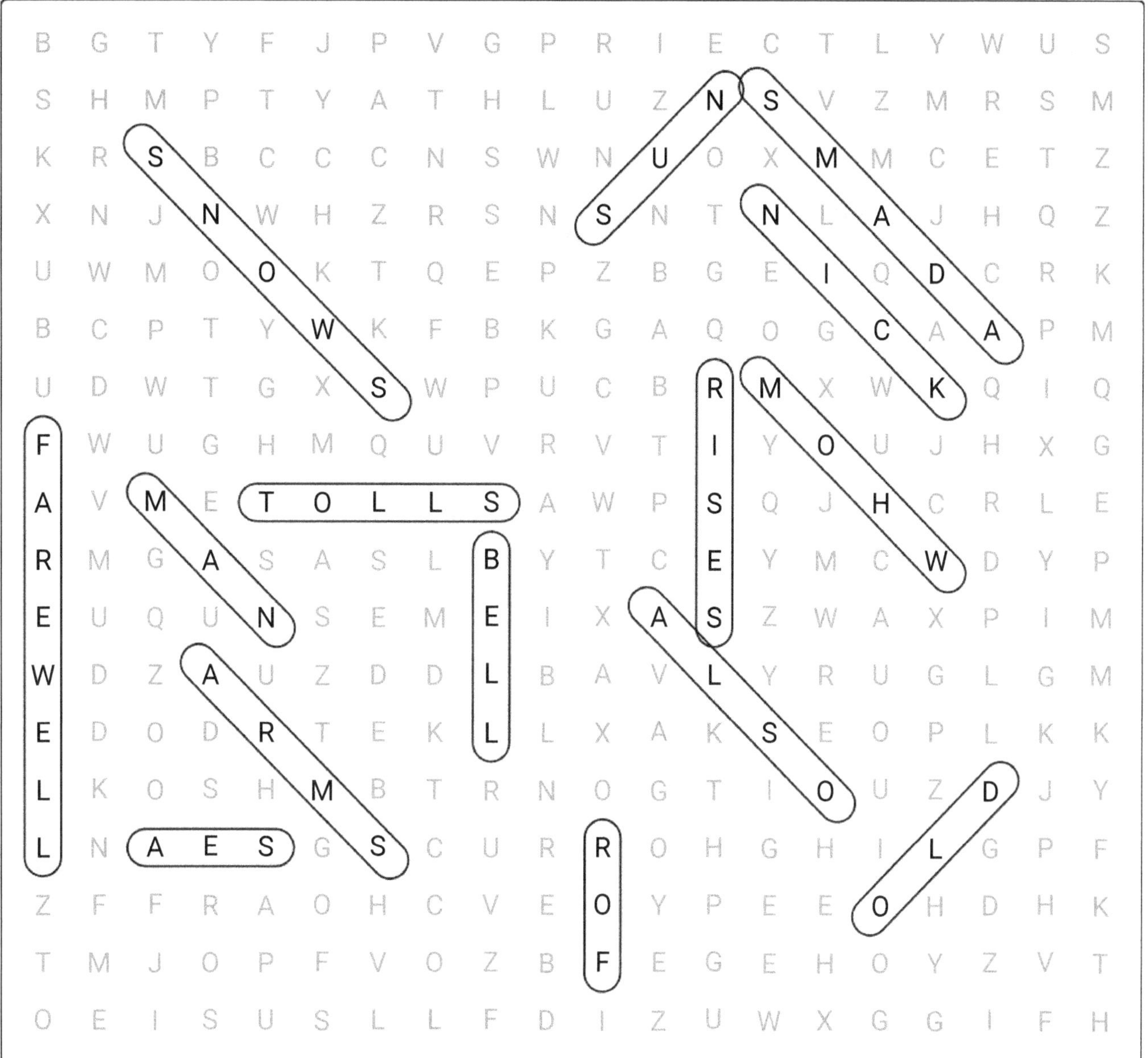

About Ernest Hemingway

Ernest Hemingway, an American writer, is esteemed for his terse, minimalist prose and deeply affecting narratives. His exploration of themes such as love, war, and the human experience has cemented his place as one of the most influential authors of the 20th century.

Trivia Questions

➢Q1. In which Ernest Hemingway novel does the character Santiago strive to catch a colossal marlin?

➢Q2. In Ernest Hemingway's "The Sun Also Rises," what is the name of the central character?

➢Q3. Which Ernest Hemingway novel features a character named Robert Jordan engaged in the Spanish Civil War?

➢Q4. In Ernest Hemingway's "A Farewell to Arms," what is the name of the main character?

➢Q5. Which Ernest Hemingway novel centres around a character named Harry on a hunting expedition in Africa?

➢Q6. Which Ernest Hemingway novel follows a character named Nick during a fishing trip in Michigan?

➢Q7. In Ernest Hemingway's "For Whom the Bell Tolls," what is the name of the central character?

➢Q8. Which Ernest Hemingway novel features a character named David Bourne on a fishing trip in France?

➢Q9. In which Ernest Hemingway novel does the character Jake Barnes struggle to deal with his war injury?

➢Q10. In Ernest Hemingway's "Islands in the Stream," what is the name of the main character, a painter residing in the Bahamas?

Turn the page upside down to see the answers.

A1. "The Old Man and the Sea." A2. Jake Barnes. A3. "For Whom the Bell Tolls." A4. Frederic Henry. A5. "The Short Happy Life of Francis Macomber." A6. "The Big Two-Hearted River." A7. Robert Jordan. A8. "The Garden of Eden." A9. "The Sun Also Rises." A10. Thomas Hudson.

Anne Rice

```
C D Q P W C D U X U A N O J Q B F E W H
T Y Q U M D L U E E R K A E K B A D I D
A R B F A M N F T R E E O L V T A N Q T
T Q W U T Q N Z D N T S C I Z O T T M D
S W J S P Q T T F Q P S O Y D E O A X E
E D I L M B G I P T L Z I O R S Z L E B
L X G T M E T U Y E L D O V V Y A H T J W
P D J C C P R N D M X L I M R G T O J Q
N P U Y H H A Y T X B E M M E C T S U K
A L X M R R I M P R W U A E R L T E T N
L N P K P K N T D M N R A A C E K A M
J A V G N F S E G B D I E U M N D X W U
V O A J I D N P N A P S I Z S S E V I L
R X H Y C W V W A M U B I M E P Q L U V
A T R S L I X H A B H O U R S S T K Z D
R Z Q F E T Z V R N O H X O L H S L Z A
H F L I S H A O G P T H A J F D B B K M
Y R S L Z G U E P J W D E N M A D M Z L
```

Armand	Interview	Ramses
Blood	Lestat	Taltos
Chronicles	Lives	Vampire
Damned	Mummy	Witching
Hour	Queen	With

SOLUTION

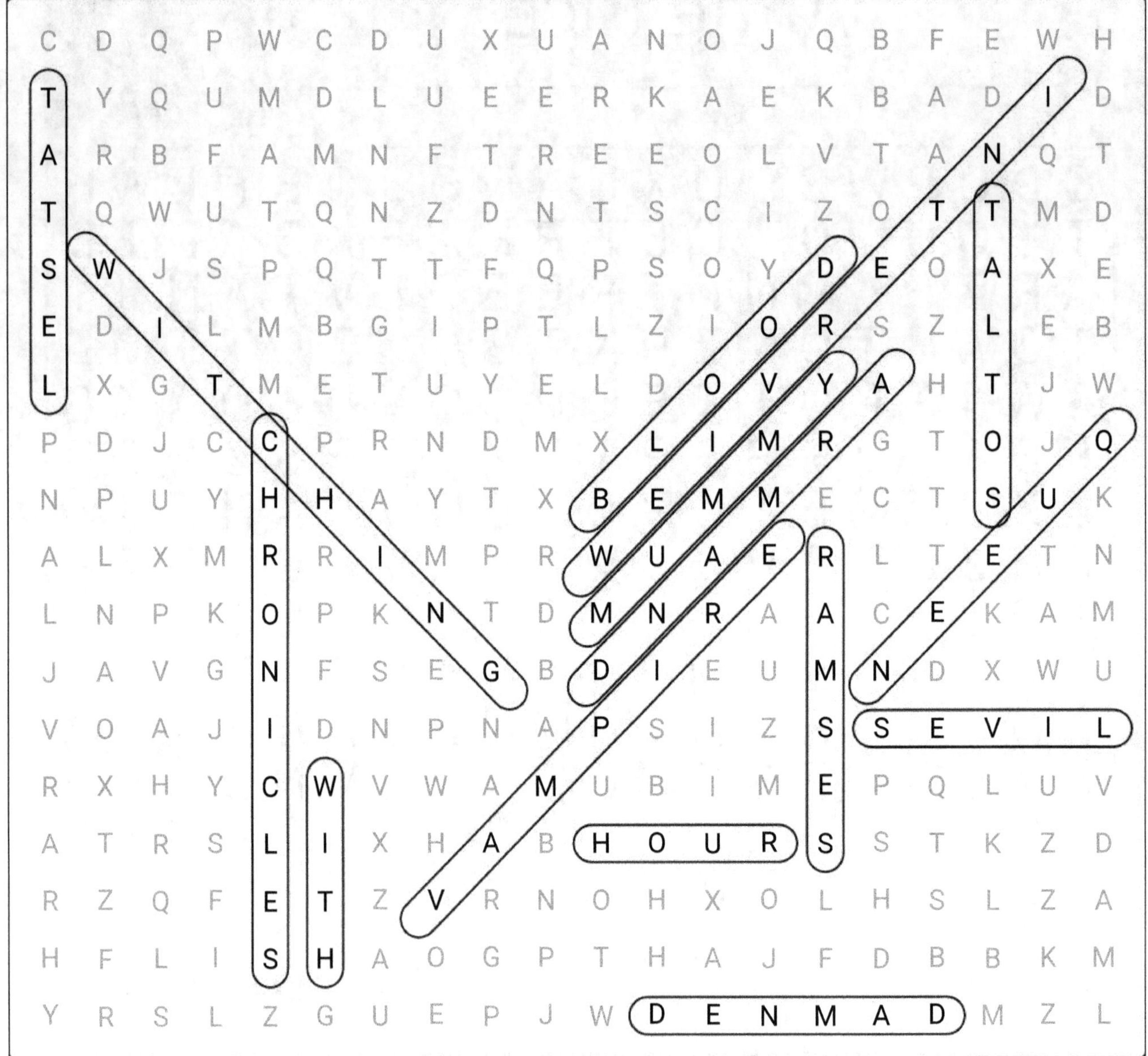

About Anne Rice

American author Anne Rice is best known for her gothic fiction, particularly her "Vampire Chronicles" series. Her vivid imagination and evocative storytelling have enthralled readers, making her a prominent figure in the realm of supernatural and horror fiction.

Trivia Questions

➤Q1. Which of Anne Rice's novels is about a vampire named Louis de Pointe du Lac?

➤Q2. What is the name of the character in Anne Rice's novel "The Witching Hour"?

➤Q3. Which of Anne Rice's novels is about a young woman named Pandora who is turned into a vampire?

➤Q4. What is the name of the character in Anne Rice's novel "Taltos"?

➤Q5. Which of Anne Rice's novels is about a vampire named Lestat de Lioncourt?

➤Q6. Which of Anne Rice's novels is about a group of witches who are trying to save the world from an evil force?

➤Q7. What is the name of the character in Anne Rice's novel "The Vampire Armand"?

➤Q8. Which of Anne Rice's novels is about a man named David Talbot who is telling the story of the vampire Marius?

➤Q9. Which of Anne Rice's novels is about a vampire named Quinn Blackwood who is trying to start a new life?

➤Q10. What is the name of the character in Anne Rice's novel "Merrick" who is a witch and a vampire hunter?

Turn the page upside down to see the answers.

A1. "Interview with the Vampire." A2. Rowan Mayfair A3. "Pandora." A4. Ashlar. A5. "The Vampire Lestat." A6. "The Mayfair Witches." A7. Armand. A8. "Blood and Gold." A9. "Blackwood Farm." A10. Merrick Mayfair.

Dr. Seuss

```
R P U Y M K V Z A M Q I E D X B B Y W R
G C H S J P N J P P P J N L T F V F T G G
J F A M U L B E R R Y Q T Y B R O O O X
L G U B I Z P I C S U R R W S M Q Y X L
U R N H S P F S T U W W E H V G K K B L
T I H H Z S C B F V F A Y P T G N I H T
Q N V V I M F K X M Y T N F I S H H Z U
K C F O M L Q K G X X D D Q F G I R T C
Y H N E U W K S C S V O Z B X D L W P T
T U R T L E D V A A N M G W B N R I M T
C H E A R S B I W Y T E F W U T I I N C
M R X R W D Q N H O C M E B E L E M L C
W H A T E E N L O J G U F T V Z W I F G
S K D W O R M O O N J E J E C F S H U Q
J B Q K U F Z T T R P Q G P J H N K C L
L M K E I Z M Y S R A A Y J R N E H R Z
E S S T R E E T R Y O X N T Y I Y S N H
O S U M Q M W W X B E H K B J X I N G U
```

Cat	Horton	Street
Fish	Lorax	Thing
Grinch	Mulberry	Turtle
Hat	Red	Who
Hears	Sneetches	Yertle

SOLUTION

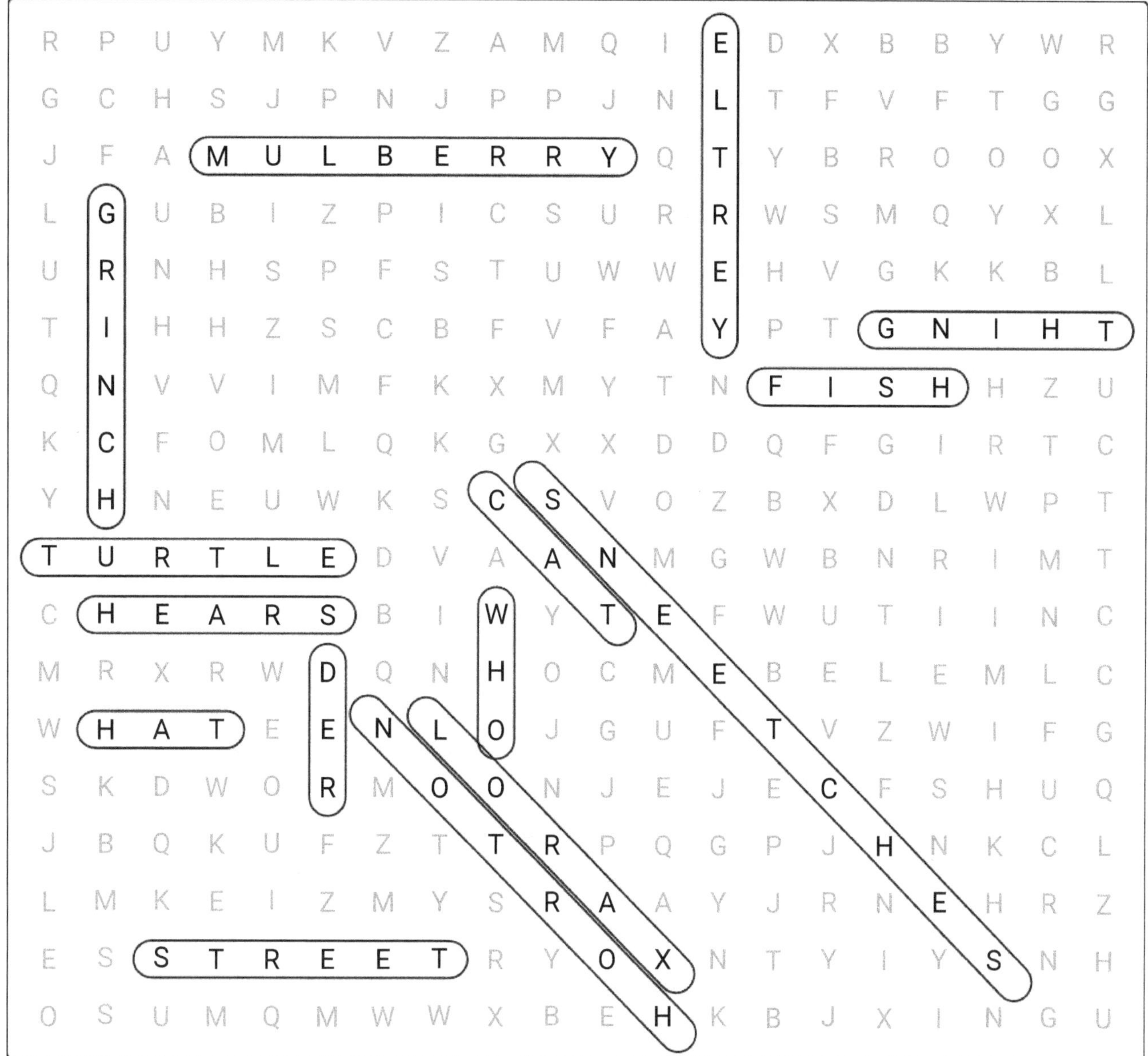

About Dr. Seuss

Dr. Seuss, an American author and illustrator, is beloved for his whimsical, imaginative children's books that feature playful rhymes and memorable characters. His timeless stories have inspired generations of young readers, solidifying his place as a cherished figure in children's literature.

Trivia Questions

➤Q1. What is the name of the character in Dr. Seuss' book "Green Eggs and Ham"?

➤Q2. Which of Dr. Seuss' books is about a character named the Lorax who speaks for the trees?

➤Q3. What is the name of the character in Dr. Seuss' book "The Cat in the Hat"?

➤Q4. Which of Dr. Seuss' books is about a character named Sam-I-Am who is trying to convince someone to try green eggs and ham?

➤Q5. What is the name of the character in Dr. Seuss' book "Horton Hears a Who!"?

➤Q6. Which of Dr. Seuss' books is about a character named the Grinch who hates Christmas?

➤Q7. What is the name of the character in Dr. Seuss' book "Oh, the Places You'll Go!"?

➤Q8. Which of Dr. Seuss' books is about a character named Thidwick who is a moose with antlers?

➤Q9. What is the name of the character in Dr. Seuss' book "Yertle the Turtle"?

➤Q10. Which of Dr. Seuss' books is about a character named the Sneetches who learns a lesson about prejudice?

Turn the page upside down to see the answers.

A1. Sam-I-Am. A2. "The Lorax." A3. The Cat in the Hat. A4. "Green Eggs and Ham." A5. Horton the Elephant. A6. "How the Grinch Stole Christmas!" A7. The reader (no specific name). A8. "Thidwick the Big-Hearted Moose." A9. Yertle the Turtle. A10. "The Sneetches."

Khaled Hosseini

```
U K V Y L N S K B F P D O Y D E E A B X
F J R R J A H H M G N I V I S J A Q T M
S E S N Z E L M G G I D D S S T H B X O
E V A N D P R A Y E R N W B F W F H F U
P L S T H S O J Q C E E M M G P R R Z N
V Y M X X G Q B O L I L S R Q H E S P T
M J K O C M N Y P E Y P S N I N Q Q G A
N H M G U Q M S I X C S J D N Q V W Y I
W P Y L A N R G M D J I L U E H O R H N
J S X F L S T N D S W X R C Q O H L X S
S U K T X L N A X A D O L O T A H O F Y
I N O H O U I A I X Y O F Y Y X E C W A
E S W O K L E W L N K S V G W R A N E S
K D K U P S C R O V S E C G S W H P S J
I E D S K R F C H O M F T Y U Q A T P E
F V X A W N H B C K G D N J N S M M I T
L A O N B R B W E P T I R Q S X K Z U I
F S C D G V W K B J K D Z O T B Y S Z K
```

And	Mountains	Splendid
Echo	Prayer	Suns
Echoed	Runner	Suns
Kite	Sea	Thousand
Mountains	Splendid	Will

SOLUTION

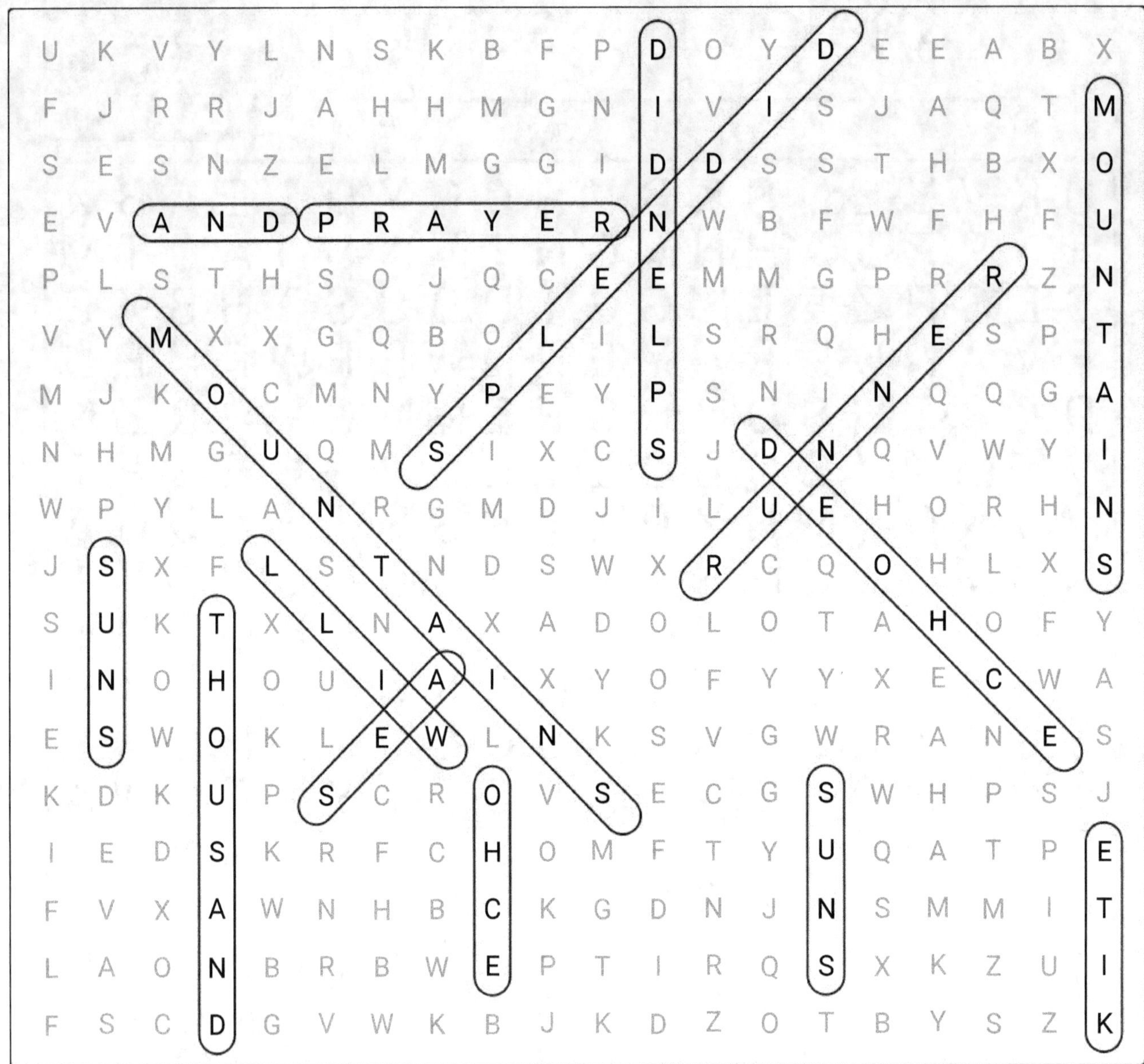

About Khaled Hosseini

Afghan-American author Khaled Hosseini is known for his heart-wrenching novels that depict the struggles of ordinary people in his native Afghanistan. His compassionate storytelling and richly drawn characters have resonated with readers worldwide, earning him widespread acclaim.

Trivia Questions

➢Q1. Which of Khaled Hosseini's novels is about a young boy named Amir and his friendship with a Hazara boy named Hassan?

➢Q2. What is the name of the character in Khaled Hosseini's novel "A Thousand Splendid Suns"?

➢Q3. Which of Khaled Hosseini's novels is about a doctor named Abdullah who is trying to save his family in war-torn Afghanistan?

➢Q4. What is the name of the character in Khaled Hosseini's novel "And the Mountains Echoed"?

➢Q5. Which of Khaled Hosseini's novels is about a young boy named Pari who is separated from his sister and his family?

➢Q6. Which of Khaled Hosseini's novels is about a man named Nabi who is a servant to a wealthy family?

➢Q7. What is the name of the character in Khaled Hosseini's novel "Sea Prayer" who is a Syrian father trying to protect his son?

➢Q8. Which of Khaled Hosseini's novels is about a man named Timur who is telling his life story to his son?

➢Q9. Which of Khaled Hosseini's novels is about a man named Markos who is trying to save his family during the Greek-Turkish War?

➢Q10. What is the name of the character in Khaled Hosseini's novel "The Kite Runner" who is searching for redemption?

Turn the page upside down to see the answers.

A1. "The Kite Runner," A2. Mariam, A3. "A Kingdom of the Wind," A4. Abdullah. A5. "And the Mountains Echoed," A6. "The Tea Girl of Hummingbird Lane," A7. Marwan. A8. "The Angel's Ego," A9. "The Mirror Maker" A10. Amir.

Jeffrey Archer

```
Y Z K T N A D B T B G H O Y Q X T P M M
X X Q U P O J F J G J T E R C E S I O K
Q U G J N L T P R O D I G A L Y H D D P
L O C U Q F D F A V I W E B W O G C T T
B C K E A K R T I K M E E S L A F H A A
I O E T J M P S U L S A B Q R A H R P I
G J H K C V A W K K C Y E V L K X O J O
P E A S V C E P E E I D N E N X M N X N
R Q H U I W M P K J X M Y I C E Z I C V
L F D E A N T Q K M E D D P Q M M C K X
F A O S M T S R W J G G A J A B E L A E
S T P J O R N T L B Y R Z U Y K G E N E
H E P F U M E T T G D G F F G M B S E A
M G T F F U V N K H K B L G V H E O O I
L E R D A P A P I N E Z U Z K N T R X C
S K S M E H E V C S K Q N R J B U E I F
B L R M Q W H H T W I D U F Y C K K R D
W G R P R I S O N E R L C P S R N A L I
```

Abel	Daughter	Kept
Be	False	Prisoner
Best	Father	Prodigal
Chronicles	Heaven	Secret
Clifton	Kane	Sins

SOLUTION

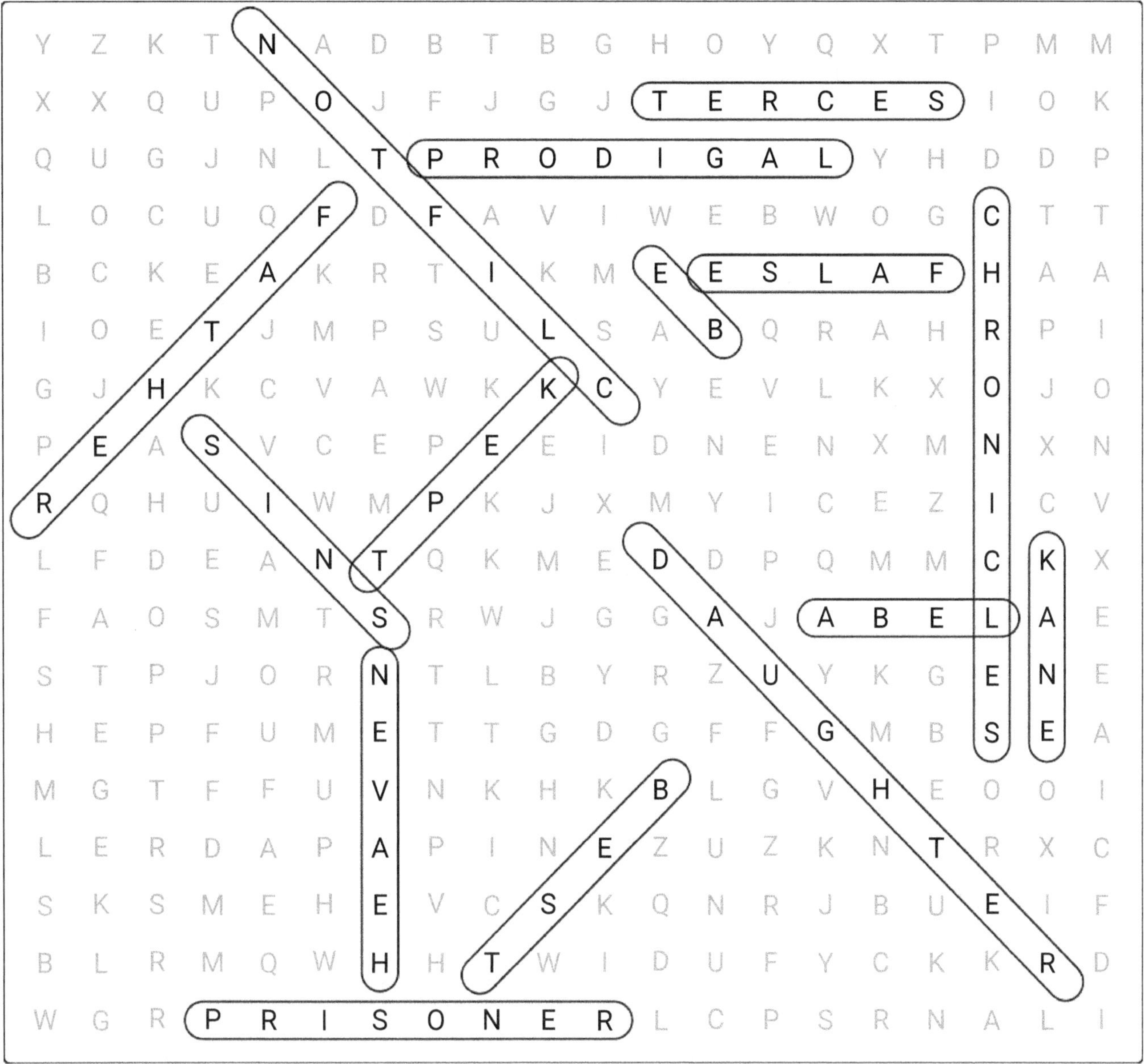

About Jeffrey Archer

British author Jeffrey Archer is recognized for his thrilling political dramas and suspenseful crime novels. His engaging storytelling, intricate plots, and memorable characters have made him a popular and respected figure in contemporary fiction.

Trivia Questions

➤Q1. Which of Jeffrey Archer's novels is about a man named Harry Clifton who rises from poverty to become a successful author?

➤Q2. What is the name of the character in Jeffrey Archer's novel "Kane and Abel"?

➤Q3. Which of Jeffrey Archer's novels is about a man named Charlie who is falsely accused of a crime?

➤Q4. What is the name of the character in Jeffrey Archer's novel "First Among Equals"?

➤Q5. Which of Jeffrey Archer's novels is about a man named Adam Scott who is investigating the death of his father?

➤Q6. Which of Jeffrey Archer's novels is about a man named James Keogh who is trying to clear his name after being falsely accused of a crime?

➤Q7. What is the name of the character in Jeffrey Archer's novel "A Prisoner of Birth"?

➤Q8. Which of Jeffrey Archer's novels is about a man named Alexander Karpenko who is on the run from the KGB?

➤Q9. Which of Jeffrey Archer's novels is about a woman named Florentyna Kane who becomes the first female president of the United States?

➤Q10. What is the name of the character in Jeffrey Archer's novel "Not a Penny More, Not a Penny Less" who is seeking revenge against a con artist?

Turn the page upside down to see the answers.

A1. "The Clifton Chronicles." A2. William Lowell Kane and Abel Rosnovski. A3. "False Impression." A4. Charles Seymour A5. "The Fourth Estate." A6. "Paths of Glory." A7. Danny Cartwright. A8. "Heads You Win." A9. "The Prodigal Daughter." A10. Harvey Metcalfe.

Jack Canfield

```
E X I L M E X Q F J D H A W A X Z F Y B
Y F A Q C O I G M W R Y L H O J Y K H N
U Z F A C T O R Z P J O A A C Q C O E E
M I W T H K D Z Y I H J D F Q W I K P N
O K R X W B P S C O V U D A M H C M E S
O H W M L G U G U N K X I R A I W Y E M
E X A B K P M M A E S M N V H O D C Y W
M V T O D R I U X W G T Z C M M V Y P O
Z C U E K I R M X I S L K E K T L E K L
W X I Y R N H M J N Y T N S A I A O M M
T Z W T P C R A Q K E V O I U C N P W I
F A M P E I E J Q A O U T R E C B N D V
D C V O K P A S T O P I Q J I H C C E D
Z N T T M L Z M M U L A Q B P E L E N R
C H P S D E P U O U T Q E B M R S I S J
Y O O L E S V S L H S R B S L C K K F S
H U H I P P U D J B A E S H L F N V N E
L E E W S L C O H D O P J A P I J C F R
```

Aladdin	Life	Soup
Chicken	Peace	Stories
Dare	Principles	Success
Factor	Secret	Win
Inner	Soul	Women

SOLUTION

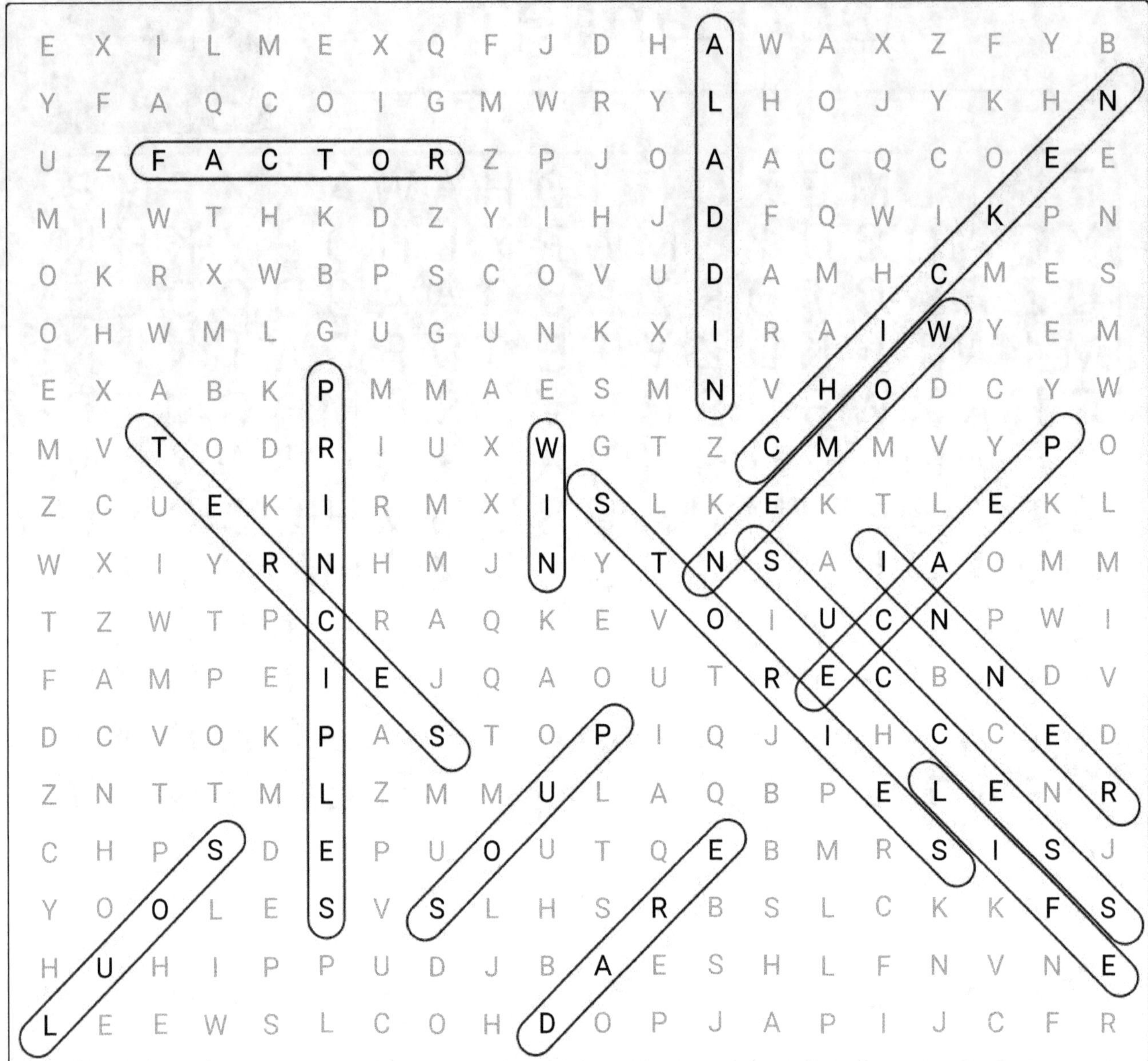

About Jack Canfield

American author Jack Canfield is celebrated for his motivational and self-help works, particularly the best-selling "Chicken Soup for the Soul" series. His uplifting stories and insightful guidance have inspired countless readers, making him a prominent figure in the personal development genre.

➢Q1. Who is the co-author of the "Chicken Soup for the Soul" series with Jack Canfield?

➢Q2. Which of Jack Canfield's books is about the power of positive thinking?

➢Q3. What is the name of the character in Jack Canfield's novel "The Success Principles"?

➢Q4. Which of Jack Canfield's books is about the law of attraction?

➢Q5. Which of Jack Canfield's books is about the importance of taking action towards your goals?

➢Q6. Which of Jack Canfield's books is about how to create wealth and abundance in your life?

➢Q7. What is the name of the character in Jack Canfield's novel "The Aladdin Factor"?

➢Q8. Which of Jack Canfield's books is about how to overcome obstacles and achieve success?

➢Q9. Which of Jack Canfield's books is about how to find and follow your life purpose?

➢Q10. Which of Jack Canfield's books is about how to improve your relationships with others?

Turn the page upside down to see the answers.

A1. Mark Victor Hansen. A2. "The Power of Focus." A3. Jack Canfield (it's a self-help book). A4. "The Key to Living the Law of Attraction." A5. "The Success Principles." A6. "The Abundance Principle." A7. Aladdin. A8. "The Success Principles." A9. "The Purpose Principles." A10. "The Relationship Principles."

Malcolm Gladwell

```
L T C K N F C A X N L C R S O R M Q P H
R P Y X T Y C O D L Z T X A T E J O O R
Z Z G O I P L G G T Z K J X S L V O R X
B K O P P M H L A B A D C R Z T N F P U
E L L H P H E O F Z I Q E I H T A B V Y
G S I F I H D R J V R I P S J I X S A O
W W A S N S H F A P L D M X T L V U D Q
W N T J G W X D N T X B O E B X H I G M
I I H J O R I Y U T A F S G B H F W L G
D G D H T Z I O J F U E B I G F U M Y G
Z Y G P O H X Q E C A N B K E R J U B R
Q O S T G B N I P H C D O R Z S G T A R
B N J E V C G X Q Q X H E P A E F J J E
R R U P Y F N J Z H H N B W D L J O Q D
N Y G B L I N K X U C M T H I N G S Q E
D Q Y E Y M A K E E Q A T A H W V H F M
D T G U Y E Z K U R I K Q P V Y Z O H E
U F A T R T O B N K T N I O P Z M X G R
```

Big	Goliath	Point
Blink	How	Saw
David	Little	Things
Difference	Make	Tipping
Dog	Outliers	What

SOLUTION

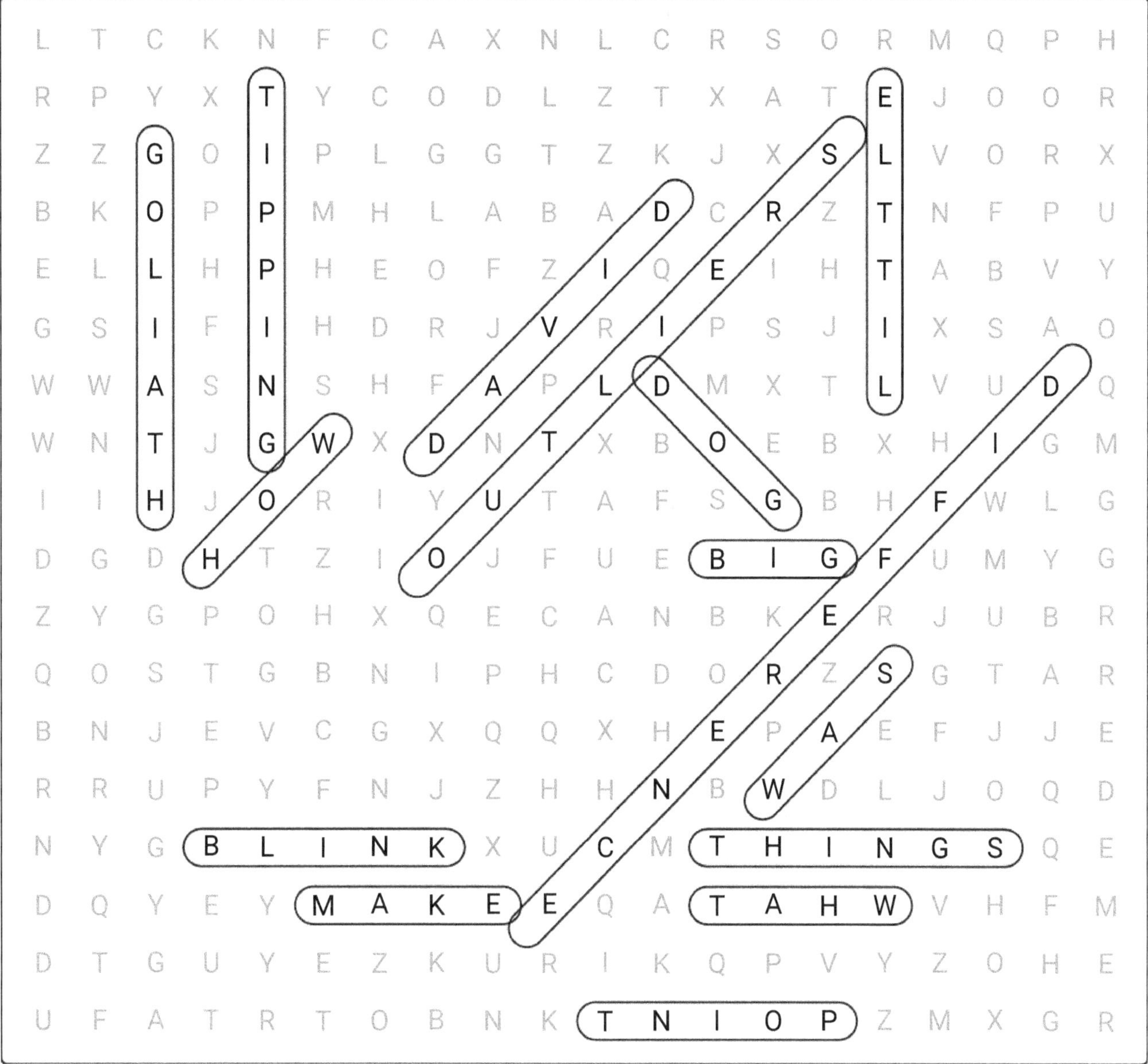

About Malcolm Gladwell

Canadian journalist and author Malcolm Gladwell is renowned for his thought-provoking nonfiction works that examine social phenomena and human behaviour. His ability to translate complex ideas into accessible and engaging narratives has made him a leading voice in contemporary popular psychology and sociology.

➢Q1. Which of Malcolm Gladwell's books is about the power of small actions and how they can create big changes?

➢Q2. What is the name of the character in Malcolm Gladwell's book "David and Goliath"?

➢Q3. Which of Malcolm Gladwell's books is about how successful people got to where they are?

➢Q4. What is the name of the character in Malcolm Gladwell's book "Blink"?

➢Q5. Which of Malcolm Gladwell's books is about how we make decisions and judgments?

➢Q6. Which of Malcolm Gladwell's books is about how people become experts in their fields?

➢Q7. What is the name of the character in Malcolm Gladwell's book "Outliers"?

➢Q8. Which of Malcolm Gladwell's books is about how we perceive and react to the world around us?

➢Q9. Which of Malcolm Gladwell's books is about how we communicate with others?

➢Q10. What is the name of the character in Malcolm Gladwell's book "What the Dog Saw" who is a dog trainer?

Turn the page upside down to see the answers.

A1. "The Tipping Point." A2. David. A3. "Outliers." A4. None (it's a non-fiction book). A5. "Thinking, Fast and Slow." A6. "Outliers." A7. None (it's a non-fiction book). A8. "The Power of Thinking Without Thinking." A9. "Talking to Strangers." A10. Cesar Millan.

Roald Dahl

```
T D G Y S H J R M I U D M R A G C E E S
U K F F K I D I S J T M K D F I Y L D O
Q I B K F L A H V A Z J T V T T N E Q N B
Q C O Y M O R V U D W W J S E Z R R A B
N Z H T E Y X W Q M A L A J A U L D B X
J R B A L O H D F Q L T X L R C L S C X
Y W I J R J V I F Q N T F P T I V A O O
R J O U Y L E R F A L H E V T R G Z M K
O X V I F M I H F I C A I A T B P V Q L
T G C L M M R E X A H M M H Z W L K M R
C T I I R T E B E G W C K Q F L I Z R P
A K X D M H S P A F V O J P O K G T M T
F R D K X G I A N T U U A O F O U Z S S
K Z Y M W X H W D W A Q M I X L S C V W
W I T C H E S E J A U T E S P L T K I T
H D W K O Z P B M I J R S E H R C G D M
E B K K N O F P N R R O Y A Y D V B Y Y
H F J G D X K G G I Z T D C Z K P F U N
```

Bfg	Fantastic	Mr
Charlie	Fox	Peach
Dahl	Giant	Trot
Esio	James	Twits
Factory	Matilda	Witches

SOLUTION

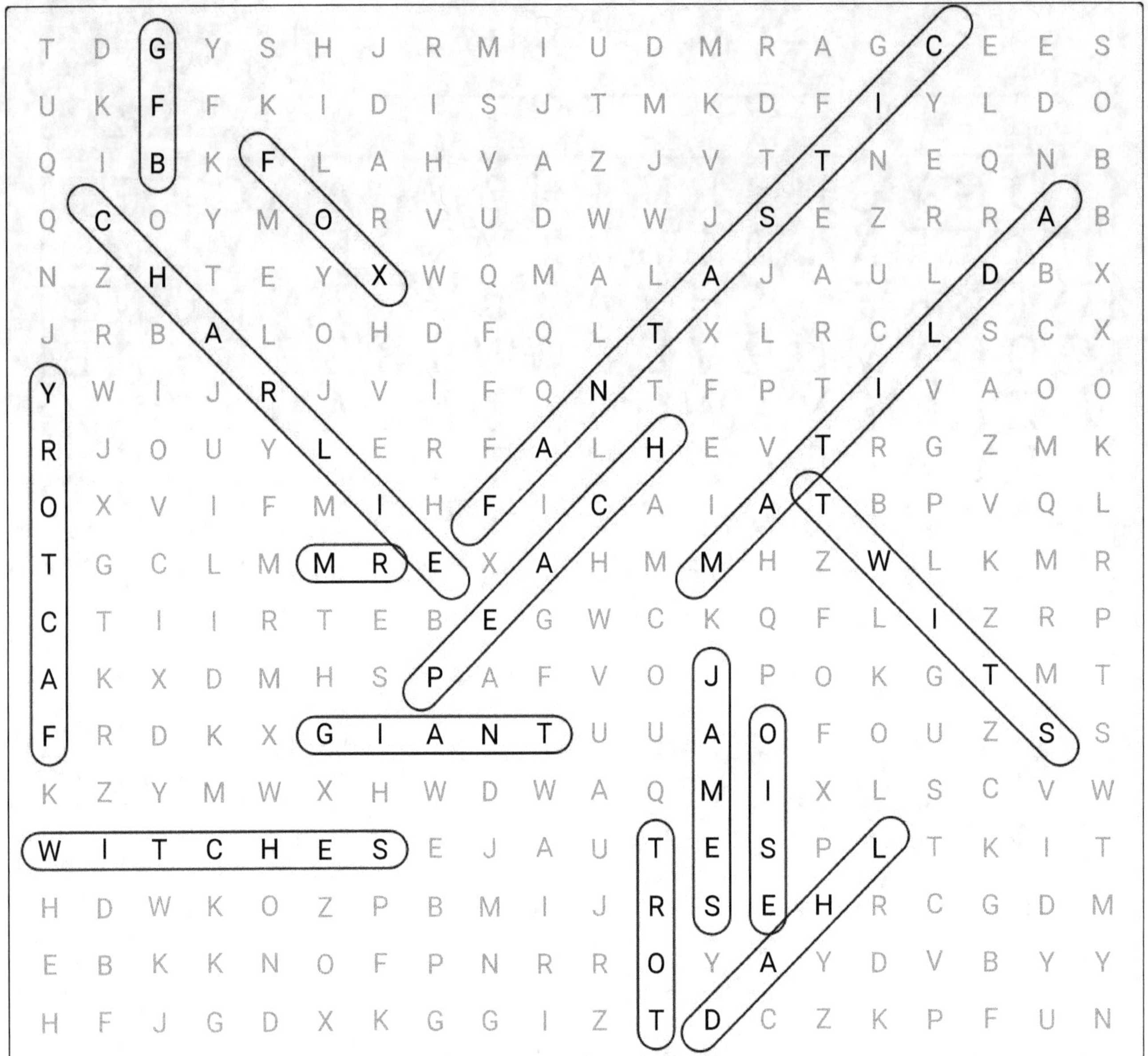

About Roald Dahl

British author Roald Dahl is cherished for his imaginative and whimsical children's stories, which often feature elements of the fantastical and macabre. His timeless tales and unforgettable characters have captured the hearts of readers of all ages, making him an enduring figure in children's literature.

Trivia Questions

➢Q1. What is the name of the character in Roald Dahl's book "Matilda" who has telekinetic powers?

➢Q2. Which of Roald Dahl's books is about a boy named Charlie who wins a golden ticket to visit a chocolate factory?

➢Q3. What is the name of the character in Roald Dahl's book "James and the Giant Peach"?

➢Q4. Which of Roald Dahl's books is about a group of animals who go on a journey to save a young boy from his evil aunts?

➢Q5. What is the name of the character in Roald Dahl's book "The BFG" who is a giant?

➢Q6. Which of Roald Dahl's books is about a girl named Sophie who befriends a giant and tries to stop other giants from eating children?

➢Q7. What is the name of the character in Roald Dahl's book "The Witches" who is turned into a mouse?

➢Q8. Which of Roald Dahl's books is about a girl named Mary who discovers a magical garden?

➢Q9. What is the name of the character in Roald Dahl's book "Danny the Champion of the World" who goes on a pheasant hunting adventure with his father?

➢Q10. Which of Roald Dahl's books is about a group of foxes who outsmart three farmers?

Turn the page upside down to see the answers.

A1. Matilda Wormwood. A2. "Charlie and the Chocolate Factory." A3. James Henry Trotter. A4. "Fantastic Mr. Fox." A5. The Big Friendly Giant (BFG). A6. "The BFG." A7. Luke Eveshim. A8. "The Secret Garden" (Dahl wrote the introduction). A9. Danny. A10. "The Fantastic Mr. Fox."

Wilbur Smith

```
S Q E N X E G E R T T D A R K H O C T C
K Q V N E E Z E O G V S U A B X O V H B
R J J K W A E A S O H D G A E Y Y D U Z
Q H Q P K Q T J L H J S N W Q Y W P N V
K A O I P I D F P N U N S X Y G T N D P
N R K K A K B S F X E T P W X O I A E C
N Y I T W G H G H R X H H H W P T C R X
M I E V T V M L M I G N A D C V D C S E
G D B P E K X A F K E O H U N T S M A N
P M I M W R N D L D Q T S R G S A M R L
B I R D S C K Y N G G X U B A O N C N P
D O Q W R R M U Q U E S T B T R D I D P
I D F B K I O F C A Y M W E W C Y A C F
G U J Q M S B D P E T B C H M F M E F P
V W V P D F F N R A S G R A T S F D M Y
K K O P T O G P U K J K M E R E D E G A
H E U Q G V U H V S D R A P O E L J U P
A P A R T H E I D H Z D A B T Z O G F D
```

Apartheid	Huntsman	Sound
Bannerman	Leopard	Star
Birds	Prey	Sunbird
Dark	Quest	Taita
God	River	Thunder

SOLUTION

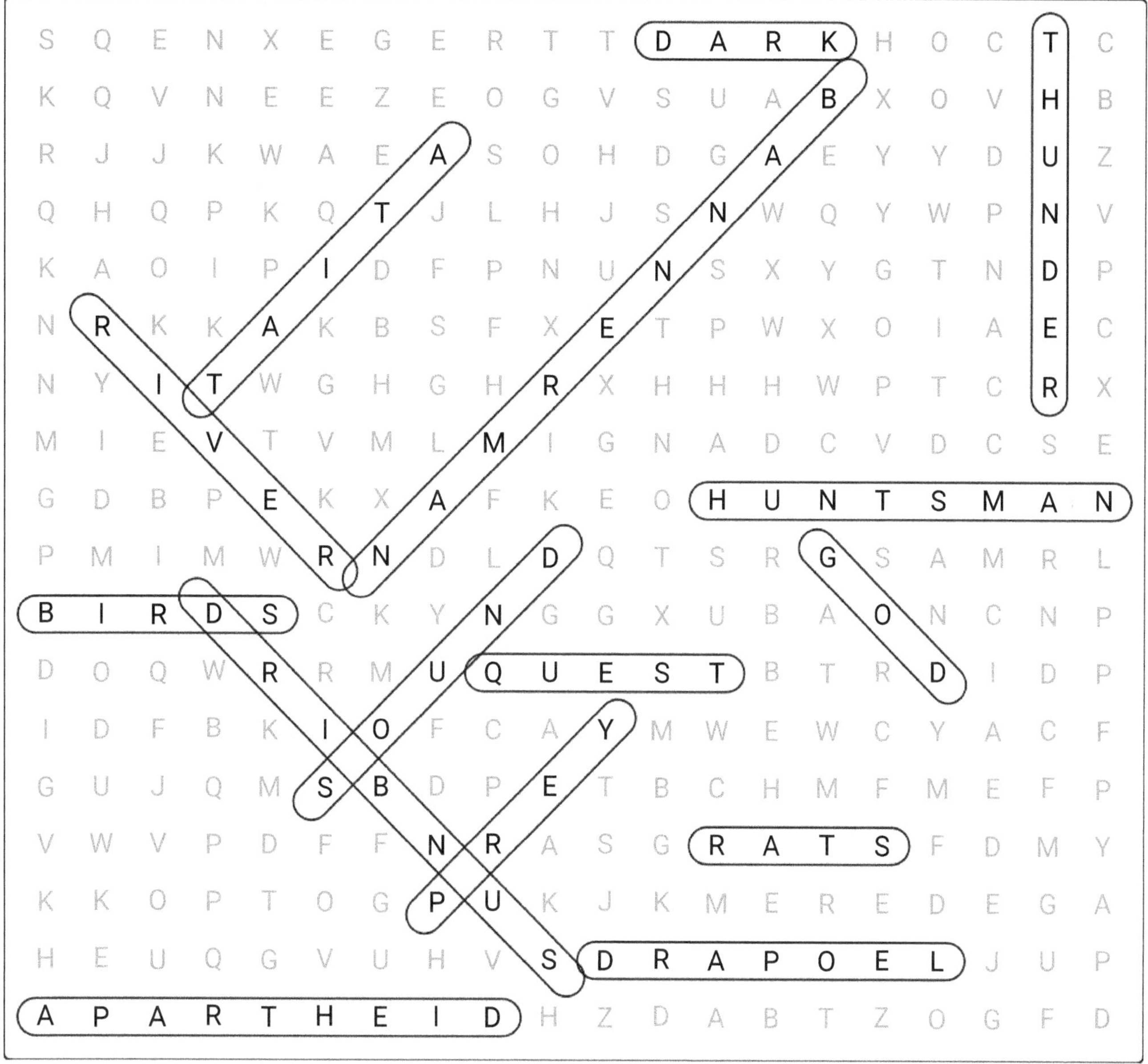

About Wilbur Smith

South African writer Wilbur Smith is acclaimed for his sweeping historical novels and thrilling adventure stories, often set against the backdrop of his native continent. His vivid storytelling and extensive research have made him a popular and respected figure in the world of adventure fiction.

Trivia Questions

➢Q1. Which of Wilbur Smith's novels is about an Egyptian Pharaoh named Taita?

➢Q2. What is the name of the character in Wilbur Smith's novel "River God" who is a slave in ancient Egypt?

➢Q3. Which of Wilbur Smith's novels is about a man named Sean Courtney and his family in Africa?

➢Q4. What is the name of the character in Wilbur Smith's novel "The Seventh Scroll" who is trying to find the tomb of an ancient queen?

➢Q5. Which of Wilbur Smith's novels is about a man named Nicholas Berg who is a pilot during World War I?

➢Q6. Which of Wilbur Smith's novels is about a man named Jim Courtney who is a pilot during World War II?

➢Q7. What is the name of the character in Wilbur Smith's novel "Warlock" who is a pharaoh's daughter?

➢Q8. Which of Wilbur Smith's novels is about a man named Leon Courtney who is a soldier in Africa during World War I?

➢Q9. Which of Wilbur Smith's novels is about a man named Craig Mellow who returns to Africa to find his family's estate in ruins?

➢Q10. What is the name of the character in Wilbur Smith's novel "The Sunbird" who is an archaeologist searching for a lost city?

Turn the page upside down to see the answers.

A1. "The Warlock Series." A2. Taita. A3. "The Courtney Series." A4. Royan Al Simma. A5. "The Triumph of the Sun." A6. "Birds of Prey." A7. Lostris. A8. "When the Lion Feeds." A9. "The Dark of the Sun." A10. Ben Kazin.

Mark Twain

```
M Q U O R I V E R U T E P Q E T G Q A X
F I X M K F I N N O C E N T S U F W R Y
M C T J Z I N S G G O H T P M C M U K I
G F R Q A M U M H B T P M D C I H Z E Y
I B H F R Y Q B J W Y I E O V T D L N Y
R M N I F W Y V P U C C E O R C N R E U
O X K N X D N R R D N V X A W E Y N A Q
G Z J N A H I E R S A W Y E R N R P R I
K F G O Q N P D Y E G A Q R V N X W P U
D O R E C U N Z Z L B F V Z D O N P X L
R B S E A V G E C R F E R D O C I N O E
A N A P K I N G E R U M L Y D S D L C Z
E Y Y O P F I X J O U Y E K S M L J S G
I U Z I C V H B S T G E N I C B B X C C
T E Z V H R G A E L K Q S M V U K V J A
F F O G U E U W W N E S M O Q E H U W E
U D M O T K O D A L I Y C Z Q J F I C G
P I F S O Y R Y Y M M W K L I H X Q D L
```

Abroad	Innocents	River
Arthur	King	Roughing
Connecticut	Mississippi	Sawyer
Finn	Pauper	Tom
Huckleberry	Prince	Yankee

SOLUTION

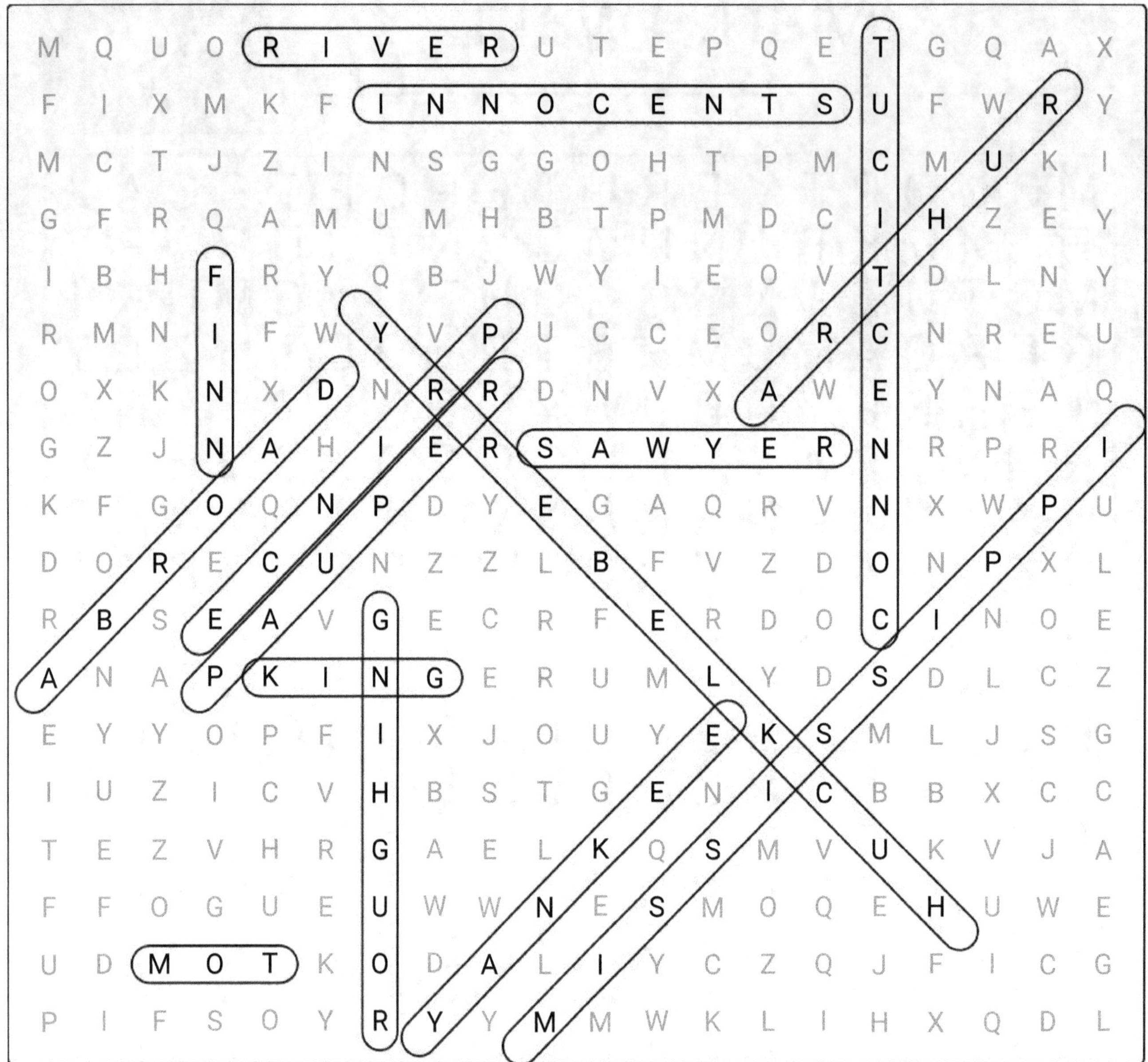

About Mark Twain

American author Mark Twain is celebrated for his witty and satirical works, which often provide a biting commentary on society and human nature. His engaging storytelling and memorable characters, such as Tom Sawyer and Huckleberry Finn, have secured his place as a leading figure in 19th-century American literature.

Trivia Questions

➢Q1. What is the name of the character in Mark Twain's novel "The Adventures of Huckleberry Finn"?

➢Q2. Which of Mark Twain's novels is about a man named Hank Morgan who travels back in time to King Arthur's court?

➢Q3. What is the name of the character in Mark Twain's novel "The Adventures of Tom Sawyer"?

➢Q4. Which of Mark Twain's novels is about a man named Edward Tudor who switches places with a pauper named Tom Canty?

➢Q5. Which of Mark Twain's novels is about a group of boys who form a club and have adventures together?

➢Q6. Which of Mark Twain's novels is about a man named Pudd'nhead Wilson who tries to solve a murder mystery?

➢Q7. What is the name of the character in Mark Twain's novel "A Connecticut Yankee in King Arthur's Court"?

➢Q8. Which of Mark Twain's novels is about a man named Adam who is the first man on Earth?

➢Q9. Which of Mark Twain's novels is about a young boy named Johnny who runs away from home and becomes a pirate?

➢Q10. What is the name of the character in Mark Twain's novel "The Prince and the Pauper" who switches places with a prince?

Turn the page upside down to see the answers.

A1. Huckleberry Finn. A2. "A Connecticut Yankee in King Arthur's Court." A3. Tom Sawyer. A4. "The Prince and the Pauper." A5. "The Adventures of Tom Sawyer." A6. "Pudd'nhead Wilson." A7. Hank Morgan. A8. "The Diaries of Adam and Eve." A9. "The Adventures of Tom Sawyer Abroad." A10. Tom Canty.

C.s. Lewis

```
L W P A X Y G H G N O A H A D S X G U C
X A H T V V A W A L I O D Z T I T L V L
B T S S L R E U Q N Y S Y B T O T L T H
Z C X T U U Y H H Q A F M O T E L B H H
B M Y T P W O N F V D I C Y Z P Q D C B
Z M V K S G O O H Z K T P A Z X N A C S
I L L V N E Z V Z C P L R S X P J W N I
Q G Y I F W M R Z H M H I E A C L N E C
S C R E W T A P E A R U D O A C Z B A U
J F Z F R J A L U I A Y Y E N D O B I M
S Y Y D G K P Z E R O U T C Q R E S Y W
T K T F N L S Y M H A R P W D T Q R J C
E C J E X R T I B I S P X R M Y S R L U
C R C X E Q F T N A N I A K H T A E I M
M L R T J B Z R U F T W L C J V D V W U
N Z T N F T A Q Q K N T T E C K I L L C
Z E D W M N K Z K F H I L E N K V I W R
L V J J E A L M P X W B Z E G T M S N E
```

Battle	Letters	Silent
Caspian	Lion	Silver
Chair	Narnia	Treader
Dawn	Out	Wardrobe
Last	Screwtape	Witch

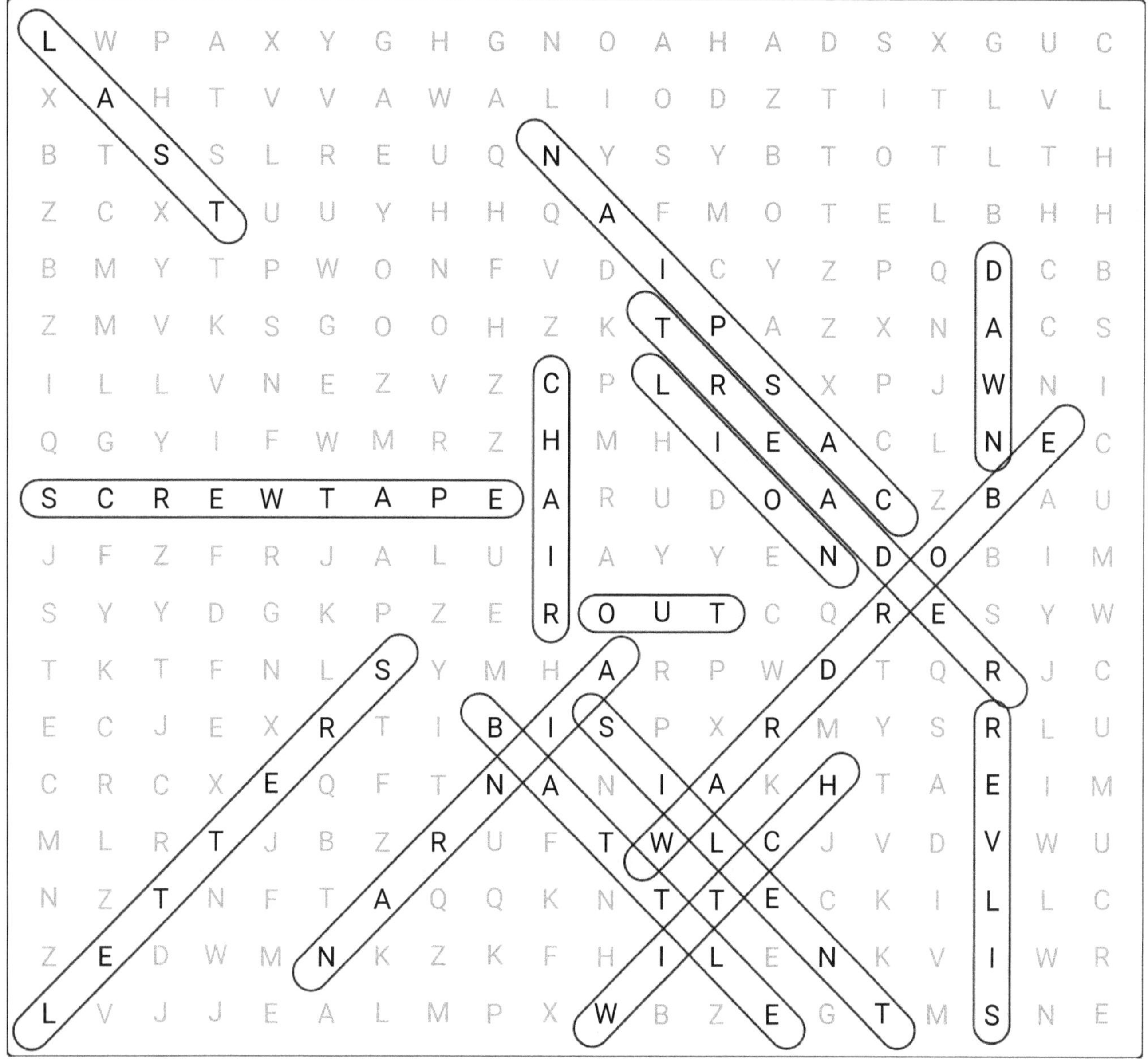

About C.s. Lewis

British author C.S. Lewis is renowned for his Christian allegories and captivating fantasy novels, including "The Chronicles of Narnia" series. His thought-provoking themes and imaginative storytelling have made him a beloved figure in both religious and secular literature.

➢Q1. Which of C.S. Lewis's novels is about a magical land called Narnia?

➢Q2. What is the name of the character in C.S. Lewis's novel "The Lion, the Witch and the Wardrobe"?

➢Q3. Which of C.S. Lewis's novels is about a man named Ransom who travels to Mars?

➢Q4. What is the name of the character in C.S. Lewis's novel "The Screwtape Letters"?

➢Q5. Which of C.S. Lewis's novel is about a group of people who are on a journey to find a kidnapped prince?

➢Q6. Which of C.S. Lewis's novels is about a man named Digory who travels to a magical world?

➢Q7. What is the name of the character in C.S. Lewis's novel "The Great Divorce" who takes a journey to Heaven and Hell?

➢Q8. Which of C.S. Lewis's novel is about a man named Elwin Ransom who travels to Venus?

➢Q9. Which of C.S. Lewis's novels is about a group of animals who go on a journey to save a kidnapped prince?

➢Q10. What is the name of the character in C.S. Lewis's novel "Till We Have Faces" who is a queen?

Turn the page upside down to see the answers.

A1. "The Chronicles of Narnia." A2. Lucy Pevensie. A3. "Out of the Silent Planet." A4. Screwtape. A5. "The Silver Chair." A6. "The Magician's Nephew." A7. None (it's a non-fiction book). A8. "Perelandra." A9. "The Horse and His Boy." A10. Psyche.

William Shakespeare

```
W I Y T B J U L I E T K H Q E L L J F A
A W G A F Q E L Z H D F L V N R M G C N
Y D X H C Z H Z E T U U Q H P D N Q A N
X W O C W T G Q I A B S E F N I D A J C
B E S M E K E Q M B R C E W H I J Q J Q
C O I B N O Y V F O H K P T Y G G V R J
M B C M K H B R X M O Z O E P Z N H B M
Z A L U V E N I C E G N G W Q E E M T X
M D C Z W J S W L O R L L S G H E R T S
M U C H V B O J I Y O T H E L L O N C A
O A F T G Z T H O W C Q C X L C A E X L
E I W T X H H C A S Q W C K V H H P G J
M I B E D A T V V H O M C U C R B T T L
O T O S E M U F H R W W L R W Q Y W X V
R H S D C L O E H A Z Z E J Q Z I M H D
K W K Z A E B Y W I K M N F M L G Z Q U
J U U E L T A L R L Y P K I N G C B A N
A A M I O R O R E M M U S D I M D C W C
```

About	Lear	Night's
Ado	Macbeth	Nothing
Hamlet	Merchant	Othello
Juliet	Midsummer	Romeo
King	Much	Venice

SOLUTION

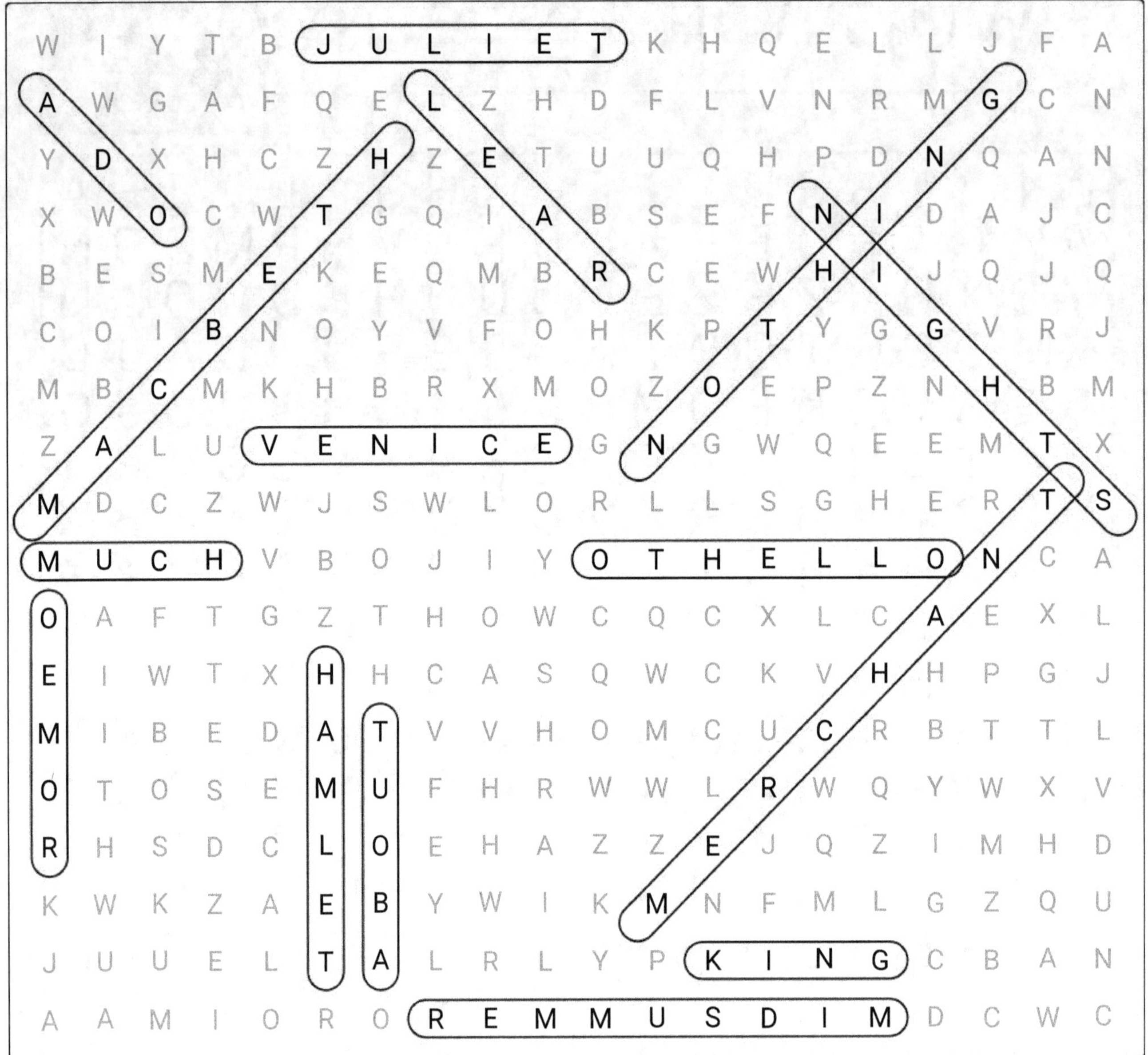

About William Shakespeare

English playwright and poet William Shakespeare is revered for his profound exploration of the human experience, brought to life through his timeless plays and sonnets. His masterful command of language and keen insight into the complexities of human nature have made him one of the most influential figures in world literature.

Trivia Questions

➢Q1. In which English town was William Shakespeare born?

➢Q2. What is the name of the theatre in London associated with William Shakespeare's plays?

➢Q3. Which two monarchs ruled England during the majority of Shakespeare's lifetime?

➢Q4. How many plays are generally attributed to William Shakespeare?

➢Q5. What are the three main genres of plays written by Shakespeare?

➢Q6. Which Shakespeare play features the famous line "To be, or not to be: that is the question"?

➢Q7. Which of Shakespeare's plays is considered the longest?

➢Q8. What is the name of the group of actors that performed most of Shakespeare's plays?

➢Q9. Which Shakespeare play is set in the ancient city of Ephesus?

➢Q10. Who is the famous historical figure portrayed in three of Shakespeare's plays?

Turn the page upside down to see the answers.

A1. Stratford-upon-Avon A2. The Globe Theatre A3. Queen Elizabeth I and King James I A4. 37 A5. Tragedy, Comedy, and History A6. "Hamlet" A7. "Hamlet" A8. The Lord Chamberlain's Men (later renamed the King's Men) A9. "The Comedy of Errors" A10. Henry V

Jhumpa Lahiri

```
L D Y D R S L D L O N G I N G E K Q L M
V N E A F T E G E H G F A N C Z Q U R I
I W F R Y O Y I X M R O S O H N N O Q N
Z U U L O X Q L D E O J L F V S W C X V
T S C S A B M D T A A T Y S B R D D O Y
Y P C R E L T E P H L B S H P S T H I I
T Q W S S X R C O L U A S U Z E H Z D B
F V W O X P Y S L X R I M S C K G N I Y
F H A H R E S T N I A L P M O C T P J Y
M L N E E D X P K E I W D V L Y A B D Y
J E T Z B R S H A Q O W E Z M M Q N E O
P N D S X L E R S F N Q K R S B J D U T
I F E V E R T A K O D N A L W O L B X H
N T Y Z G H P S B O K X K F S F N T O E
B W V E A Y Z T D O X T G A N A S F R R
I B A D S L H V B B U E Z I K I Z E C F
R N A M E S A K E I D T X C L L Y B P S
P L S C V I M T F R Z Z S Y C T Z H G R
```

Complaints	Longing	Other
Earth	Lowland	Sexy
In	Maladies	Unaccustomed
Interpreter	Namesake	Whereabouts
List	No	Words

SOLUTION

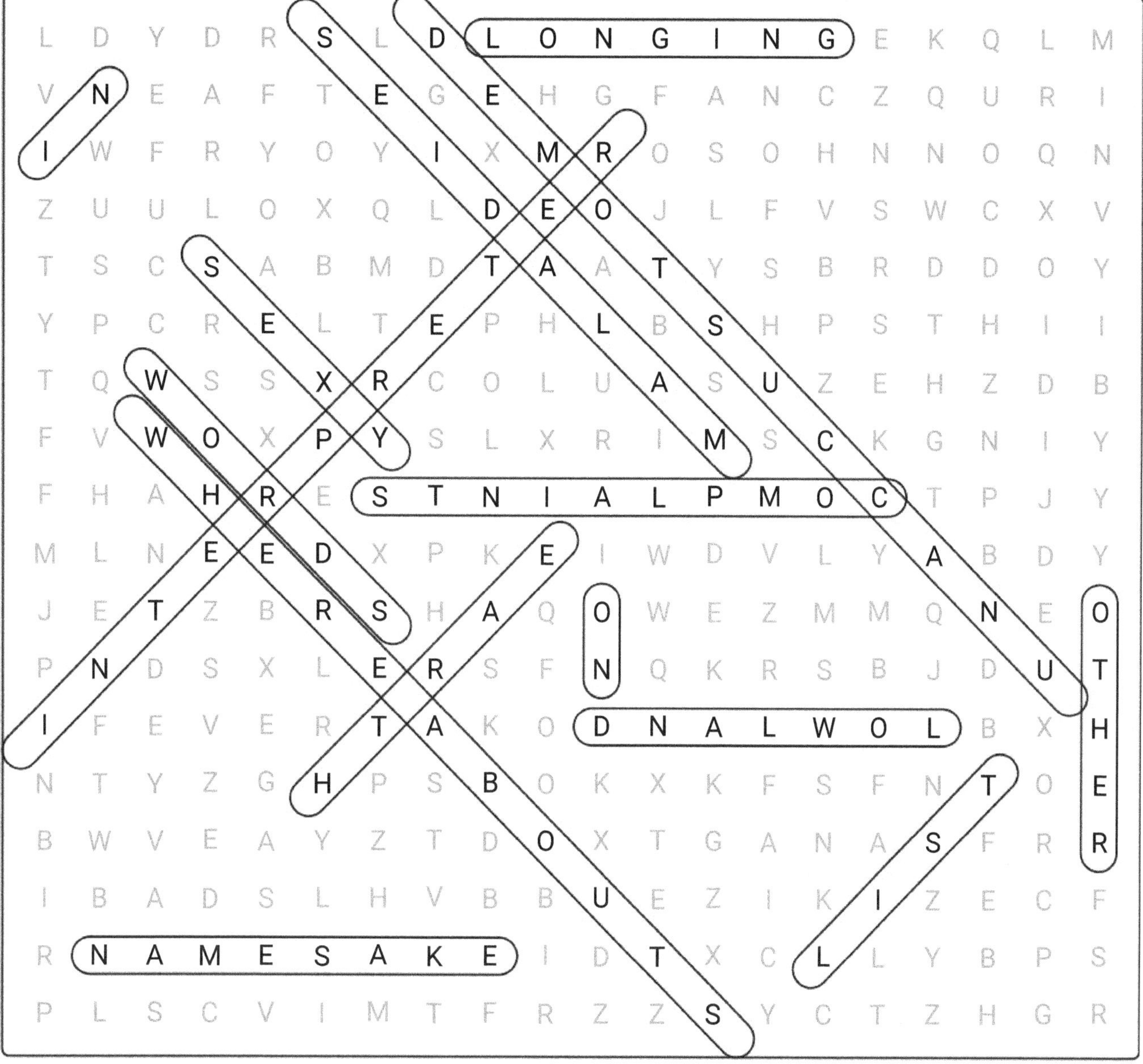

About Jhumpa Lahiri

Indian-American author Jhumpa Lahiri is known for her evocative stories that explore themes of identity, culture, and the immigrant experience. Her rich prose and deeply affecting narratives have earned her critical acclaim and numerous literary awards.

Trivia Questions

➢Q1. What is the name of the character in Jhumpa Lahiri's novel "The Namesake" who struggles with his identity as an Indian-American?

➢Q2. Which of Jhumpa Lahiri's novels is about a family of Bengali immigrants in the United States?

➢Q3. What is the name of the character in Jhumpa Lahiri's novel "The Lowland" who is involved in a political uprising in India?

➢Q4. Which of Jhumpa Lahiri's novels is about a woman named Ashima who moves to the United States with her husband?

➢Q5. What is the name of the character in Jhumpa Lahiri's novel "Unaccustomed Earth" who is a successful lawyer in Seattle?

➢Q6. Which of Jhumpa Lahiri's novels is about a woman named Miranda who travels to Italy and becomes involved in a love affair?

➢Q7. What is the name of the character in Jhumpa Lahiri's short story "Interpreter of Maladies" who is a tour guide in India?

➢Q8. Which of Jhumpa Lahiri's novels is about a woman named Gauri who struggles with her identity as an Indian-American?

➢Q9. Which of Jhumpa Lahiri's novels is about a woman named Hema who moves to the United States to attend college?

➢Q10. What is the name of the character in Jhumpa Lahiri's short story "A Temporary Matter" who experiences a power outage with his wife?

Turn the page upside down to see the answers.

A1. Gogol Ganguli. A2. "The Interpreter of Maladies." A3. Subhash. A4. "The Namesake." A5. Ruma. A6. "The Lost Decade." A7. Mr. Kapasi. A8. "The Mistress of Spices." A9. "The Treatment of Bibi Haldar."A10. Shukumar.

Judy Blume

```
N Q V I T S Q C G N X B S R N O Y J Y C
I P X L L U Y F I S X K F H S T X Q P J
F U D G E M O A L O L O K O T R F S B W
Q U T Y U M V K G Z B Z X L R R U T Z T
C N Q K R E F C O R B L T I E E U D D V
S Z O E S R R A E S R Y C P S J V O R F
Q T X Z Z Q R I E S U Y P R L E X E F U
E N G N I H T O N I N P E G R Y X V R Z
C M B F Q M R C V W T T E G N D P A U D
J E E J V V M C R O S Q Y R Q Q Q Q T B
T E F L G U X I X I B B E C F G R A D E
M A R G O D M Y S I A W F D G U I M H Z
K C L Y J N W F O D F S S T B Z D S F T
M Y Q E T D Y X X U Q C S H Y G M G J T
O C R P S T F O X O R O E E C G W J E L
O C P I K X K B M I T E B R L C U I C F
N D B T E R A G R A M J Z E A L Z Y U D
F E Q B D I M X L C T S R Z H C L P L U
```

Are	Grade	Summer
Forever	Margaret	Superfudge
Fourth	Me	Tales
Fudge	Nothing	There
God	Sisters	You

SOLUTION

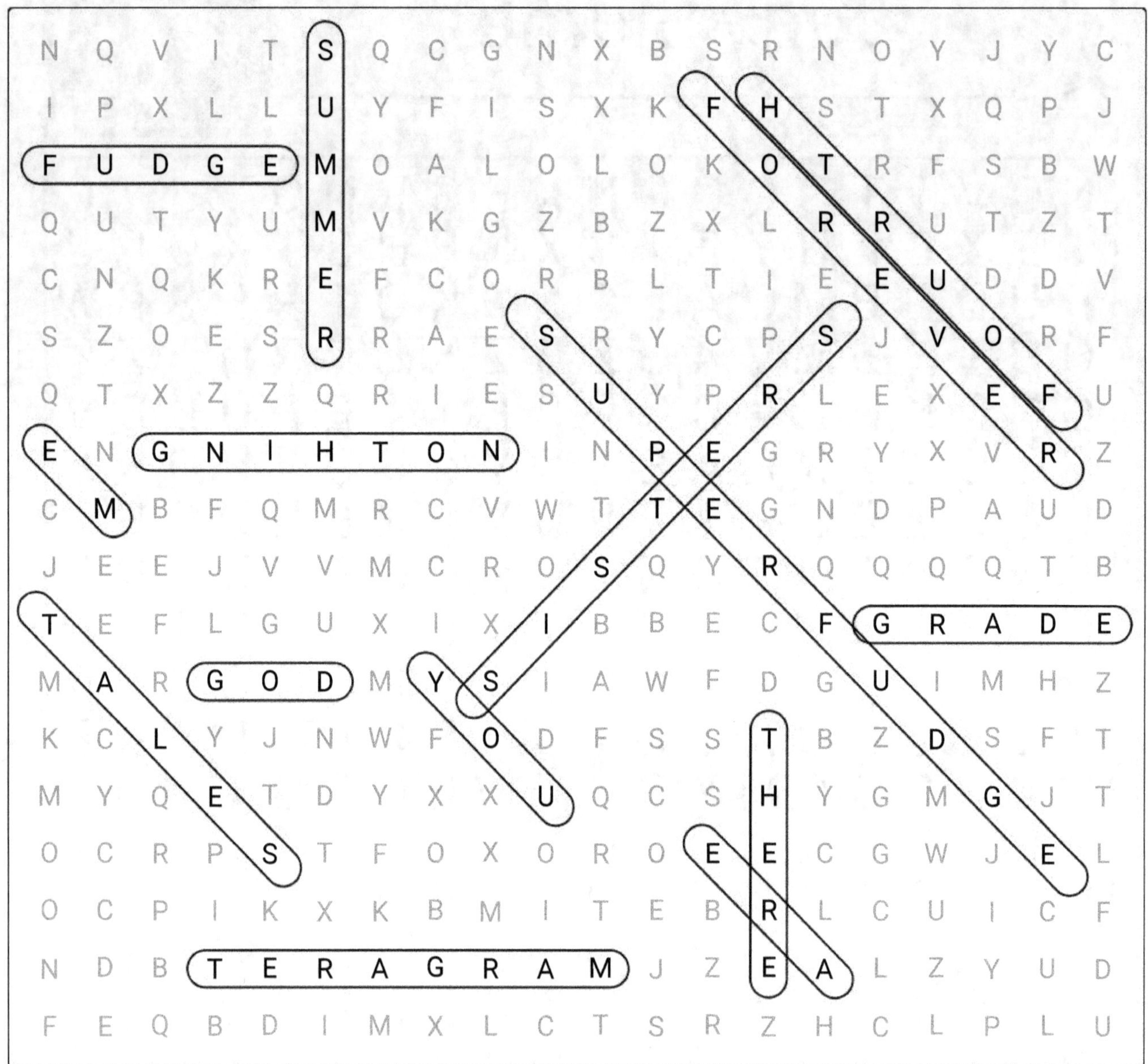

About Judy Blume

American author Judy Blume is beloved for her relatable and heartfelt young adult novels, which often tackle themes of adolescence, friendship, and self-discovery. Her honest storytelling and engaging characters have made her a cherished figure in the world of children's and young adult literature.

Trivia Questions

➢Q1. In which year was Judy Blume's first children's novel, "The One in the Middle Is the Green Kangaroo," published?

➢Q2. What is the title of Judy Blume's novel that was inspired by her own experience with breast cancer?

➢Q3. Which Judy Blume book focuses on the impact of a plane crash on the lives of three generations of a family?

➢Q4. What was Judy Blume's profession before she became a successful author?

➢Q5. Which Judy Blume novel, released in 1981, addresses the topic of divorce and its effect on a young girl?

➢Q6. In which U.S. state was Judy Blume born?

➢Q7. What is the name of the organisation Judy Blume co-founded, which is dedicated to protecting the freedom to read and write?

➢Q8. Judy Blume's books have been translated into how many languages, approximately?

➢Q9. In 1996, which of Judy Blume's novels was adapted into a feature film?

➢Q10. In 2004, Judy Blume received which prestigious award for her contribution to American letters?

Turn the page upside down to see the answers.

A1. 1969 A2. "Deenie" A3. "In the Unlikely Event" A4. Teacher A5. "It's Not the End of the World" A6. New Jersey A7. The National Coalition Against Censorship (NCAC) A8. Over 30 languages A9. "Fudge-A-Mania" A10. National Book Foundation's Medal for Distinguished Contribution to American Letters

Alexander Pushkin

```
G L W S X N V N T A S W K Q D J G R L B
N P S J J F R I Y N C P B E L K I N O S
T B C W O T K K D U E T A G T Y P B A I
Z T M Z R N S N M G B E G D K T D M R N
R T R A J V E E G T G E U O E P K E O O
C R Z R O V N G U Z A T Q Q G S I I H W
P O Y R E R I J I G N C D V I L L O V P
M P B Y O T O V X N E H W D A L M J U Q
J U C G G Y S U R A Q N M S E W O G F Z
D J A A Y G L A J C U Z E B S V A L S Q
M C N J P E N B M U R O E L B C N X E R
B O R I S J G B A N H R I K H O D S L P
C J F J I B C O D U O E N E W D H Z A Y
N U S X E K O C D U I I V R Q V P W T J
S V R N S U V I K U X S T A A L G P G V
W R E Y X B J F W F N O B A W W H K K A
H F X Z C D C T Y H J O I E T T M T T R
Z A X A Z M P Q W R G B V A P S I H J M
```

Belkin	Gypsies	Rebellion
Boris	Mozart	Salieri
Dubrovsky	Onegin	Spades
Eugene	Pugachev's	Stationmaster
Godunov	Queen	Tales

SOLUTION

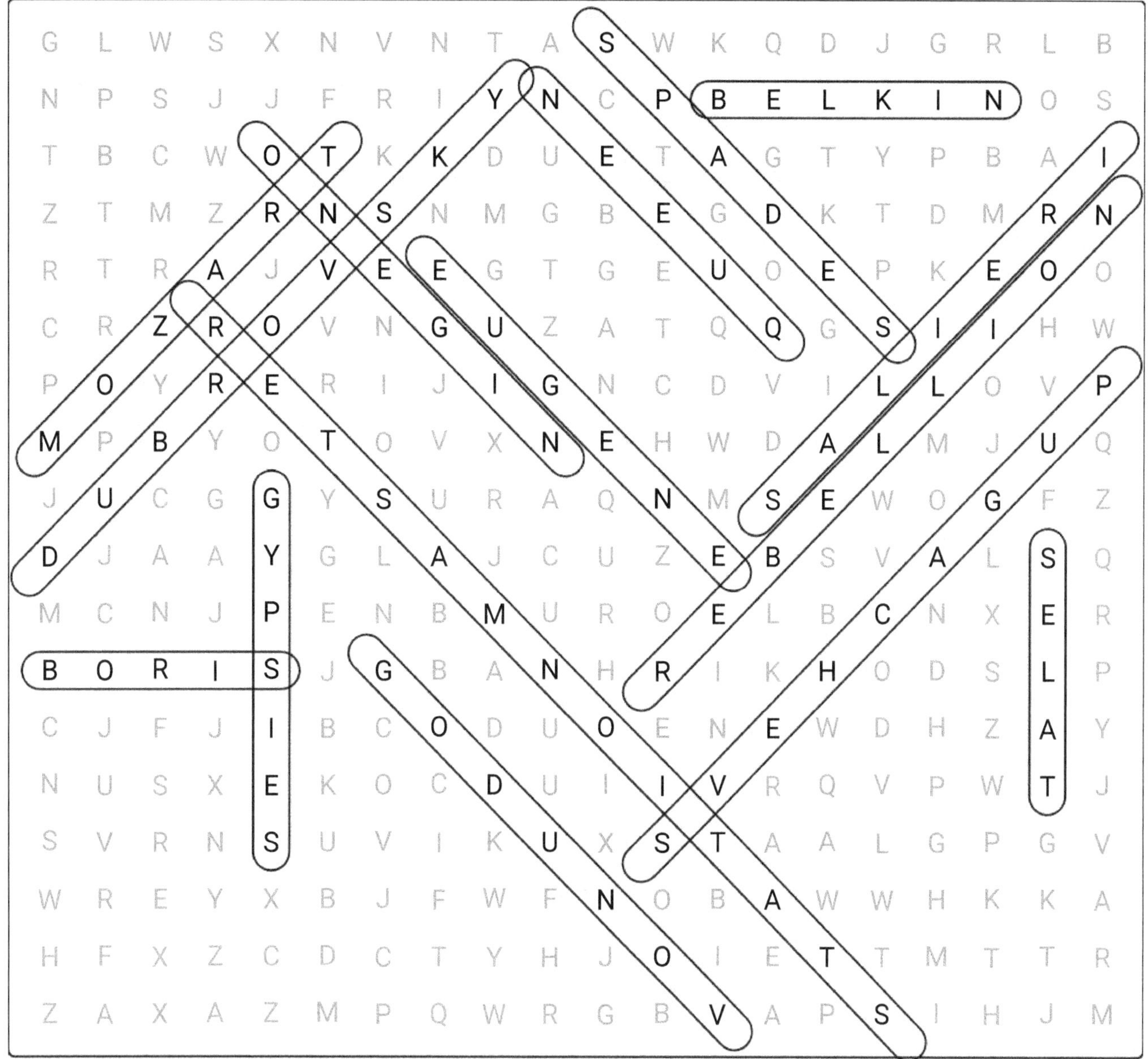

About Alexander Pushkin

Russian poet and author Alexander Pushkin is esteemed for his groundbreaking contributions to Russian literature, including his mastery of both prose and poetry. His innovative storytelling and richly drawn characters have left an indelible mark on the literary world.

Trivia Questions

➢Q1. What is the name of the character in Alexander Pushkin's novel in verse "Eugene Onegin" who rejects the love of a young woman named Tatyana?

➢Q2. Which of Alexander Pushkin's works is a play about a man named Boris Godunov who becomes Tsar of Russia?

➢Q3. What is the name of the character in Alexander Pushkin's story "The Queen of Spades" who becomes obsessed with a gambling secret?

➢Q4. Which of Alexander Pushkin's works is a fairy tale about a prince who sets out on a quest to rescue a princess?

➢Q5. What is the name of the character in Alexander Pushkin's novel "The Captain's Daughter" who falls in love with a girl named Masha?

➢Q6. Which of Alexander Pushkin's works is a historical novel about the reign of Peter the Great?

➢Q7. What is the name of the character in Alexander Pushkin's play "The Miserly Knight" who becomes obsessed with money?

➢Q8. Which of Alexander Pushkin's works is a short story about a man named Ivan who meets the devil?

➢Q9. What is the name of the character in Alexander Pushkin's story "The Shot" who becomes obsessed with seeking revenge?

➢Q10. Which of Alexander Pushkin's works is a poem about a soldier who falls in love with a gypsy woman?

Turn the page upside down to see the answers.

A1. Eugene Onegin. A2. "Boris Godunov." A3. Hermann. A4. "Ruslan and Ludmila." A5. Pyotr Grinyov. A6. "The Bronze Horseman." A7. Miser. A8. "The Queen of Spades." A9. Silvio. A10. "The Gypsies."

Nicholas Sparks

```
F N V O C H O I C E Q R F Y G D Q C T X
U T E M K I E E U D R O N G N O S O Z K
H A V E N Z S N K C J G N W N B B I B D
J G V D T T B C N N B R J E Z I V Z U R
S U R B A Y J A Y R Q Y C G U N B I I E
D S L V J L Z O T V T Z N B Q L T J Z M
I A E Q V F W A L K M N O T E B O O K E
N F C P H L Z E G J J B P L A X S B K M
H E R C T X X B H Q E N U V F R R E D B
W R H Z R B C O U M E S S A G E Y S W E
I I O H N Z F T K Z Y L E U C U N T J R
L A S T D W P T P U G W J Q E N R R S H
I H S H Q S O L T N Q D Z O G Z O D U J
L Y A T B L M E I Q H X V I B T N K I X
V B J T D F U D X O E F D I S E W O O B
D S L X V Y D C T W O T A H I E B K A K
L E O V Z E A O K Z B Z H R X R X J S J
A Q R Z W V Z U U Y R I F S D Q N H R X
```

Best	Last	Remember
Bottle	Lucky	Safe
Choice	Message	Song
Friends	Notebook	Walk
Haven	One	Wedding

SOLUTION

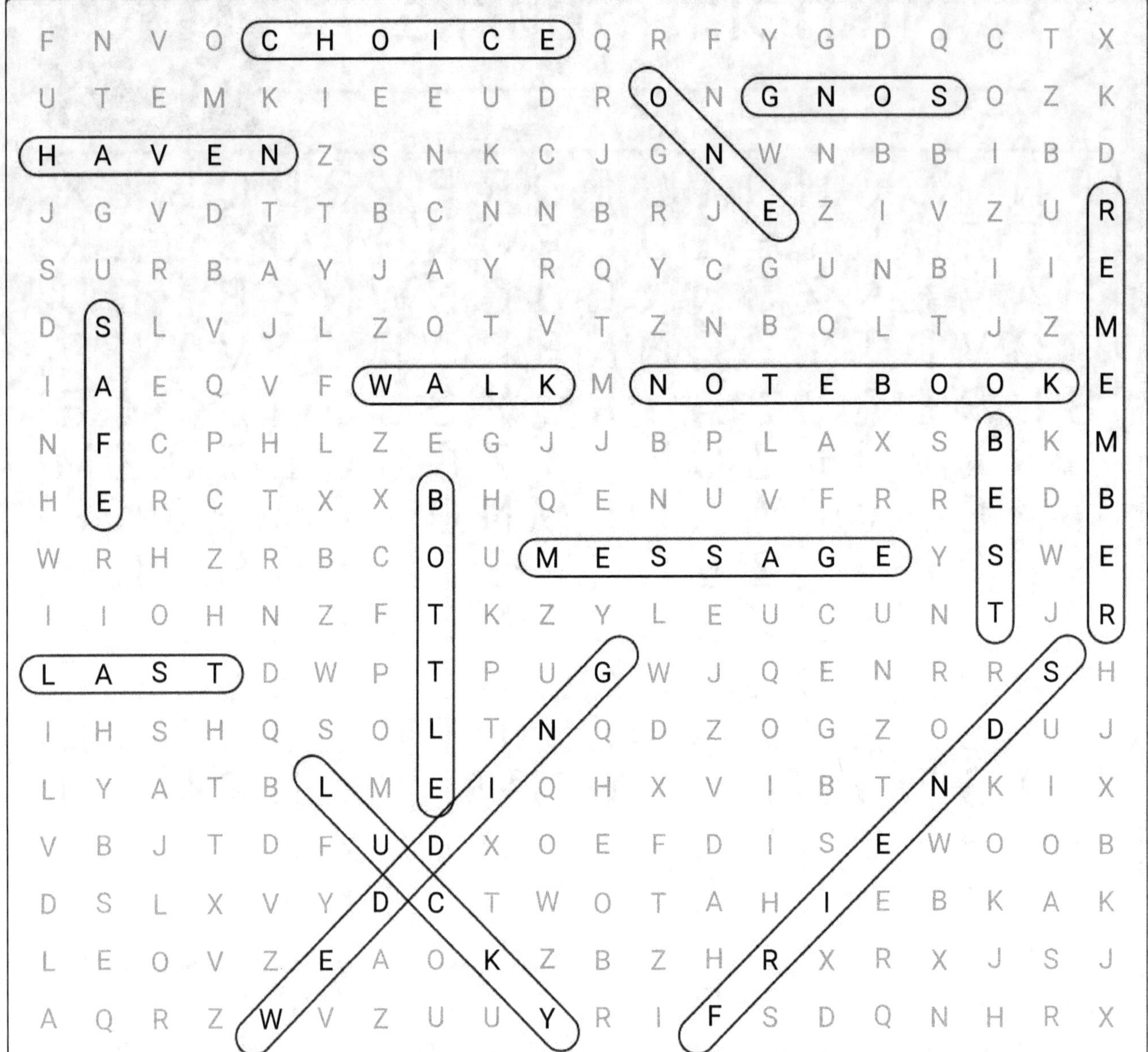

About Nicholas Sparks

American novelist Nicholas Sparks is recognized for his emotionally charged romance novels, which often explore themes of love, loss, and destiny. His heartfelt storytelling and relatable characters have endeared him to readers around the world, making him one of the most successful authors in the genre.

Trivia Questions

➢Q1. What is the name of the character in Nicholas Sparks's novel "The Notebook " who falls in love with a woman named Allie?

➢Q2. Which of Nicholas Sparks's novels is about a man named Travis who falls in love with his neighbor Gabby?

➢Q3. What is the name of the character in Nicholas Sparks's novel "Dear John" who falls in love with a woman named Savannah?

➢Q4. Which of Nicholas Sparks's novels is about a man named Landon who falls in love with a girl named Jamie who has leukemia?

➢Q5. What is the name of the character in Nicholas Sparks's novel "A Walk to Remember" who is a minister's daughter?

➢Q6. Which of Nicholas Sparks's novels is about a woman named Julie who goes on a journey to find her missing husband?

➢Q7. What is the name of the character in Nicholas Sparks's novel "Message in a Bottle" who finds a love letter in a bottle on the beach?

➢Q8. Which of Nicholas Sparks's novels is about a man named Logan who falls in love with a woman named Beth?

➢Q9. What is the name of the character in Nicholas Sparks's novel "The Lucky One" who believes a photo of a woman he found in Iraq brought him good luck?

➢Q10. Which of Nicholas Sparks's novels is about a man named Russell who becomes involved in a love triangle with two women named Elizabeth and Lexie?

Turn the page upside down to see the answers.

A1. Noah Calhoun. A2. "The Choice." A3. John Tyree. A4. "A Walk to Remember." A5. Jamie Sullivan. A6. "Safe Haven." A7. Theresa Osborne. A8. "The Lucky One." A9. Logan Thibault. A10. "The Best of Me."

Michael Connelly

```
B W U M S A I L E O H C E B X L U H F P
G B L A C K W U I G D A R K N E S S V Q
T S B G U Q E K C N P Y B K X I F J A B
T R M Y P A M Q D G C Z M L D D D B H E
E F O O E I S O P P L O M B O H N N J Y
E N E S S A R B R S U F L G J N T I S E
C T J Q X C N H J E I F S N R G D Q H F
N R W T B H B T E V L H C I E T Q E X P
V P W R C V Z D H C Y Z A N Y W U S E J
K Z O S W M X C F A O S R F W T D Y J N
F E O P D F U K J T N N E G A V U Q W V
M B F H Y Y B M C G B S C P L W X S V F
T T E O U T M I R R Y B R R H I C X X J
U F W N X C D U Y U S O O T E R K S R H
M L I H L R L J E N R N W G O T J J D L
L U B G E Q E V R X I E V M K V E S H M
Q Z L V U S W R P D U S E A H T U T E A
S Q F Q W A A X T W L D N O R M K A X R
```

Black	Concrete	More
Blonde	Darkness	Poet
Bones	Echo	Scarecrow
Bosch	Lawyer	Than
Brass	Lincoln	Verdict

SOLUTION

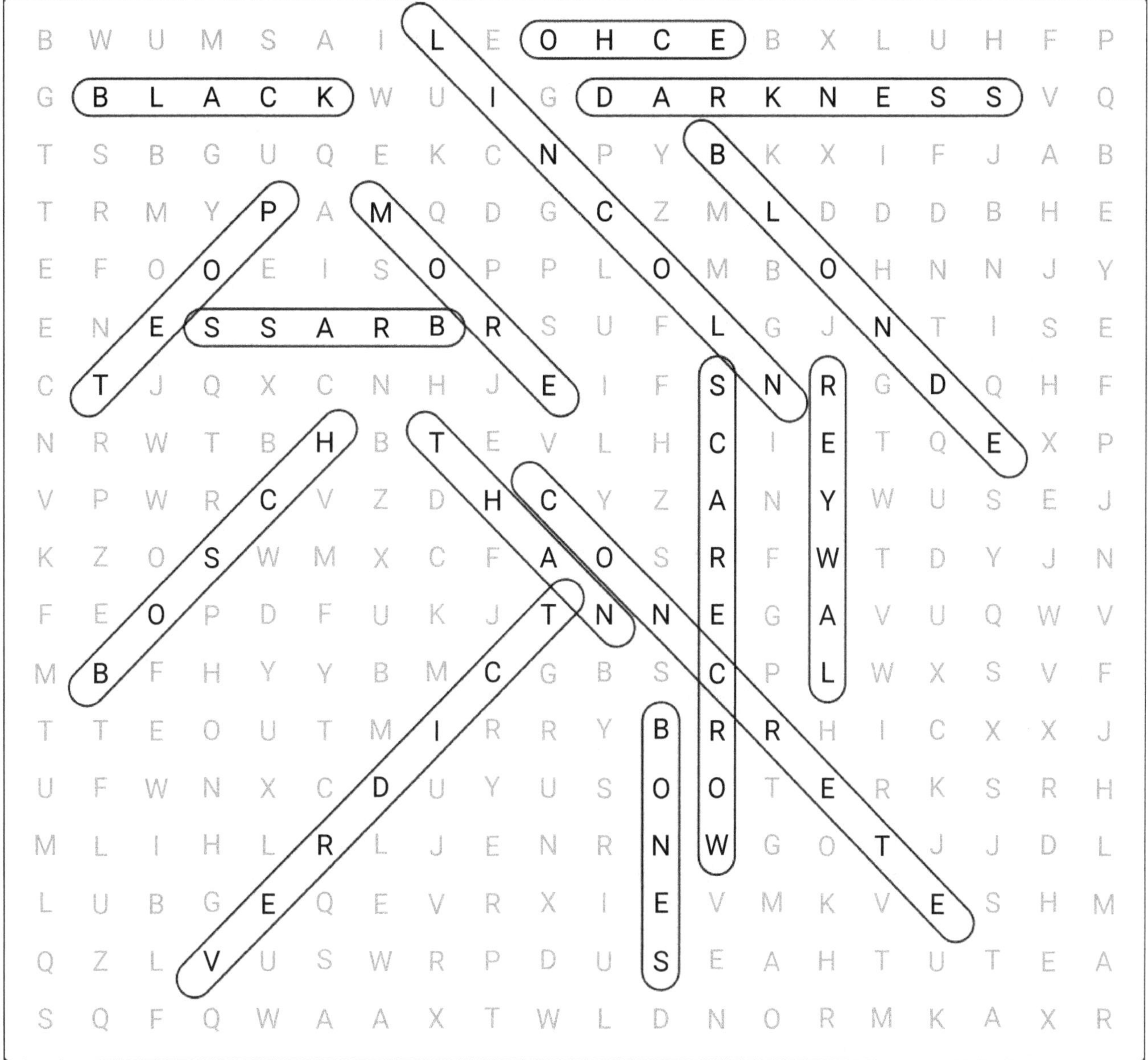

About Michael Connelly

American author Michael Connelly is celebrated for his gripping crime novels and detective stories, which often feature intricate plots and well-drawn characters. His ability to create suspenseful, page-turning narratives has made him a popular and respected figure in the world of crime fiction.

➢Q1. What is the name of the character in Michael Connelly's series of detective novels who works for the Los Angeles Police Department?

➢Q2. Which of Michael Connelly's novels is about a lawyer named Mickey Haller who defends a wealthy client accused of murder?

➢Q3. What is the name of the character in Michael Connelly's novel "The Poet" who investigates a series of murders?

➢Q4. Which of Michael Connelly's novels is about a detective named Harry Bosch who investigates the murder of a Hollywood producer?

➢Q5. What is the name of the character in Michael Connelly's novel "The Lincoln Lawyer" who defends a client accused of assaulting a woman?

➢Q6. Which of Michael Connelly's novels is about a reporter named Jack McEvoy who investigates the murder of his twin brother?

➢Q7. What is the name of the character in Michael Connelly's novel "The Black Echo" who investigates a bank robbery that leads to a much larger conspiracy?

➢Q8. Which of Michael Connelly's novels is about a detective named Renee Ballard who works the night shift in Hollywood?

➢Q9. What is the name of the character in Michael Connelly's novel "The Drop" who investigates the murder of a man found in the trunk of a car?

➢Q10. Which of Michael Connelly's novels is about a detective named Terry McCaleb who investigates a series of murders while awaiting a heart transplant?

Turn the page upside down to see the answers.

A1. Harry Bosch. A2. "The Lincoln Lawyer." A3. Jack McEvoy. A4. "The Black Echo." A5. Mickey Haller. A6. "The Poet." A7. Harry Bosch. A8. Renee Ballard. A9. Harry Bosch. A10. "Blood Work."

Robert Ludlum

```
N R R V T J F P Y N O K D S N Y D R F I
D Q B R K Y P O J E S P Y L A C O P A F
H F E N I A T I U Q A O X N N B Y U B U
U D G X Y U U V Y E E B O U R N E I L P
B R H Q R H I N E M A N N Z U C Y R H S
U H W X I U I S B R L V F Y V L S C U L
F L Y I D E N T I T Y A N C Q T A T B E
Z I T J T F C C F T M O U R I H S F D Q
A R I I C D J J I G I U V O F R C O E H
G I A U M K Z P I S H D C E M S C T U Z
D R V R P A E S S L M D X X A S B L A H
H O U N K E T E U Q K C N B T N U C E W
T N X V P S R U B Y H A C N A H S C O R
Y R V Y V G Y H M A M R I Q R S X E Z A
W Y S Z O G S K N T D G D L E T J Z M N
R C E R E E H G L A K T U Y S Z Y R Y W
F L P E R Q E A O U O Y G T E G H Z W V
D M O S L B H M L U W L O C O T O R P F
```

Altman	Code	Protocol
Apocalypse	Exchange	Rhinemann
Aquitaine	Identity	Sigma
Bourne	Matarese	Ultimatum
Circle	Progression	Watch

SOLUTION

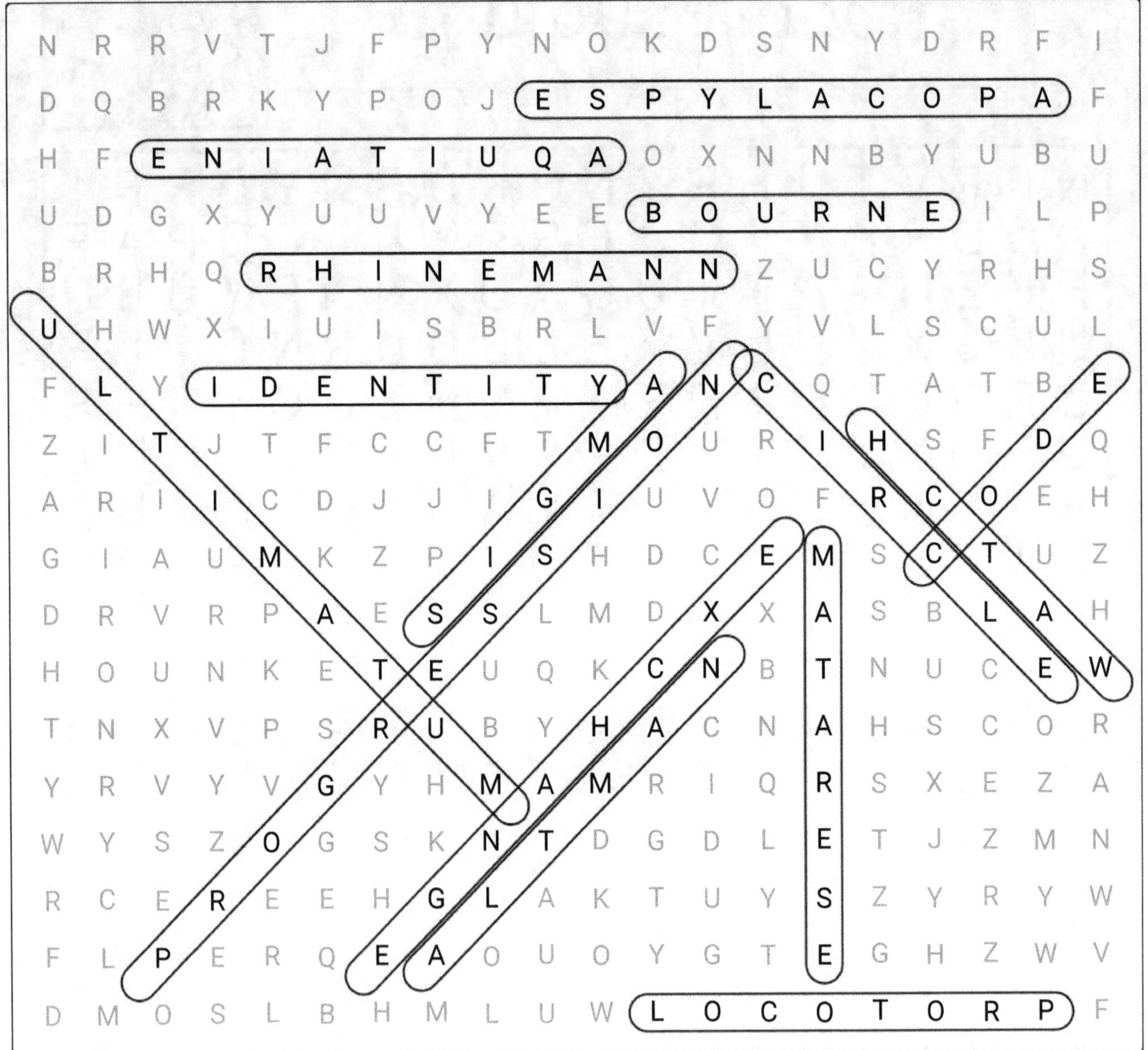

About Robert Ludlum

American novelist Robert Ludlum is renowned for his thrilling espionage and conspiracy novels, which often feature complex plots and high-stakes action. His engaging storytelling and suspenseful narratives have made him a popular and respected figure in the spy fiction genre.

➢Q1. What is the name of the character in Robert Ludlum's novel "The Bourne Identity" who suffers from amnesia and tries to uncover his identity?

➢Q2. Which of Robert Ludlum's novels is about a man named Michael Havelock who investigates the murder of his girlfriend?

➢Q3. What is the name of the character in Robert Ludlum's novel "The Sigma Protocol" who investigates a conspiracy involving a secret organization?

➢Q4. Which of Robert Ludlum's novels is about a man named Jason Bourne who is forced to confront his past as a CIA assassin?

➢Q5. What is the name of the character in Robert Ludlum's novel "The Scorpio Illusion" who is a former CIA agent?

➢Q6. Which of Robert Ludlum's novels is about a man named John Grady who becomes involved in a conspiracy involving a powerful corporation?

➢Q7. What is the name of the character in Robert Ludlum's novel "The Parsifal Mosaic" who becomes involved in a conspiracy involving the KGB?

➢Q8. Which of Robert Ludlum's novels is about a man named David Webb who must confront his past as Jason Bourne?

➢Q9. What is the name of the character in Robert Ludlum's novel "The Altman Code" who becomes involved in a conspiracy involving a biotech company?

➢Q10. Which of Robert Ludlum's novels is about a man named Nicholas Bryson who becomes involved in a conspiracy involving the CIA and the KGB?

Turn the page upside down to see the answers.

A1. Jason Bourne. A2. "The Hades Factor." A3. Ben Hartman. A4. "The Bourne Supremacy." A5. Adam Stone. A6. "The Apocalypse Watch." A7. Michael Havelock. A8. "The Bourne Ultimatum." A9. Jon Smith. A10. "The Janson Directive."

Terry Pratchett

```
J X V D P L X W P G M M Y T J L Z K C B
I Q V F C G T O X U H S U E U G R M N N
U M Z D E R X Z Y S O R N C E O A F D K
J K D O J F I B V M G S U E P Q I D B Y
J B F C A T B S M T F O B R F J B V B F
J A C H I N G T Y Z A K O V P H S C K F
G T D P K N H P Z P T M U R L T Y A J A
L K J K U V S Z A S H V B L I A E M M S
J B T K G V Y M E K E O U U P E B U O L
X A Y S O N G H N B R D W Z W D S X P P
R Z Q T A I C A T V I I F U I Y L K O Q
X C I F U T B A Z S N S V V G N C W S S
M P F X I N F Q G J C C A I T D A F T V
R I V W D A I O S N E W I T M W Z Q A I
T O D K Q M I I O X W O Y S X E H K L W
W J R Q I N L V H W I R O I D U S S P Q
J R K D G J E A V N L W O P R Q R P V
R J L T G N Q K E Q D D P M Y Z Q P U C
```

Aching	Hogfather	Sam
Ankh-morpork	Lipwig	Tiffany
Death	Moist	Vimes
Discworld	Postal	Von
Going	Rincewind	Witches

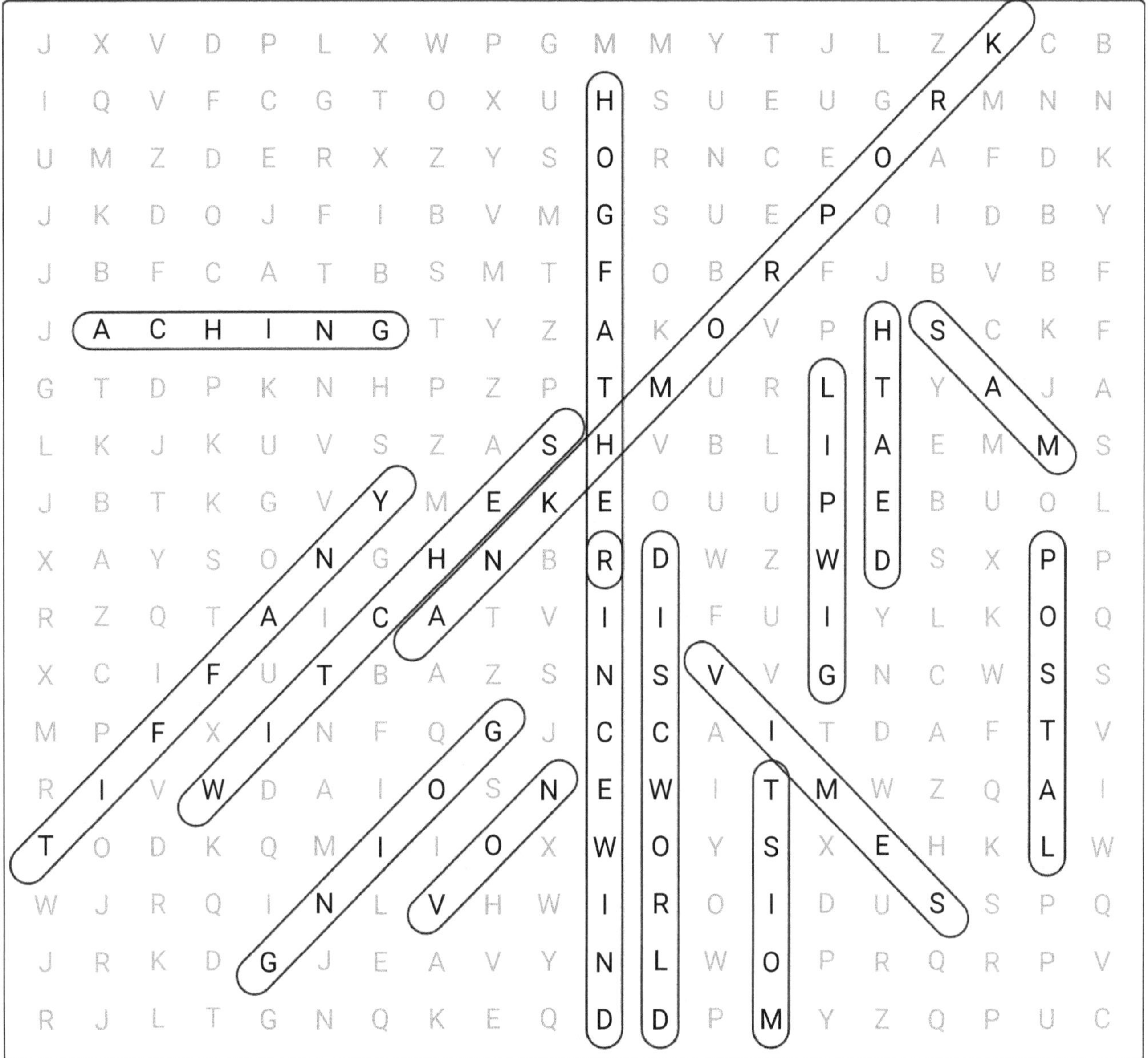

About Terry Pratchett

British author Terry Pratchett is celebrated for his satirical and humorous fantasy series, "Discworld." His clever wit and imaginative storytelling have captivated readers, making him a beloved figure in the world of fantasy literature.

Trivia Questions

➤Q1. What is the name of the character in Terry Pratchett's Discworld series who is the head of the Ankh-Morpork City Watch?

➤Q2. Which of Terry Pratchett's novels is about a young girl named Tiffany Aching who becomes a witch?

➤Q3. What is the name of the character in Terry Pratchett's novel "Small Gods" who is the only believer in a god who has been reduced to the form of a tortoise?

➤Q4. Which of Terry Pratchett's novels is about a boy named Maurice who leads a group of rats on a pied piper-style adventure?

➤Q5. What is the name of the character in Terry Pratchett's novel "Going Postal" who is hired to revive a failing post office in Ankh-Morpork?

➤Q6. Which of Terry Pratchett's novels is about a young man named Mort who becomes an apprentice to Death?

➤Q7. What is the name of the character in Terry Pratchett's novel "Pyramids" who becomes a pharaoh in the desert kingdom of Djelibeybi?

➤Q8. Which of Terry Pratchett's novels is about a group of witches who must prevent a fairy queen from taking over their kingdom?

➤Q9. What is the name of the character in Terry Pratchett's novel "The Color of Magic" who becomes the first tourist of the Discworld?

➤Q10. Which of Terry Pratchett's novels is about a group of dwarves who must find a new home after their mine collapses?

Turn the page upside down to see the answers.

A1. Samuel Vimes. A2. "The Wee Free Men." A3. Brutha. A4. "The Amazing Maurice and His Educated Rodents." A5. Moist von Lipwig. A6. "Mort." A7. Pteppic. A8. "Lords and Ladies." A9. Twoflower. A10. "The Fifth Elephant."

Virgil

```
V H T V G O L D E N W X L J Z U N S N R
A R H K L B F C B Z R P K N I U S U S O
V N H T K E Z T O K A W U B V N X T G M
V U D Y T P P M Q N C F C N R T P S Y E
L K D N J L Q O V J S Y X I E L O U C V
D Z A L T R I T F J U B O U G H B G U N
J D X E L E M P I R E G M E F B F U T I
N B Y Y L C G O P X E R R U Q Y O A K T
F P T D A J S W X R G E O R G I C S B A
Q L W M A G L E U F S P O D F G T J O L
W G W U V V O T U K X I X W Y P N O V P
O I R O T U A J X G S C Y L D S N A L D
P O N Z Q R E I I C O Q Z B C R G P B N
K Z S Z E H N J C H E L V G E K O R V K
L N J T W B E G I Z I T C F L E L S I J
V A I I N A I G P K F U N E T Z D I N X
T L F R V I D Q V P Y I F O H F L M O D
M R W Q E N J O S I C I L Y H O P Z M U
```

Aeneid	Empire	Latin
Augustus	Epic	Literature
Bough	Georgics	Poet
Dante	Golden	Rome
Eclogues	Inferno	Sicily

SOLUTION

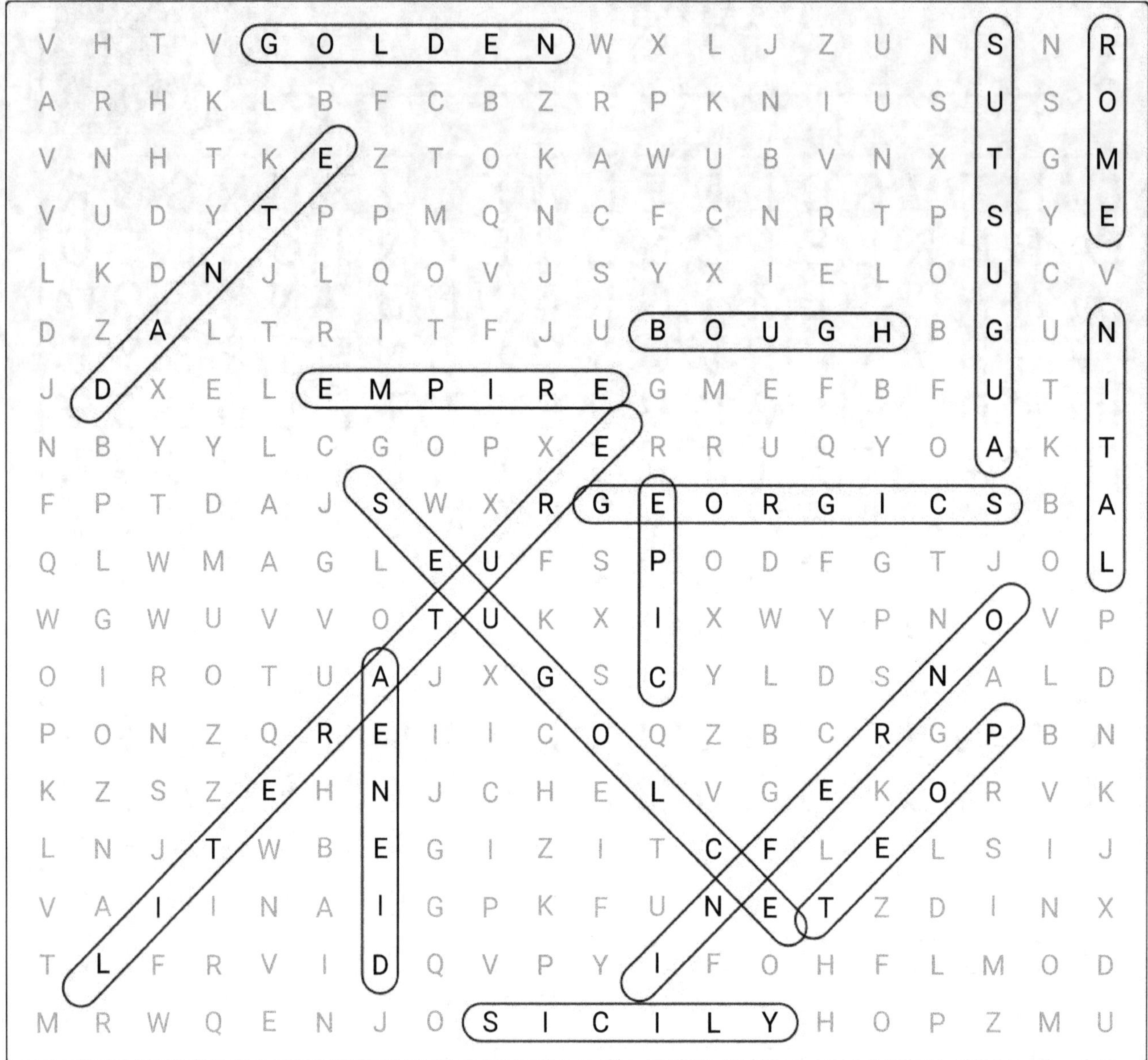

About Virgil

Ancient Roman poet Virgil is esteemed for his epic works, including the "Aeneid," which explores the founding of Rome. His masterful command of language and timeless themes have made him an enduring figure in the history of world literature.

Trivia Questions

➢Q1. What is the name of the character in Virgil's epic poem "The Aeneid" who is a Trojan prince and founder of Rome?

➢Q2. Which of Virgil's works is a collection of pastoral poems that celebrate the beauty of the countryside?

➢Q3. What is the name of the character in Virgil's poem "Georgics" who is a farmer and provides instruction on farming?

➢Q4. Which of Virgil's works is a poem about a young boy named Iulus who learns about the history of Rome?

➢Q5. What is the name of the character in Virgil's poem "Culex" who is a shepherd boy that dreams of being stung by a gnat and transformed into a warrior?

➢Q6. Which of Virgil's works is a poem about a man named Orpheus who descends into the underworld to rescue his wife?

➢Q7. What is the name of the character in Virgil's poem "Eclogues" who is a shepherd that sings about his love for a woman named Alexis?

➢Q8. Which of Virgil's works is a poem about the love affair between Dido, Queen of Carthage, and Aeneas?

➢Q9. What is the name of the character in Virgil's poem "Aetna" who is a volcano that erupts and speaks about its own creation?

➢Q10. Which of Virgil's works is a poem about the epic battle between two shepherds, Damon and Alphesiboeus?

Turn the page upside down to see the answers.

A1. Aeneas. A2. "Eclogues." A3. Georgics. A4. "Culex." A5. Culex. A6. "Orpheus." A7. Tityrus. A8. "The Aeneid." A9. Aetna. A10. "The Battle of the Shepherds."

Arthur Conan Doyle

```
V E Y J G W I X Z F H U H T S X A C S X
C X J R L Q A Y N F Z E A C L G Q R B K
B T V J J N Q T Y R F P W I E E N N L J
C R T C R N G D S R K S D N A S Z R R L
X A E Z T E U T J O E C P G G G D X X T K
D O L C A T D G P L N L O S U W I F W H
C R R J S D D H L C G T N L E A C V M C
X D A Q G T V I E N G S V O R W C C D D
Z I C K Z U V E P A X S U I R E P H A U
P N S A L R L T N S D A C S W E H S N C
S A V Y E J L Z B T C E X B O Y Q S C G
O R Q K E C P I K X U E D N U O H U I W
K Y S H N H G F S R K M E N D V K N S
A A S Y O J H V Q U A A E S C G F P G T
B D K L V A M S N O P I S H U D R H F
K B M P E X C J Z F Q S I F Q S I G N B
A E X H W A Y A Y J F R I R P V F A P X
S N S R T W V R I R M H B L T X L D W Q
```

Adventures	Holmes	Scarlet
Baskervilles	Hound	Sherlock
Dancing	League	Sign
Extraordinary	Men	Study
Four	Red-headed	Watson

SOLUTION

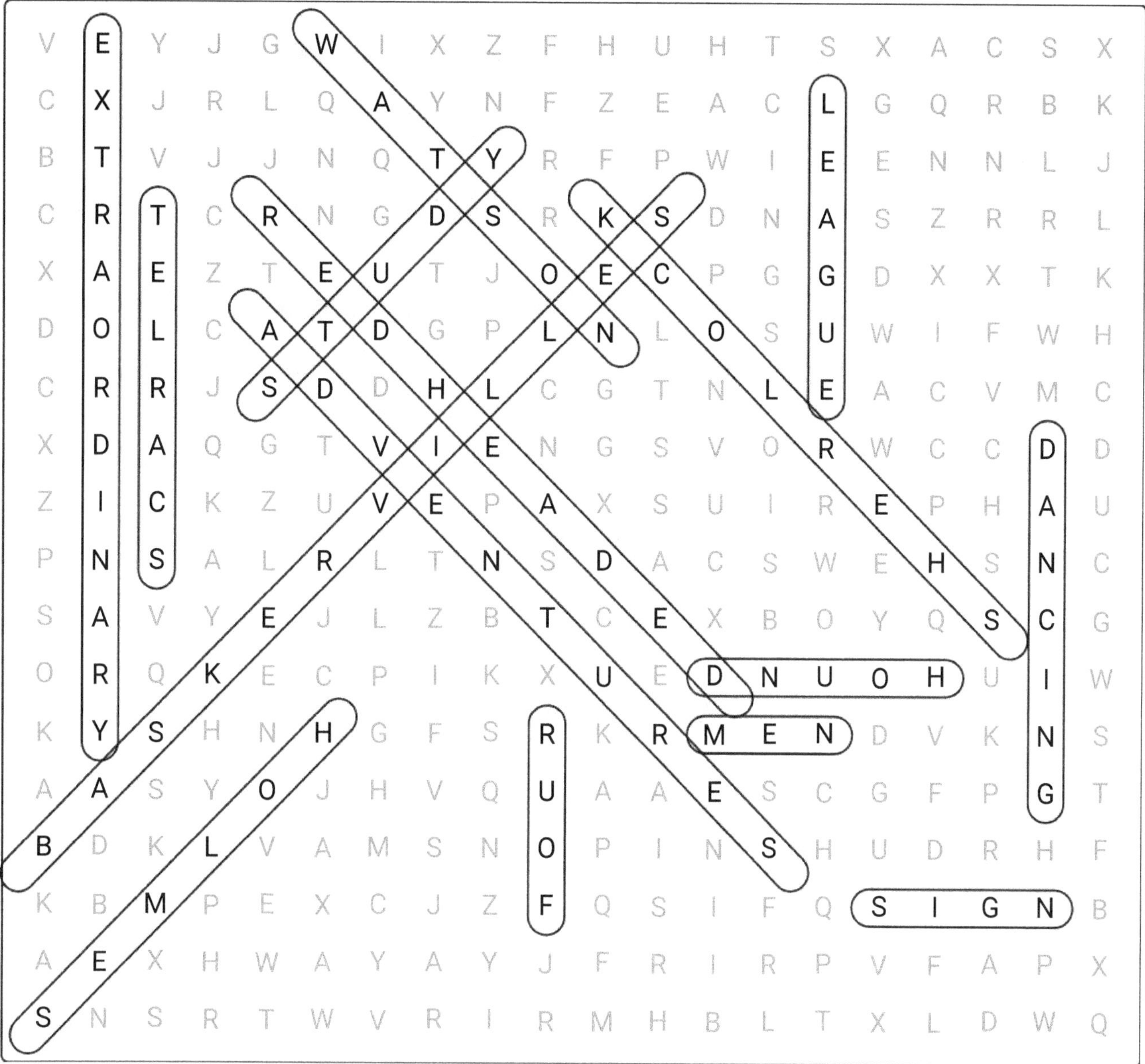

About Arthur Conan Doyle

Scottish author Arthur Conan Doyle is best known for his creation of the iconic detective Sherlock Holmes. His inventive mysteries and memorable characters have captivated readers and inspired countless adaptations, making him a leading figure in the world of crime fiction.

Trivia Questions

➢Q1. What is the full name of the author who created the famous detective character Sherlock Holmes?

➢Q2. In which Scottish city was Arthur Conan Doyle born?

➢Q3. Which historical fiction novel by Arthur Conan Doyle is set during the Hundred Years' War?

➢Q4. What profession did Arthur Conan Doyle's father, Charles Altamont Doyle, practice?

➢Q5. Arthur Conan Doyle was a strong advocate for which pseudoscientific belief?

➢Q6. Which character created by Arthur Conan Doyle is a brilliant but eccentric scientist and explorer?

➢Q7. Which collection of short stories published in 1892 features a mix of horror, detective, and speculative fiction?

➢Q8. How many times did Arthur Conan Doyle attempt to "kill off" the character of Sherlock Holmes?

➢Q9. What was the title of Arthur Conan Doyle's first published work?

➢Q10. In which year was Arthur Conan Doyle knighted by King Edward VII?

Turn the page upside down to see the answers.

A1. Sir Arthur Ignatius Conan Doyle A2. Edinburgh A3. "The White Company" A4. Artist (Illustrator) A5. Spiritualism A6. Professor George Edward Challenger A7. "Tales of Terror and Mystery" A8. Once (in "The Final Problem") A9. "Mysteries and Adventures" (also published as "The Gully of Bluemansdyke and Other Stories") A10. 1902

Alexandre Dumas

```
P U K O P M Y J N S N C N F V G F X J S
V D J Y X E R I X N I Q R F X V O I E Z
C M K W S Z C R A O V E C P W D P M L N
U J O Z V W X R V R E P X T T U L I P E
X V Z N Q N Q D I I L K K A O Q S H B C
A V O Y T H B O U S T E S Q U E E N S K
P A R V A E P J X W T Z F E K P V F O L
M B R A G E L O N N E O V T O H X N P A
T A D M U S K E T E E R S I L N R O N C
D J N R U Q T I T L N I S D C R M W G E
O O V H O E Y T V Z P H G M Y O G J B T
R S P D H F N H P M E Q F A E X M A E C
L E D A Y U Y P C V S U I S F M L T Z X
B P P P O H D K L A H Y M K F S J G E A
P H J C Z B C I B M I R K D A O N H U X
E B V C K A G R J M N O X M P H V M U X
T N R V L X Q W N X Q B O K O A E S A W
X T L B E M V A D P F U L S A F N D J K
```

Balsamo	Iron	Musketeers
Black	Joseph	Necklace
Bragelonne	Man	Queen's
Count	Mask	Tulip
Cristo	Monte	Vicomte

SOLUTION

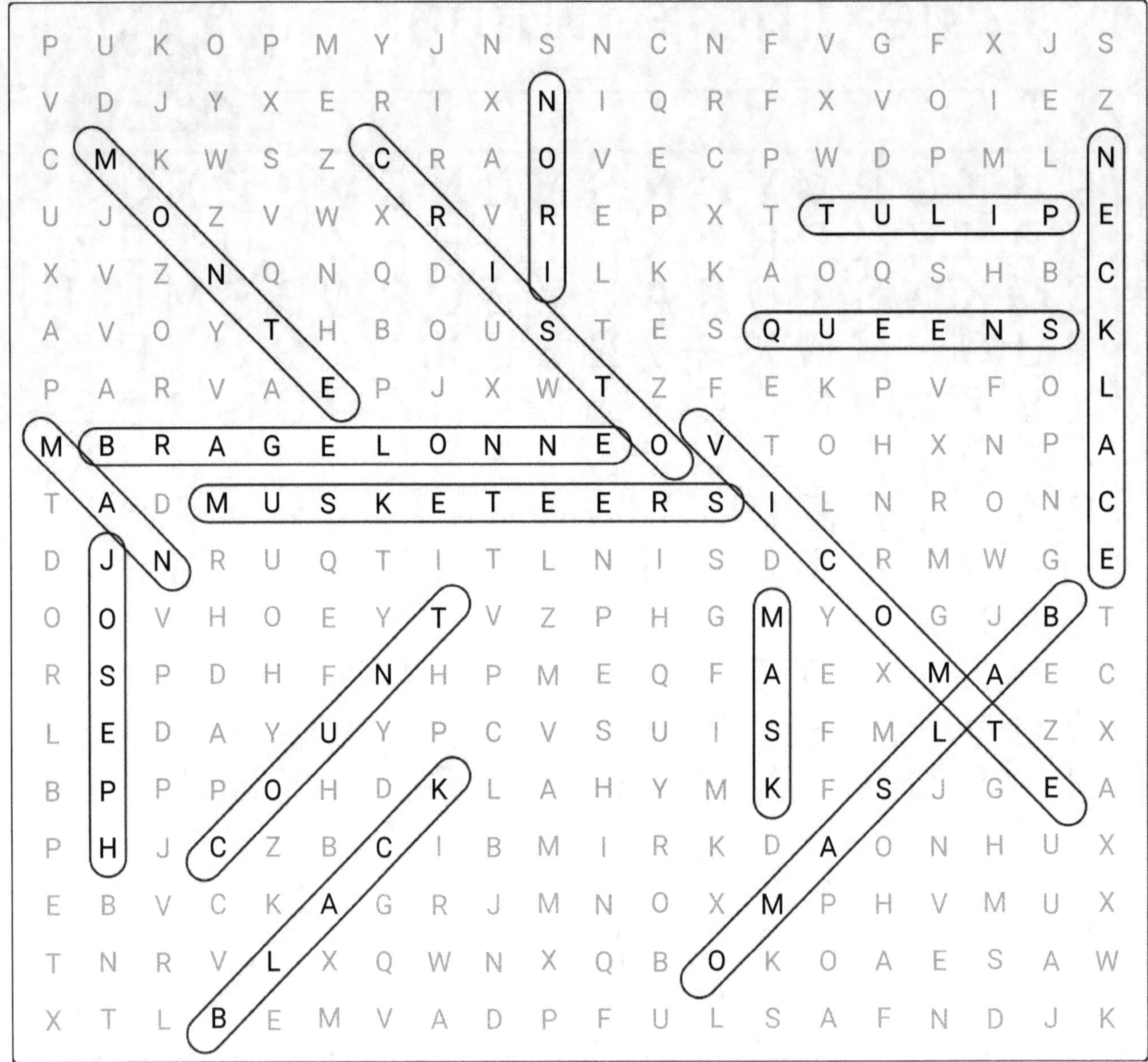

About Alexandre Dumas

French author Alexandre Dumas is acclaimed for his sweeping historical novels, including "The Count of Monte Cristo" and "The Three Musketeers." His engaging narratives and vivid characters have made him a popular and enduring figure in world literature.

Trivia Questions

➢Q1. What is the full name of the author known as Alexandre Dumas?

➢Q2. Which historical adventure novel by Alexandre Dumas features the character Edmond Dantès?

➢Q3. Which series of novels written by Alexandre Dumas follows the adventures of a group of swordsmen in 17th-century France?

➢Q4. What was Alexandre Dumas's primary occupation before he became a successful writer?

➢Q5. In which French city was Alexandre Dumas born?

➢Q6. Alexandre Dumas is often referred to as "Dumas, père" to distinguish him from his son. What did his son also achieve fame for?

➢Q7. Which play by Alexandre Dumas, père, was adapted into the opera "La Traviata" by Giuseppe Verdi?

➢Q8. How many volumes are in Alexandre Dumas's lesser-known work "The Valois Romances"?

➢Q9. Which Dumas novel features the character Balsamo, a magician and alchemist?

➢Q10. In which year was "The Three Musketeers" first published as a serialised novel?

Turn the page upside down to see the answers.

A1. Alexandre Dumas Davy de la Pailleterie A2. "The Count of Monte Cristo" A3. The D'Artagnan Romances A4. Playwright A5. Villers-Cotterêts A6. Writing, particularly as a playwright A7. "La Dame aux Camélias" (The Lady of the Camellias) A8. Eight A9. "Joseph Balsamo" (also known as "Memoirs of a Physician") A10. 1844

Zane Grey

```
X C K X F N T D C G J E L O Q X E C G P
Y U M V M Y B F H L E O W E S T E R N B
G Q N P Q M P U G T X P M T K X E J O O
E E M D I C N U Z U J A K L P P D P R Q
D E H X E I X T R W V F D W P F T U O T
C N Y F O R N D V P E T R A I L M N M E
T Z L N K P W V M T L G I E M S R X S D
B N G H P D S P O M S E A S G W N A K A
G U Q M D P T A U G R T E T L A C T G G
C S N N D Y A P N P M B S H I L S A E P
T R X C T H R I T I X U O S Y R G G X C
E E E N K N G X A H S I N A P S E M B Z
T D X T Z G Q K I Y T C W R W T Y H M T
X I K C I H L N N A N H F L T J P D C G
G R L D Q L X T G W O K G Q E O Q O Z N
T I Y W O C N W D Y H P X I Y B B R O P
W R E N T D X U Z H Z H B H L L V M H I
A L E W R E D N U H T V F R G F P F U N
```

Diggings	Purple	Thunder
Heritage	Riders	Trail
Light	Sage	Under
Lone	Spanish	Union
Mountain	Star	Western

SOLUTION

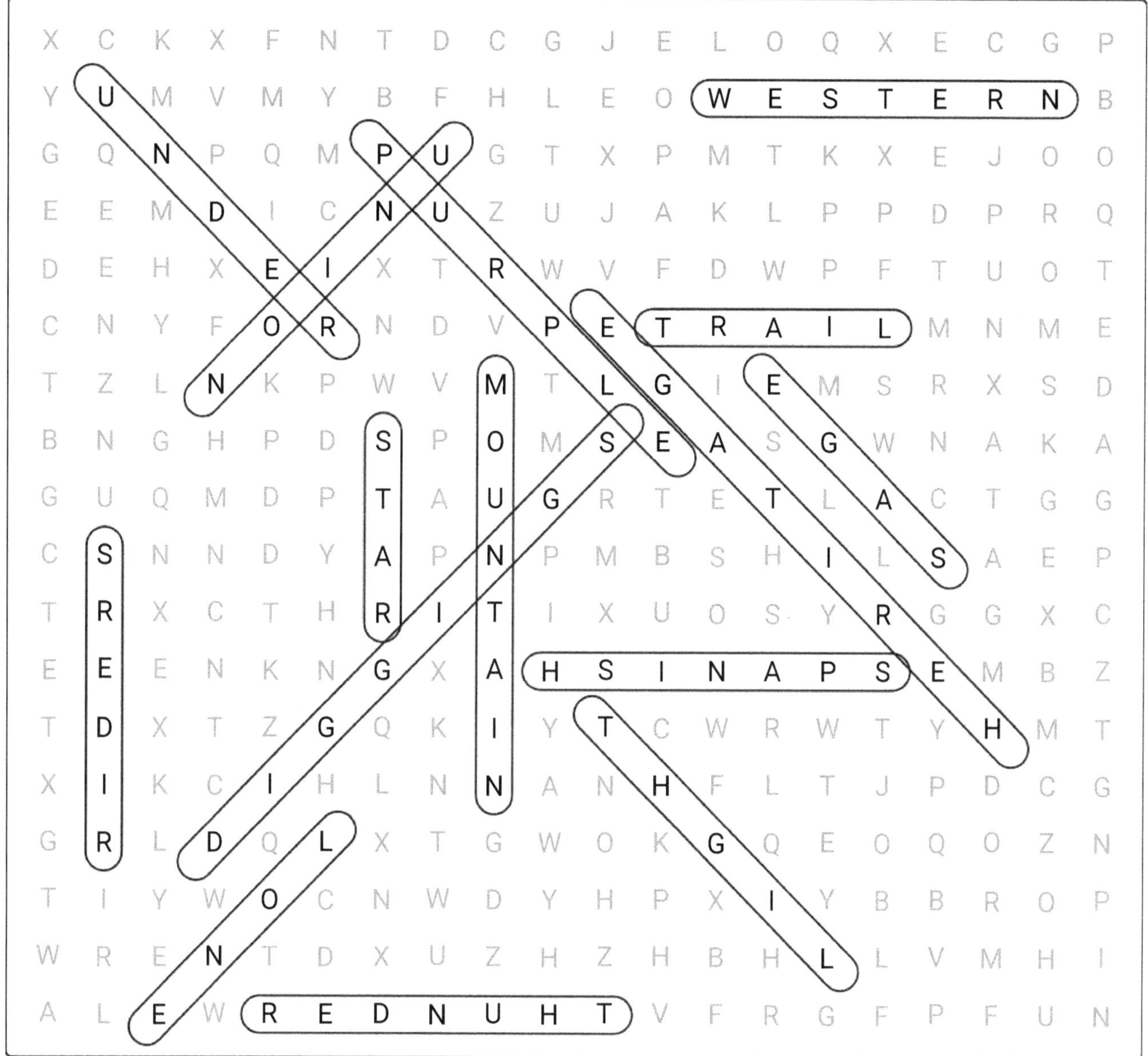

About Zane Grey

American author Zane Grey is recognized for his captivating Western novels, which often feature rugged landscapes and authentic portrayals of frontier life. His evocative storytelling and memorable characters have made him a defining figure in the Western genre.

Trivia Questions

➢Q1. What was Zane Grey's full name?

➢Q2. Zane Grey is best known for writing novels in which genre?

➢Q3. What was the title of Zane Grey's first published novel?

➢Q4. Before becoming a writer, what profession did Zane Grey initially pursue?

➢Q5. In which U.S. state was Zane Grey born?

➢Q6. Which Zane Grey novel, published in 1912, is considered his best-known work?

➢Q7. What was Zane Grey's major in college, where he also played baseball?

➢Q8. Besides writing novels, Zane Grey was passionate about which outdoor sport?

➢Q9. Which Zane Grey novel was inspired by his 1927 fishing trip to Australia and New Zealand?

➢Q10. In which year did Zane Grey pass away?

Turn the page upside down to see the answers.

A1. Pearl Zane Grey A2. Western A3. "Betty Zane" A4. Dentistry A5. Ohio A6. "Riders of the Purple Sage" A7. Dentistry A8. Fishing A9. "The Vanishing American" A10. 1939

Herman Melville

```
M Q C I R N R C K E U Z G Q I A V Y L U
T X C A A S J O Y H I N D J S A L Q I D
A I V E L W O M A N I K H Y V S I K M N
R S C V O J V H N L N B Y R U I A N Z N
U O C A B Z A L A A B A R T L E B Y O R
Q O V R B B L H N G D S B T P Z D V N B
Z B J H I E W T H O R C T B F Z F Q F Q
H U G J A V U E U M O B Y D I C K B B U
R J V M S C E Q B O W S F P E L N I E E
Q U H F K V E N M X D H C B I D W O N E
T S H E U P J K E Q U T W H I T E R Z Q
I V T N Z V U K X R U H H Y S K I U C U
I M M F B E P X O V Y Y C Y R U Q B D E
S Z J I G V L T F I N D E R N J Z Z H G
Y B N A A R P A C I F I C R A B D H C I Y
F E Y U Q C Z V I Y H P D Y G P S H V B
U O G B B V S S Y J C Q P P D F L R T L
V G O W E S A F D N S V S D A W N D X U
```

Ahab	Moby-dick	Queequeg
Bartleby	Nantucket	Scrivener
Dawn	Ocean	Voyage
Grey	Pacific	Whaling
Ishmael	Pequod	White

SOLUTION

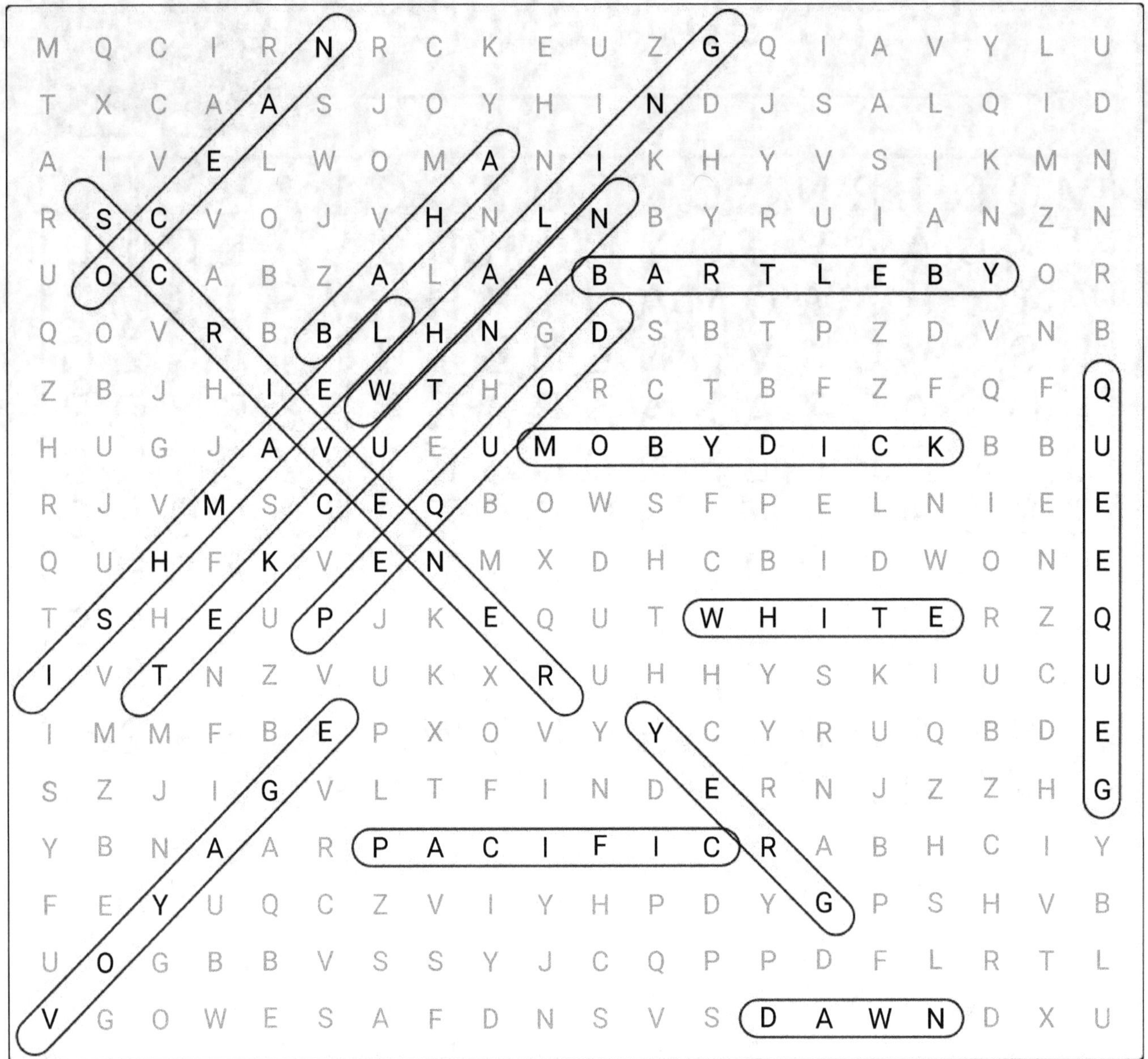

About Herman Melville

American novelist Herman Melville is esteemed for his profound works, including "Moby-Dick," which explores themes of obsession, revenge, and the human condition. His masterful storytelling and richly drawn characters have made him a celebrated figure in 19th-century American literature.

Trivia Questions

➢Q1. What is the name of the character in Herman Melville's novel "Moby-Dick" who is a sailor seeking revenge on a white whale?

➢Q2. Which of Herman Melville's novels is about a man named Bartleby who works as a scrivener and refuses to do his job?

➢Q3. What is the name of the character in Herman Melville's novel "Billy Budd" who is a sailor that is falsely accused of mutiny?

➢Q4. Which of Herman Melville's novels is about a man named Ishmael who signs up for a whaling voyage and befriends a harpooner named Queequeg?

➢Q5. What is the name of the character in Herman Melville's novel "Redburn" who is a young sailor on his first voyage to Liverpool?

➢Q6. Which of Herman Melville's novels is about a man named Pierre Glendinning who discovers a family secret and falls in love with his half-sister?

➢Q7. What is the name of the character in Herman Melville's novel "The Confidence-Man" who is a con artist that preys on passengers on a steamboat?

➢Q8. Which of Herman Melville's novels is about a man named Captain Ahab who becomes obsessed with hunting a white whale?

➢Q9. What is the name of the character in Herman Melville's novel "Israel Potter" who is an American Revolutionary War veteran that becomes a sailor?

➢Q10. Which of Herman Melville's novels is about a man named John Gentian who is a painter that becomes involved in a utopian community?

Turn the page upside down to see the answers.

A1. Captain Ahab. A2. "Bartleby, the Scrivener." A3. Billy Budd. A4. Ishmael. A5. Wellingborough Redburn. A6. "Pierre; or, The Ambiguities." A7. The Confidence-Man. A8. "Moby-Dick." A9. Israel Potter. A10. "The Paradise of Bachelors and The Tartarus of Maids."

Louis L'amour

```
S G Y I G R P S A J N J H U H F C H B Y
X R Q A P W Z A Z R O F L S G T Q B X M
H U C V H L A X G M R U A K M T V D R U
C E M P T Y S Z E Q T R N B L B K R P V
D O V N V Z X V J A H Y D N P Q Y N J P
E B M D I R E V I R L F V E C C T K T T
U S J S G J X S I A G O P E K J G O D R
E H P X T Q O I B Q A N D I G N L N Y U
L K X M W O D M U K R V J E A J Z B X K
D N J D V O C J D A I M G T H B F D J A
D N K T M C C K M R M T S G R B G G C A
A A B W N S L E E V U U V U P E L M K F
S M X E N A A B N B M U N G Q P X L B
V D C F L C N E I M P T E S G K W X H G
R A N S K K N V A E L H T N H N Z F P I
S B L J I E Q W T R I H J B D X C D S E
W O I S P T W S G A T T Z L C C F H K E
A D L A W T A Q K W O F Q M A K J A M H
```

Bend	Land	North
Comstock	Law	River
Empty	Lode	Sackett
Fury	Man	Saddle
Guns	Mustang	War

SOLUTION

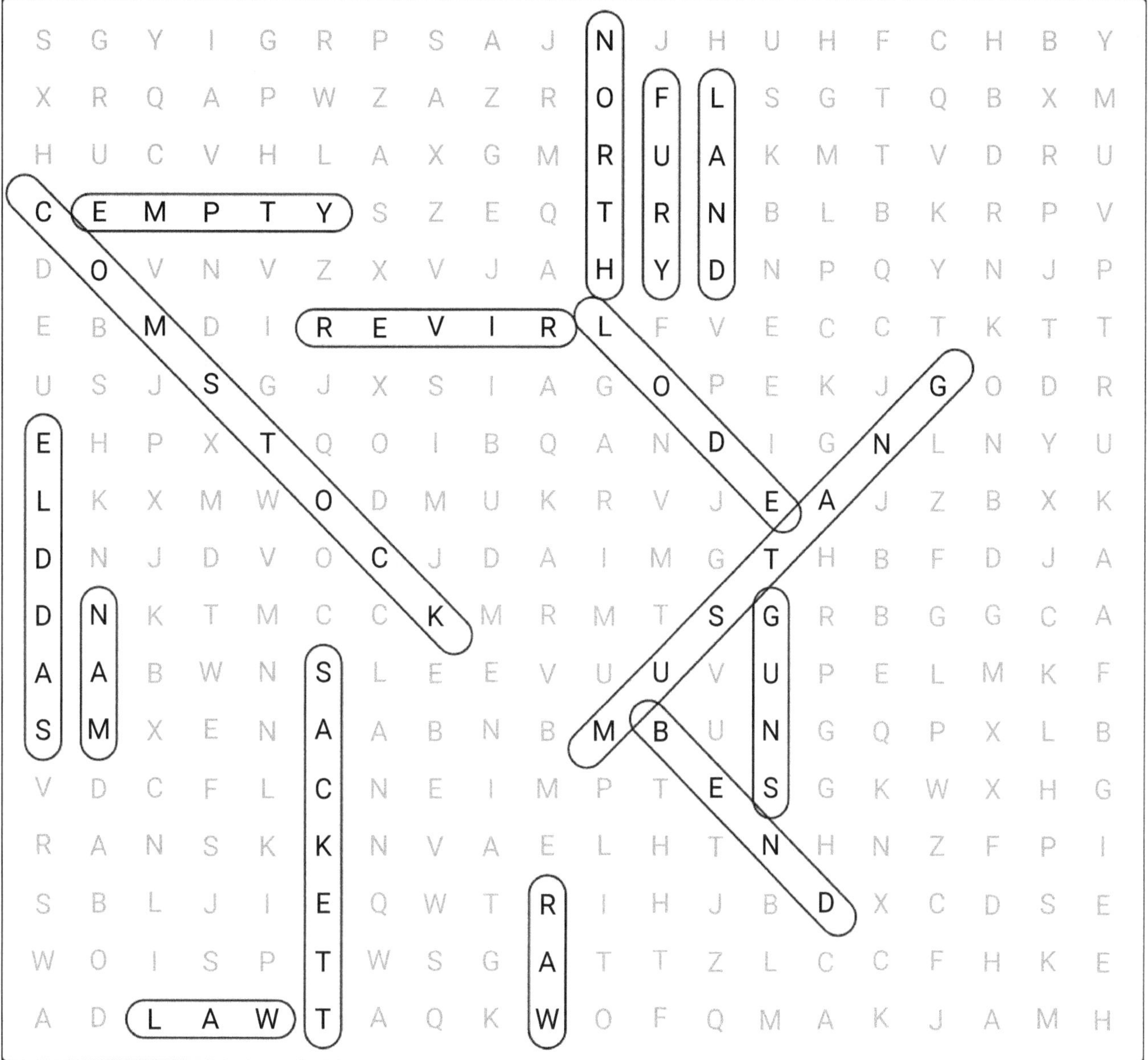

About Louis L'amour

American writer Louis L'Amour is known for his action-packed Western novels and short stories, which often feature themes of courage, honour, and perseverance. His vivid storytelling and compelling narratives have made him a beloved figure in the world of Western literature.

Trivia Questions

➢Q1. What was Louis L'Amour's full birth name?

➢Q2. In which U.S. state was Louis L'Amour born?

➢Q3. Louis L'Amour is best known for writing novels in which genre?

➢Q4. What was the title of Louis L'Amour's first published novel?

➢Q5. Which series of Louis L'Amour's books focuses on the fictional Sackett family?

➢Q6. How many books did Louis L'Amour write throughout his career, approximately?

➢Q7. Which prestigious award did Louis L'Amour receive from the U.S. Congress in 1984?

➢Q8. Louis L'Amour's novels were also popular in other formats. What were these formats?

➢Q9. What was the title of Louis L'Amour's first collection of short stories?

➢Q10. In which year did Louis L'Amour pass away?

Turn the page upside down to see the answers.

A1. Louis Dearborn LaMoore A2. North Dakota A3. Western A4. "Westward the Tide" A5. The Sackett series A6. Over 100 A7. Congressional Gold Medal A8. Audiobooks and films A9. "Night Over the Solomons" A10. 1988

David Baldacci

```
L O R T N O C K A U T K A N H S D B V K
C D V H C Q U D T C M H B R G M M M E W
C B J B K K T Y C O B V Y D X G V S X L
X H J I E N V N Q I L L I W E V K V F G
Q U R P T O T A L L W W V K H P Z E Q E
N F R C J G V M A G Y M Z I T A G I B A
G U H I M T Y S G R Z P N M E H B Q P
O F H V L A T Q O D Q I Q N I P G O I E
Y C L U B I N M I E Z V V O U G Y R J I
R D H P T M E A J R L T F C V V X U A F
Q D D Q R M N R G F Z Y M E D E Z E N T
C V O T R Y C C R U T N P N U Z A U M H
K G L C Y U A W L W G M V T M K K S T B
R K J S P J M X T S I M P L E L F U L U
H K J T S K E E S V J W M G S S R U S Z
S I C N J P L L L B V X C H H K T C I A P
A L J C R D A I X K W A A E Y L C Z Q X
N D G Y O Q Z M C D S W F X O Z Q U V N
```

Camel	Man	Simple
Club	Memory	Target
Control	Mile	Total
Innocent	Robie	Truth
Last	Shaw	Will

SOLUTION

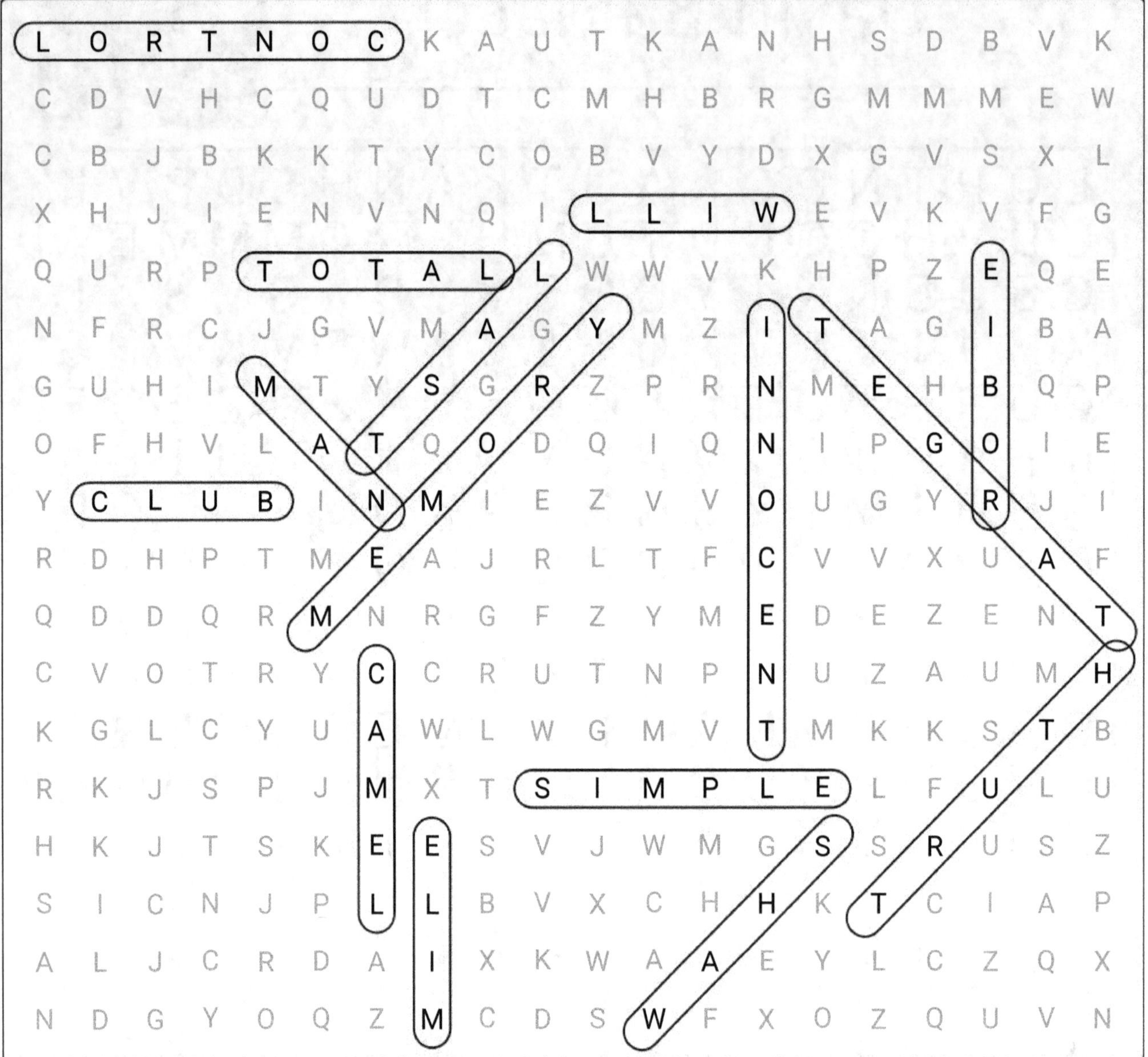

About David Baldacci

American author David Baldacci is celebrated for his gripping crime novels and political thrillers, which often feature intricate plots and suspenseful action. His engaging storytelling and well-drawn characters have made him a popular and respected figure in the world of contemporary fiction.

Trivia Questions

➢Q1. In which year was David Baldacci's first novel, "Absolute Power," published?

➢Q2. What is the name of the series by David Baldacci that features the character Amos Decker, a detective with a perfect memory?

➢Q3. Before becoming a successful author, what was David Baldacci's profession?

➢Q4. Which David Baldacci novel features characters Michelle Maxwell and Sean King, former Secret Service agents turned private detectives?

➢Q5. In which U.S. state was David Baldacci born and raised?

➢Q6. What is the name of the 2018 David Baldacci novel that introduces Atlee Pine, an FBI agent in search of her sister?

➢Q7. How many copies of David Baldacci's books have been sold worldwide, approximately?

➢Q8. In David Baldacci's novel, which character embarks on a festive cross-country train journey?

➢Q9. What is the name of the foundation David Baldacci and his wife created to support literacy efforts worldwide?

➢Q10. In which year was the film adaptation of David Baldacci's novel "Absolute Power" released?

Turn the page upside down to see the answers.

A1. 1996 A2. The Memory Man series A3. Lawyer A4. "Split Second" A5. Virginia A6. "Long Road to Mercy" A7. Over 130 million copies A8. "The Christmas Train" A9. The Wish You Well Foundation A10. 1997

William Goldman

```
U N Y D G Y D H X P S W Y K U A W L C P
W R N E D B X K T O F C W F W H F Y A V
S K H Z V N T Y A X Q Z R J Z W J D S E
O V P O M Z T U A Z L X T E Q H S S S Z
R U P P A U M X F B U E O S E C B J I X
N M N F N H T H Y U Q I N A F N L D D E
S U B P R I N C E S S M B E C Y P F Y M
D P Q A B M E Z Y O P O V U B L O L U D
B V I X D Q S M B E Y D C P O V C A A Y
F U Q Q K V W Z G S M L I Z W L Z F D Y
J D T H O E E D H D S V X K T V S E T E
L W E C H D I N I S I G F S A L D A T W
A L V Y H R R T T B U A Z L Q I E V Y R
V Z B F B I A Q C U R R C Q R H F O I F
H G B D O Y Q W A N R V K B H C A O N D
Z Z I N O B O D Y P L E I T R K N W X P
T H J B E C N A D N U S S H O V K E G A
B F M K L C A O G B N O H T A R A M F K
```

Adventures	Cassidy	Marathon
Boys	Far	Nobody
Bride	Heat	Princess
Bridge	Kid	Screenplay
Butch	Man	Sundance

SOLUTION

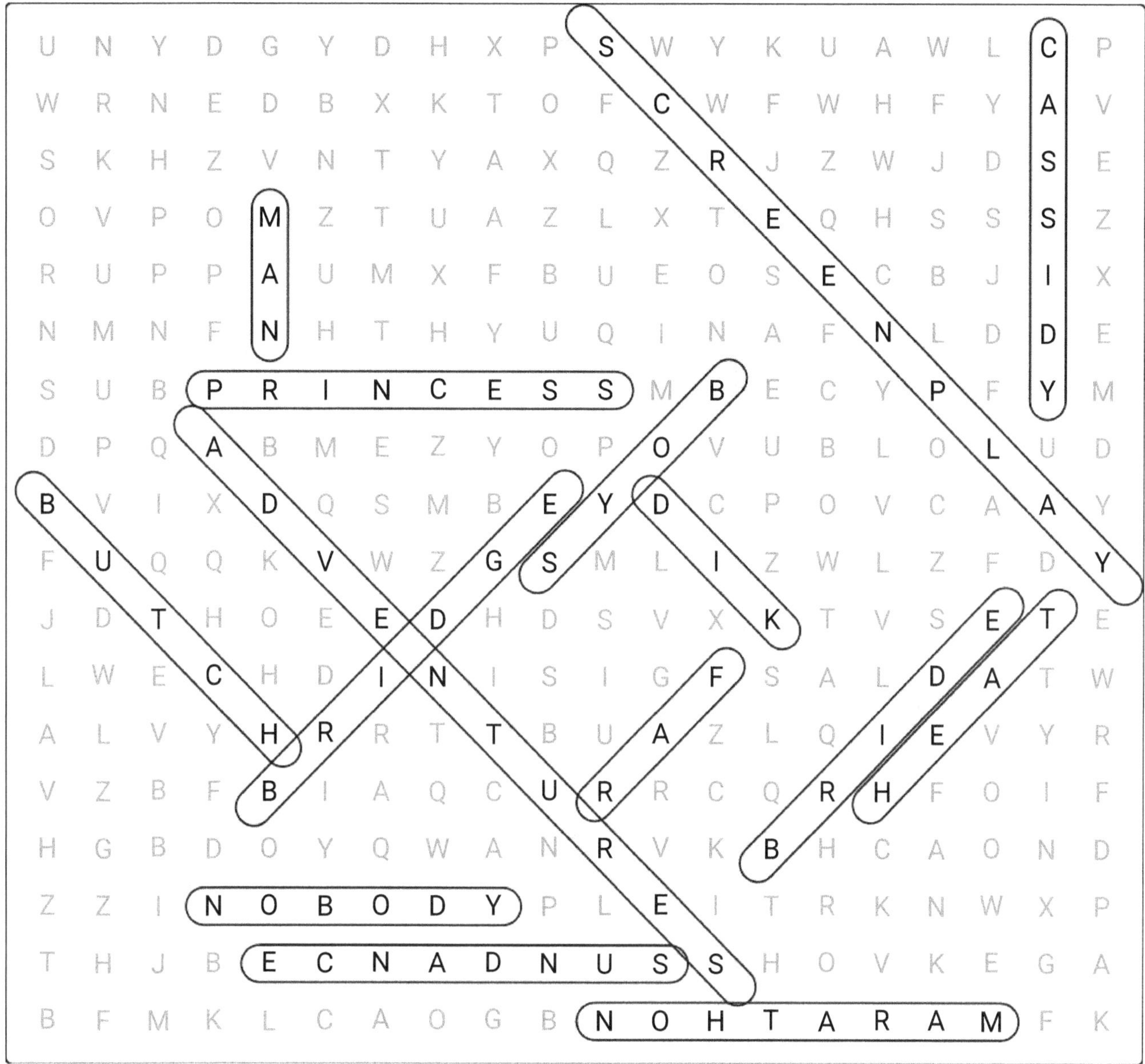

About William Goldman

American novelist and screenwriter William Goldman is acclaimed for his versatile writing, which includes works of fiction, drama, and screenplays. His inventive storytelling and memorable characters have made him a celebrated figure in both literature and the film industry.

Trivia Questions

➢Q1. In William Goldman's novel "The Princess Bride," what is the name of the farmhand who falls in love with a princess?

➢Q2. Which William Goldman novel revolves around a character named Tom, who gets caught up in a dispute between two circus proprietors?

➢Q3. In William Goldman's novel "Magic," what is the name of the ventriloquist grappling with mental illness?

➢Q4. Which William Goldman novel features a character named Lord Lavender who gets entangled in a plot to overthrow the English government?

➢Q5. In William Goldman's "Soldier in the Rain," what is the name of the soldier stationed in Korea?

➢Q6. Which William Goldman novel follows a character named Eddie as he becomes part of a plan to steal a fortune in gold?

➢Q7. In William Goldman's novel "Heat," what is the name of the screenwriter working on a Hollywood film?

➢Q8. Which William Goldman novel centres around a character named Harry, who becomes involved in a conspiracy to steal a priceless artefact?

➢Q9. In William Goldman's novel "Boys and Girls Together," what is the name of the struggling writer residing in New York City?

➢Q10. Which William Goldman novel features a character named Sully who becomes part of a scheme to steal an invaluable painting?

Turn the page upside down to see the answers.

A1. Westley, A2. "The Temple of Gold," A3. Corky Withers. A4. "Lord of the Flies 2." A5. Sergeant Pope. A6. "Marathon Man." A7. Harry Stoner. A8. "The Silent Gondoliers." A9. Paul Regret. A10. "The Color of Light."

Dad's Day Decoded

Dad's Day Decoded" is a fascinating section that is dedicated to uncovering 50 riveting facts about Father's Day celebrations from across the globe. This compelling exploration provides a unique insight into diverse customs, traditions, and rituals associated with the celebration of fatherhood, presenting a tapestry of cultural richness and historical significance that's sure to intrigue readers with its global perspective on a universally celebrated occasion.

1. Father's Day was first celebrated on June 19, 1910, in the state of Washington.

2. The idea of Father's Day was proposed by Sonora Dodd to honor her father, a Civil War veteran who raised six children as a single parent.

3. The first Father's Day was observed on the birthday of Sonora Dodd's father, William Jackson Smart.

4. Father's Day was officially recognized as a national holiday in the US in 1972, during Richard Nixon's presidency.

5. Unlike Mother's Day, which is the busiest day for phone calls, Father's Day is the busiest day for collect calls.

6. Neckties are the most popular Father's Day gift.

7. In Thailand, Father's Day is celebrated on the King's birthday.

8. In Australia, Father's Day is celebrated on the first Sunday of September.

9. Germany celebrates Father's Day by having men pulling wagons filled with beer into parks and woods.

10. In Russia, Father's Day is known as Defender of the Fatherland Day.

11. On Father's Day in South Africa, many families go fishing due to its pleasant winter season.

12. The world record for having the most children is 69, held by the first wife of Feodor Vassilyev, a peasant from Russia – a record certain to make Father's Day a busy one.

13. According to Hallmark, Father's Day is the fourth largest card-sending occasion.

14. The official flower for Father's Day is the rose; a red rose is worn in the lapel if your father is living, a white rose if he is deceased.

15. There are approximately 2 billion fathers worldwide.

16. In Mandarin Chinese, the phonetic pronunciation of the number eight is "ba," which also sounds like the informal word for father, "baba," making 8 a lucky number associated with Father's Day in China.

17. In Brazil, Father's Day is celebrated on the second Sunday of August in honor of Saint Joachim, the patron saint of fathers and grandfathers.

18. The US Census Bureau estimates there are over 72 million fathers across the nation.

19. There are about 2 million single fathers in the US.

20. Almost 25% of Father's Day cards are purchased by wives for their husbands.

21. In Mexico, a 21-kilometer race in Mexico City is held every Father's Day.

22. Father's Day is the fifth most popular occasion for sending personal greeting cards in the United States.

23. Over 50 countries in the world celebrate Father's Day on the third Sunday in June.

24. In Italy, Father's Day is celebrated on March 19, the Feast of Saint Joseph.

25. In Finland, Father's Day is a flag-flying day.

26. Father's Day is the busiest day of the year for collect (reverse charge) telephone calls in the UK.

27. The word "Dad" is believed to have originated in the sixteenth century from the Latin word 'Tata', a child's word for father.

28. The first presidential proclamation honoring fathers was issued in 1966 by President Lyndon B. Johnson.

29. The phrase "Happy Father's Day" is said in over 130 languages around the world, demonstrating the widespread celebration of fathers globally.

30. A popular custom on Father's Day in Japan is to gift fathers with a pair of glass beer mugs, symbolizing relaxation and enjoyment after a long day's work.

31. The Father's Day Council was founded in New York City in 1931.

32. According to a survey, the most popular gift for
Father's Day is a special outing, like dinner or a sports
event.

33. The idea to make Father's Day a national holiday
began to gain support when a bill was introduced in the
U.S. Congress in 1913.

34. "In Estonia, Father's Day ("Isadepäev") is a national
holiday, celebrated on the second Sunday of November,
and typically involves families spending quality time
together, often in the great outdoors."

35. In certain countries, such as the Netherlands and
Belgium, Father's Day is typically celebrated with
breakfast in bed prepared by children.

36. Around a quarter of all Father's Day cards are
humorous in nature, reflecting the trend of dads being the
'funny guy' in many households.

37. The city of Spokane, Washington, where Sonora Dodd
initially proposed Father's Day, is now home to a
dedicated Father's Day memorial.

38. There are almost as many pet dads in the U.S. as
there are human dads, with almost 70 million men
owning a pet.

39. More than 135 countries celebrate Father's Day every
year.

40. The first Father's Day celebration was said to be quite somber, as it was dedicated to the memory of a large group of men, many of them fathers, who had died in a mining accident in Monongah, West Virginia in December 1907.

41. In the United States, Father's Day is the busiest day for the collectible industry as many people gift their fathers memorabilia, vintage items or collectibles.

42. More than a third of the Father's Day cards purchased are for husbands.

43. There are more than 2.85 million single fathers in the United Kingdom.

44. According to the National Retail Federation, Americans were expected to spend more than $16 billion on gifts for Father's Day in 2019.

45. The most popular internet search associated with the term "Father's Day" is "When is Father's Day?"

46. In the U.S., over 93 million Father's Day cards are exchanged each year.

47. Father's Day is the fourth most popular occasion for sending greeting cards, after Christmas, Valentine's Day, and Mother's Day.

48. Most South American countries celebrate Father's Day in June, though the date can vary and may be celebrated in March, like in Bolivia.

49. The tradition of giving gifts on Father's Day started in the early 20th century in the United States as a way to honor the contributions of fathers to their families.

50. "In France, Father's Day was introduced in 1950 by a lighter manufacturer as part of a marketing campaign to sell their products. It's celebrated on the third Sunday in June, similar to many other countries."

Dad Jokes Extravaganza

Get ready for an explosion of laughter with our "Dad Jokes Extravaganza" - a whopping collection of over 800 jokes guaranteed to tickle your funny bone! This book is the perfect Father's Day gift, packed with knee-slappers, puns, and good-natured humor that will have the whole family groaning in delight. Embrace the spirit of Father's Day and keep the laughter flowing with this ultimate joke collection.

1. A son asks his father, "Dad, why do we have to be innovative?" The father replies, "Well, son, innovation is the driving force behind progress and change. It's through innovation that we find new solutions to old problems, spark creativity, and push the boundaries of what's possible. It's a way of constantly improving and adapting to the ever-evolving world." The son says, "So, when I embrace innovation, is it just my way of contributing to the forward march of humanity?"

2. A son says to his father, "Dad, when I grow up, I want to be an astronaut." The father replies, "That's an extraordinary choice, son. Remember, astronauts need to have a thirst for knowledge, physical endurance, and the courage to explore the vast unknown. Through their journeys, they inspire us to dream big and venture into uncharted territories." The son says, "I've got that, Dad. I always feel a sense of wonder and excitement when I gaze at the stars and imagine what lies beyond."

3. A father and son are watching a show about the wonders of the Serengeti. The son asks, "Dad, why is the Serengeti so captivating?" The father replies, "Well, son, the Serengeti is a pristine ecosystem teeming with diverse wildlife and natural beauty. It's a living testament to the delicate balance of nature and the interconnectedness of all living things. It reminds us of our responsibility to protect and preserve our planet's precious biodiversity." The son says, "So, when I see the Serengeti, is it just a

reminder of the importance of conservation and coexistence?"

4. A son asks his father, "Dad, why do we have to be resilient?" The father replies, "Well, son, resilience is the key to overcoming challenges and bouncing back from adversity. It's through resilience that we find the strength to persevere, learn from setbacks, and emerge stronger than before. It's a quality that empowers us to face life's ups and downs with unwavering determination." The son says, "So, when I embody resilience, is it just my way of embracing the warrior spirit within me?"

5. A son says to his father, "Dad, when I grow up, I want to be an explorer." The father replies, "That's an adventurous choice, son. Remember, explorers need to have curiosity, bravery, and a thirst for discovery. Through their explorations, they expand our knowledge of the world and inspire us to venture into the unknown." The son says, "I've got that, Dad. I always feel a sense of exhilaration when I embark on new journeys and uncover hidden treasures."

6. A father and son are watching a show about the wonders of the Great Wall of China. The son asks, "Dad, why is the Great Wall of China so impressive?" The father replies, "Well, son, the Great Wall of China is a testament to human ingenuity, determination, and the power of unity. It stretches for thousands of miles, standing as a symbol

of China's rich history and the collective strength of its people." The son says, "So, when I see the Great Wall, is it just a reminder of the remarkable feats that can be accomplished when we come together?"

7. A son asks his father, "Dad, why do we need to be adaptable?" The father replies, "Well, son, adaptability is the key to thriving in a rapidly changing world. It's through adaptability that we embrace new circumstances, learn new skills, and navigate unexpected challenges. It's a way of staying flexible and resilient in the face of uncertainty." The son says, "So, when I embrace adaptability, is it just my way of riding the waves of change and seizing new opportunities?"

8. A son says to his father, "Dad, when I grow up, I want to be a teacher." The father replies, "That's a noble choice, son. Remember, teachers have the power to shape young minds, inspire a love for learning, and ignite the flame of curiosity. Through their guidance and mentorship, they have the opportunity to make a lasting impact on future generations." The son says, "I've got that, Dad. I always feel a sense of fulfillment when I see the spark of understanding in a student's eyes."

9. A father and son are watching a show about the wonders of the Mayan civilization. The son asks, "Dad, why are the Mayan ruins so fascinating?" The father

replies, "Well, son, the Mayan ruins hold the secrets of an ancient civilization that flourished centuries ago. They are a testament to the ingenuity, advanced knowledge, and cultural richness of the Mayan people. They remind us of the enduring legacy of human history." The son says, "So, when I see the Mayan ruins, is it just a glimpse into the achievements and wisdom of our ancestors?"

10. A son asks his father, "Dad, why do we have to be compassionate?" The father replies, "Well, son, compassion is the bridge that connects us to the hearts of others. It's through compassion that we understand and empathize with their joys, sorrows, and struggles. It's a way of showing kindness, support, and love to those around us, fostering a sense of unity and shared humanity." The son says, "So, when I embody compassion, is it just my way of spreading warmth and healing in a world that sometimes feels cold?"

11. A son says to his father, "Dad, when I grow up, I want to be a chef." The father replies, "That's a flavorful choice, son. Remember, chefs need to have a passion for culinary arts, creativity, and the ability to tantalize taste buds with their delicious creations. Through their culinary skills, they can bring joy and nourishment to people's lives." The son says, "I've got that, Dad. I always feel a sense of fulfillment when I create a delectable dish that brings smiles to people's faces."

12. A father and son are watching a show about the wonders of the Inca civilization. The son asks, "Dad, why are the Inca ruins so awe-inspiring?" The father replies, "Well, son, the Inca ruins hold the stories of a magnificent civilization that thrived in the Andes. They are a testament to the Inca's architectural prowess, cultural richness, and their deep connection with the natural world. They remind us of the power of human creativity and the impermanence of empires." The son says, "So, when I see the Inca ruins, is it just a reminder of the fleeting nature of human achievements and the importance of cherishing our cultural heritage?"

13. A son asks his father, "Dad, why do we have to be patient?" The father replies, "Well, son, patience is the art of waiting gracefully. It's through patience that we cultivate inner peace, resilience, and understanding. It's a way of recognizing that some things take time to unfold and that the best outcomes often require patience and perseverance." The son says, "So, when I practice patience, is it just my way of surrendering to the rhythm of life and trusting in the process?"

14. A son says to his father, "Dad, when I grow up, I want to be an engineer." The father replies, "That's a brilliant choice, son. Remember, engineers have the power to transform ideas into reality, solve complex problems, and improve the world we live in. Through their innovative

thinking and technical expertise, they shape the future and create a better tomorrow." The son says, "I've got that, Dad. I always feel a sense of fulfillment when I see the tangible impact of my engineering designs."

15. A father and son are watching a show about the wonders of the Louvre Museum. The son asks, "Dad, why are the artworks in the Louvre so captivating?" The father replies, "Well, son, the artworks in the Louvre hold the expressions of human creativity, emotions, and stories from different periods of history. They are a testament to the power of artistic expression and the enduring legacy of artists throughout the ages." The son says, "So, when I see the artworks in the Louvre, is it just a glimpse into the kaleidoscope of human imagination and the beauty that can be created with a brushstroke?"

16. A son asks his father, "Dad, why do we need to be courageous?" The father replies, "Well, son, courage is the inner strength that propels us forward in the face of fear or uncertainty. It's through courage that we take risks, pursue our dreams, and stand up for what we believe in. It's a way of embracing life's challenges and discovering the depth of our own capabilities." The son says, "So, when I embrace courage, is it just my way of unlocking the doors to my full potential?"

17. A son says to his father, "Dad, when I grow up, I want to be a writer." The father replies, "That's a captivating

choice, son. Remember, writers have the power to weave words into captivating stories, inspire minds, and transport readers to different worlds. Through their narratives, they give a voice to emotions, ideas, and the human experience." The son says, "I've got that, Dad. I always feel a sense of magic and fulfillment when I let my imagination dance on the pages."

18. A father and son are watching a show about the wonders of the Taj Mahal. The son asks, "Dad, why is the Taj Mahal so breathtaking?" The father replies, "Well, son, the Taj Mahal is a marvel of architectural beauty and a symbol of enduring love. It stands as a testament to human craftsmanship, intricate detailing, and the power of immortalizing emotions through art." The son says, "So, when I see the Taj Mahal, is it just a reminder of the beauty that can be born from love and devotion?"

19. A son asks his father, "Dad, why do we have to be grateful?" The father replies, "Well, son, gratitude is the practice of acknowledging and appreciating the blessings in our lives. It's through gratitude that we cultivate a positive mindset, foster happiness, and deepen our connections with others. It's a way of recognizing the abundance that surrounds us and finding joy in the present moment." The son says, "So, when I express gratitude, is it just my way of counting my blessings and cherishing the beauty of each day?"

20. A son says to his father, "Dad, when I grow up, I want to be a psychologist." The father replies, "That's a profound choice, son. Remember, psychologists have the opportunity to understand the complexities of the human mind, offer support, and help people navigate their emotional well-being. Through their expertise, they provide insights and facilitate positive change." The son says, "I've got that, Dad. I always feel a sense of fulfillment when I witness the transformation and healing that comes from understanding ourselves and others."

21. A father and son are watching a show about the wonders of the Eiffel Tower. The son asks, "Dad, why is the Eiffel Tower so iconic?" The father replies, "Well, son, the Eiffel Tower is a symbol of Paris and a testament to human engineering and creativity. It stands tall as a reminder of the power of imagination and the possibilities that arise when we dare to dream big." The son says, "So, when I see the Eiffel Tower, is it just a spark of inspiration that fuels my own dreams?"

22. A son asks his father, "Dad, why do we have to be resilient?" The father replies, "Well, son, resilience is the strength that emerges when we face adversity head-on, adapt to change, and keep moving forward. It's through resilience that we discover our own inner fortitude, learn from setbacks, and rise above the challenges that come our way." The son says, "So, when I embody resilience, is

it just my way of showing the world that I won't let circumstances define me?"

23. A son says to his father, "Dad, when I grow up, I want to be an athlete." The father replies, "That's an inspiring choice, son. Remember, athletes have the discipline, dedication, and perseverance to push their physical limits and excel in their chosen sports. Through their achievements, they inspire others to strive for greatness and demonstrate the power of determination." The son says, "I've got that, Dad. I always feel a sense of exhilaration and personal growth when I challenge my body and push my boundaries."

24. A father and son are watching a show about the wonders of the Colosseum. The son asks, "Dad, why is the Colosseum so fascinating?" The father replies, "Well, son, the Colosseum stands as a testament to the grandeur of ancient Rome and the prowess of its engineering. It's a reminder of the rich history that shapes our world today and the enduring legacy of human achievements." The son says, "So, when I see the Colosseum, is it just a glimpse into the marvels of our collective human history?"

25. A son asks his father, "Dad, why do we have to be compassionate?" The father replies, "Well, son, compassion is the gentle force that connects us to others' pain and suffering, inspiring us to offer kindness, understanding, and support. It's through compassion that

we build bridges of empathy and create a more caring and inclusive world." The son says, "So, when I embody compassion, is it just my way of being a beacon of light in someone's darkness?"

26. A son says to his father, "Dad, when I grow up, I want to be a musician." The father replies, "That's a melodious choice, son. Remember, musicians have the power to stir emotions, convey messages, and uplift spirits through the language of music. Through their melodies, they create harmony and touch the deepest corners of the human soul." The son says, "I've got that, Dad. I always feel a sense of joy and connection when I play an instrument and share my music with others."

27. A father and son are watching a show about the wonders of the Great Barrier Reef. The son asks, "Dad, why is the Great Barrier Reef so captivating?" The father replies, "Well, son, the Great Barrier Reef is a mesmerizing underwater wonderland, teeming with vibrant coral and marine life. It's a testament to the beauty and fragility of our oceans, reminding us of the importance of environmental stewardship and the interconnectedness of all living things." The son says, "So, when I see the Great Barrier Reef, is it just a reminder of the wonders that lie beneath the surface?"

28. A son asks his father, "Dad, why do we have to be resilient?" The father replies, "Well, son, resilience is the

strength that helps us weather the storms of life, bounce back from setbacks, and embrace challenges as opportunities for growth. It's through resilience that we develop inner fortitude, perseverance, and the belief that we can overcome even the toughest obstacles." The son says, "So, when I embody resilience, is it just my way of rising from the ashes and showing the world the power of a resilient spirit?"

29. A son says to his father, "Dad, when I grow up, I want to be a painter." The father replies, "That's a stroke of artistic brilliance, son. Remember, painters have the ability to translate emotions, impressions, and visions onto canvas, creating visual poetry that touches the hearts of others. Through their art, they invite us to see the world through new eyes." The son says, "I've got that, Dad. I always feel a sense of freedom and expression when I hold a paintbrush in my hand."

30. A father and son are watching a show about the wonders of the Amazon River. The son asks, "Dad, why is the Amazon River so extraordinary?" The father replies, "Well, son, the Amazon River is the lifeline of a vast ecosystem, teeming with diverse plant and animal species. It's a symbol of the interconnectedness of nature, providing sustenance, shelter, and a source of wonder for countless creatures." The son says, "So, when I see the Amazon River, is it just a reminder of the intricate tapestry of life and the need to protect our natural resources?"

31. A son asks his father, "Dad, why do we have to be courageous?" The father replies, "Well, son, courage is the fire that burns within us, empowering us to step outside our comfort zones, face our fears, and take bold leaps of faith. It's through courage that we expand our horizons, embrace growth, and unlock new realms of possibility." The son says, "So, when I embrace courage, is it just my way of living life to the fullest and embracing the adventures that await?"

32. A son says to his father, "Dad, when I grow up, I want to be an architect." The father replies, "That's a visionary choice, son. Remember, architects have the power to shape the physical world, create spaces that inspire, and harmonize aesthetics with functionality. Through their designs, they leave a lasting imprint on the landscapes we inhabit." The son says, "I've got that, Dad. I always feel a sense of pride and accomplishment when I see my architectural visions come to life."

33. A father and son are watching a show about the wonders of the Sahara Desert. The son asks, "Dad, why is the Sahara Desert so captivating?" The father replies, "Well, son, the Sahara Desert is a vast expanse of beauty and mystery. Its golden dunes, shifting landscapes, and serene emptiness remind us of the immense power of

nature and the importance of preserving the fragile balance of our planet." The son says, "So, when I see the Sahara Desert, is it just a glimpse into the enigmatic charm of the natural world?"

34. A son asks his father, "Dad, why do we have to be compassionate?" The father replies, "Well, son, compassion is the language of the heart, a way of connecting with others and offering a helping hand. It's through compassion that we create a ripple effect of kindness, understanding, and support, nurturing the seeds of love and humanity in our world." The son says, "So, when I embody compassion, is it just my way of being an instrument of peace and healing?"

35. A son says to his father, "Dad, when I grow up, I want to be a scientist." The father replies, "That's an exploratory choice, son. Remember, scientists have the curious minds, analytical skills, and thirst for knowledge that drive discoveries and push the boundaries of human understanding. Through their research, they unlock the secrets of the universe and pave the way for progress." The son says, "I've got that, Dad. I always feel a sense of wonder and excitement when I unravel the mysteries of the world through science."

36. A father and son are watching a show about the wonders of the Redwood Forest. The son asks, "Dad, why are the redwood trees so awe-inspiring?" The father

replies, "Well, son, the redwood trees stand as giants, reaching for the sky and defying the passage of time. They are a reminder of the resilience and grandeur of nature, showcasing the beauty and harmony that can be found in the embrace of towering trees." The son says, "So, when I see the redwood trees, is it just a glimpse into the magnificence and wisdom of the natural world?"

37. A son asks his father, "Dad, why do we have to be resilient?" The father replies, "Well, son, resilience is the anchor that keeps us steady amidst life's storms, the inner flame that refuses to be extinguished. It's through resilience that we find the strength to face adversity, overcome obstacles, and emerge stronger than before. It's a quality that teaches us the power of perseverance and the art of bouncing back." The son says, "So, when I embody resilience, is it just my way of showing the world that setbacks are not the end, but merely a detour on the path to success?"

38. A son says to his father, "Dad, when I grow up, I want to be a filmmaker." The father replies, "That's a cinematic choice, son. Remember, filmmakers have the power to tell compelling stories, evoke emotions, and transport audiences to different worlds. Through their lens, they capture the essence of humanity, shedding light on diverse perspectives and nurturing empathy." The son says, "I've got that, Dad. I always feel a sense of wonder

and magic when I bring my imagination to life on the silver screen."

39. A father and son are watching a show about the wonders of the Galapagos Islands. The son asks, "Dad, why are the Galapagos Islands so extraordinary?" The father replies, "Well, son, the Galapagos Islands are a living laboratory of evolution and biodiversity. They hold a treasure trove of unique species and offer a glimpse into the intricate web of life. They remind us of the delicate balance of nature and the importance of conservation." The son says, "So, when I see the Galapagos Islands, is it just a reminder of the wonders that arise when nature is left undisturbed?"

40. A son asks his father, "Dad, why do we have to be true to ourselves?" The father replies, "Well, son, being true to yourself means embracing your authentic voice, values, and passions. It's through authenticity that we find fulfillment, create genuine connections with others, and make a meaningful contribution to the world. It's a way of honoring who you are and living a life that aligns with your deepest truth." The son says, "So, when I embody authenticity, is it just my way of shining my unique light and inspiring others to do the same?"

41. A son asks his father, "Dad, why do we have dreams?" The father replies, "Well, son, dreams are a gateway to our subconscious mind. They allow us to explore our

deepest desires, fears, and aspirations, and can sometimes offer insights into our own thoughts and emotions." The son says, "So, when I dream, is it just my mind unraveling its hidden mysteries?"

42. A son says to his father, "Dad, when I grow up, I want to be an archaeologist." The father replies, "That's an adventurous choice, son. Remember, archaeologists need to have a passion for history, an eye for detail, and a love for unraveling the secrets of ancient civilizations." The son says, "I've got that, Dad. I always feel like a treasure hunter when I dig in the backyard."

43. A father and son are watching a show about the wonders of the human body. The son asks, "Dad, why do we have fingerprints?" The father replies, "Well, son, fingerprints are unique to each individual. They serve as a form of identification and help us leave our mark on the world, both literally and metaphorically." The son says, "So, when I see my fingerprints, is it just a reminder of my own uniqueness?"

44. A son asks his father, "Dad, why do we have to work?" The father replies, "Well, son, work gives us a sense of purpose, allows us to contribute to society, and provides for our needs and the needs of our loved ones. It's through work that we can grow and achieve our goals." The son says, "So, when I work, is it just my way of making a meaningful impact?"

45. A son says to his father, "Dad, when I grow up, I want to be an astronaut." The father replies, "That's an out-of-this-world choice, son. Remember, astronauts need to have courage, a strong scientific background, and a passion for exploration." The son says, "I've got that, Dad. I always feel like I'm floating among the stars when I gaze up at the night sky."

46. A father and son are watching a show about the wonders of the rainforest. The son asks, "Dad, why is the rainforest so important for the planet?" The father replies, "Well, son, the rainforest is often called the 'lungs of the Earth' because it produces a significant amount of oxygen and plays a crucial role in maintaining the balance of our planet's ecosystems." The son says, "So, when I see pictures of the rainforest, is it just a reminder of the beauty and importance of nature?"

47. A son asks his father, "Dad, why do we have to forgive?" The father replies, "Well, son, forgiveness is a powerful act of letting go of resentment, anger, or hurt. It allows us to heal, move forward, and nurture healthier relationships with others and ourselves." The son says, "So, when I forgive, is it just my way of finding peace and embracing compassion?"

48. A son says to his father, "Dad, when I grow up, I want to be a chef." The father replies, "That's a delicious choice,

son. Remember, chefs need to have creativity, culinary skills, and a passion for bringing joy through food." The son says, "I've got that, Dad. I always feel like a maestro in the kitchen, creating flavors that dance on the palate."

49. A father and son are watching a show about the wonders of the universe. The son asks, "Dad, why is the universe so vast?" The father replies, "Well, son, the universe is vast because it contains billions of galaxies, stars, and planets, all expanding and constantly evolving. It's a reminder of the infinite possibilities and mysteries that await us." The son says, "So, when I gaze at the night sky, is it just a glimpse into the grandeur of the cosmos?"

50. A son asks his father, "Dad, why do we have to be kind?" The father replies, "Well, son, kindness is like a ripple in a pond. It has the power to brighten someone's day, create a sense of belonging, and make the world a better place. It's through acts of kindness that we cultivate compassion and foster harmonious relationships." The son says, "So, when I show kindness, is it just my way of spreading warmth and positivity?"

51. A son says to his father, "Dad, when I grow up, I want to be a teacher." The father replies, "That's an admirable choice, son. Remember, teachers have the incredible opportunity to inspire and shape young minds, impart knowledge, and ignite a love for learning." The son says,

"I've got that, Dad. I always feel a sense of fulfillment when I help others understand and grow."

52. A father and son are watching a show about the wonders of the deep sea. The son asks, "Dad, why is the deep sea so mysterious?" The father replies, "Well, son, the deep sea is vast and largely unexplored. It's home to fascinating creatures and hidden wonders that continue to captivate scientists and explorers." The son says, "So, when I hear about deep-sea discoveries, is it just a reminder of the mysteries that lie beneath the surface?"

53. A son asks his father, "Dad, why do we need to be patient?" The father replies, "Well, son, patience is a virtue that allows us to stay calm in the face of challenges, wait for things to unfold in their own time, and cultivate resilience. It's through patience that we can find inner peace and navigate life's ups and downs." The son says, "So, when I practice patience, is it just my way of trusting in the process?"

54. A son says to his father, "Dad, when I grow up, I want to be an athlete." The father replies, "That's a fantastic choice, son. Remember, athletes need to have discipline, perseverance, and a love for their chosen sport. Through dedication and hard work, they can achieve remarkable feats." The son says, "I've got that, Dad. I always feel alive and free when I'm running and competing."

55. A father and son are watching a show about the wonders of the human brain. The son asks, "Dad, why is the brain so fascinating?" The father replies, "Well, son, the brain is like a complex universe within us. It's the command center that controls our thoughts, emotions, and actions, enabling us to think, feel, and experience the world around us." The son says, "So, when I learn about the brain, is it just a reminder of the marvels of our own minds?"

56. A son asks his father, "Dad, why do we need to take risks?" The father replies, "Well, son, taking risks opens doors to new experiences, growth, and personal development. It's through stepping outside our comfort zones that we discover our true potential and embrace the possibilities that life has to offer." The son says, "So, when I take a risk, is it just my way of writing my own adventure?"

57. A son says to his father, "Dad, when I grow up, I want to be a doctor." The father replies, "That's a noble choice, son. Remember, doctors need to have compassion, empathy, and a deep desire to heal and care for others. Through their expertise, they can make a significant impact on people's lives." The son says, "I've got that, Dad. I always feel a sense of purpose when I imagine myself serving others in the medical field."

58. A father and son are watching a show about the wonders of the desert. The son asks, "Dad, why is the desert so intriguing?" The father replies, "Well, son, the desert is a place of stark beauty and survival. It's a testament to the resilience of life in harsh conditions and teaches us the value of adaptation and resourcefulness." The son says, "So, when I see pictures of the desert, is it just a reminder of the strength and tenacity of nature?"

59. A son asks his father, "Dad, why do we have to be grateful?" The father replies, "Well, son, gratitude is the practice of acknowledging and appreciating the blessings, big and small, in our lives. It helps us cultivate a positive mindset, enhances our overall well-being, and deepens our connection with others." The son says, "So, when I express gratitude, is it just my way of counting my blessings and cherishing the present moment?"

60. A son says to his father, "Dad, when I grow up, I want to be a musician." The father replies, "That's a melodious choice, son. Remember, musicians need to have a passion for music, dedication to their craft, and the ability to move hearts with their melodies." The son says, "I've got that, Dad. I always feel a sense of joy and freedom when I play my instrument."

61. A father and son are watching a show about the wonders of the cosmos. The son asks, "Dad, why is space exploration important?" The father replies, "Well, son,

space exploration pushes the boundaries of human knowledge, expands our understanding of the universe, and inspires future generations to dream big and reach for the stars." The son says, "So, when I hear about space missions, is it just a reminder of our endless thirst for discovery?"

62. A son asks his father, "Dad, why do we have to be honest?" The father replies, "Well, son, honesty is the foundation of trust, integrity, and healthy relationships. It allows us to be true to ourselves and others, creating an atmosphere of authenticity and respect." The son says, "So, when I choose honesty, is it just my way of honoring the value of truth?"

63. A son says to his father, "Dad, when I grow up, I want to be a firefighter." The father replies, "That's a courageous choice, son. Remember, firefighters need to have bravery, physical strength, and a commitment to protecting and saving lives. Through their selflessness, they become everyday heroes." The son says, "I've got that, Dad. I always feel a sense of duty and responsibility when I imagine myself in their shoes."

64. A father and son are watching a show about the wonders of the savannah. The son asks, "Dad, why is the savannah so captivating?" The father replies, "Well, son, the savannah is a dynamic ecosystem teeming with

diverse wildlife, showcasing the intricate balance between predators and prey. It's a place of raw beauty and the circle of life." The son says, "So, when I see pictures of the savannah, isit just a glimpse into nature's ever-changing tapestry of existence?"

65. A son asks his father, "Dad, why do we have to be resilient?" The father replies, "Well, son, resilience is the ability to bounce back from adversity, setbacks, or challenges. It's through resilience that we grow stronger, learn valuable lessons, and persevere in the face of obstacles." The son says, "So, when I demonstrate resilience, is it just my way of showing the world that I won't be easily defeated?"

66. A son says to his father, "Dad, when I grow up, I want to be an architect." The father replies, "That's a visionary choice, son. Remember, architects need to have creativity, technical skills, and a passion for designing spaces that blend functionality with aesthetics." The son says, "I've got that, Dad. I always find inspiration in the structures that shape our surroundings."

67. A father and son are watching a show about the wonders of the ocean. The son asks, "Dad, why is the ocean so captivating?" The father replies, "Well, son, the ocean covers most of our planet and is home to a staggering array of marine life. It's a place of beauty, mystery, and immense power that continues to intrigue

and inspire us." The son says, "So, when I see the ocean, is it just a reminder of the vastness and wonders of the natural world?"

68. A son asks his father, "Dad, why do we need to be open-minded?" The father replies, "Well, son, being open-minded allows us to embrace new ideas, perspectives, and experiences. It fosters growth, understanding, and empathy, and expands our horizons." The son says, "So, when I practice open-mindedness, is it just my way of embracing the rich tapestry of human diversity?"

69. A son says to his father, "Dad, when I grow up, I want to be a social worker." The father replies, "That's a compassionate choice, son. Remember, social workers need to have empathy, strong communication skills, and a dedication to helping individuals and communities overcome challenges." The son says, "I've got that, Dad. I always feel a deep sense of fulfillment when I lend a helping hand to those in need."

70. A father and son are watching a show about the wonders of the Redwood Forest. The son asks, "Dad, why are the Redwood trees so majestic?" The father replies, "Well, son, the Redwood trees are among the tallest and oldest living beings on Earth. They stand as guardians of history, reminding us of the passage of time and the resilience of nature." The son says, "So, when I see the

Redwood Forest, is it just a glimpse into the ancient wisdom of the natural world?"

71. A son asks his father, "Dad, why do we have to be adaptable?" The father replies, "Well, son, life is full of changes and uncertainties. Being adaptable allows us to adjust, learn, and thrive in new situations. It's through adaptability that we can navigate the ever-evolving landscape of life." The son says, "So, when I embrace adaptability, is it just my way of dancing gracefully with the rhythm of life?"

72. A son says to his father, "Dad, when I grow up, I want to be a marine biologist." The father replies, "That's a fascinating choice, son. Remember, marine biologists need to have a deep love for the ocean, scientific curiosity, and a commitment to understanding and conserving marine ecosystems." The son says, "I've gotthat, Dad. I always feel a sense of wonder and awe when I explore the mysteries of the underwater world."

73. A father and son are watching a show about the wonders of the Himalayas. The son asks, "Dad, why are the Himalayas so breathtaking?" The father replies, "Well, son, the Himalayas are home to majestic peaks, serene valleys, and a rich cultural heritage. They represent the awe-inspiring beauty and the indomitable spirit of nature

and its people." The son says, "So, when I see the Himalayas, is it just a reminder of the majestic power of the Earth?"

74. A son asks his father, "Dad, why do we have to be curious?" The father replies, "Well, son, curiosity is the key that unlocks the doors of knowledge and discovery. It fuels our desire to explore, ask questions, and seek answers, leading to personal growth and the expansion of our understanding." The son says, "So, when I embrace curiosity, is it just my way of embarking on an exciting journey of learning?"

75. A son says to his father, "Dad, when I grow up, I want to be a psychologist." The father replies, "That's an insightful choice, son. Remember, psychologists need to have empathy, active listening skills, and a genuine interest in understanding and supporting others' mental well-being." The son says, "I've got that, Dad. I always find joy in helping others navigate the complexities of the human mind."

76. A father and son are watching a show about the wonders of the Galapagos Islands. The son asks, "Dad, why are the Galapagos Islands so unique?" The father replies, "Well, son, the Galapagos Islands are a living laboratory of evolution, with diverse species found nowhere else on Earth. They remind us of the interconnectedness of all living things and the importance

of preserving biodiversity." The son says, "So, when I learn about the Galapagos Islands, is it just a glimpse into the wonders of nature's creativity?"

77. A son asks his father, "Dad, why do we need to be humble?" The father replies, "Well, son, humility is the virtue that keeps us grounded, open to learning from others, and aware of our own limitations. It allows us to appreciate the strengths and contributions of others, fostering meaningful connections and personal growth." The son says, "So, when I embrace humility, is it just my way of acknowledging the vastness of knowledge and the beauty of humility?"

78. A son says to his father, "Dad, when I grow up, I want to be a filmmaker." The father replies, "That's a captivating choice, son. Remember, filmmakers need to have a creative vision, storytelling skills, and the ability to evoke emotions through their visual narratives." The son says, "I've got that, Dad. I always feel a sense of excitement and inspiration when I capture stories through the lens of a camera."

79. A father and son are watching a show about the wonders of the Antarctic. The son asks, "Dad, why is the Antarctic so mesmerizing?" The father replies, "Well, son, the Antarctic is a frozen wilderness of pristine beauty and extraordinary wildlife. It represents the delicate balance of our planet's ecosystems and reminds us of the importance

of environmental conservation." The son says, "So, when I see the Antarctic, is it just a reminder of the fragility and resilience of our planet?"

80. A son asks his father, "Dad, why do we have to be compassionate?" The father replies, "Well, son, compassion is the empathy and kindness we extend to others, especially during their times of need. It connects us on a deeper level, encourages acts of kindness, and creates a more compassionate and caring world." The son says, "So, when I show compassion, is it just my way of nurturing the bonds of humanity?"

81. A son says to his father, "Dad, when I grow up, I want to be a scientist." The father replies, "That's an inquisitive choice, son. Remember, scientists need to have a curious mind, critical thinking skills, and a passion for unraveling the mysteries of the universe." The son says, "I've got that, Dad. I always feel a sense of wonder and excitement when I conduct experiments and explore the world of science."

82. A father and son are watching a show about the wonders of the Australian Outback. The son asks, "Dad, why is the Outback so fascinating?" The father replies, "Well, son, the Outback is a vast and rugged landscape that showcases the resilience of nature and the unique adaptations of its inhabitants. It's a symbol of the untamed beauty and the spirit of the wilderness." The son says,

"So, when I see the Outback, is it just a reminder of the extraordinary diversity of life on Earth?"

83. A son asks his father, "Dad, why do we have to be authentic?" The father replies, "Well, son, authenticity is the courage to be true to ourselves, to embrace our uniqueness, and to live in alignment with our values and beliefs. It fosters genuine connections and allows us to live a life of purpose and fulfillment." The son says, "So, when I choose authenticity, is it just my way of honoring my true self?"

84. A son says to his father, "Dad, when I grow up, I want to be a veterinarian." The father replies, "That's a compassionate choice, son. Remember, veterinarians need to have a deep love for animals, medical expertise, and a dedication to the well-being of our furry friends." The son says, "I've got that, Dad. I always feel a sense of joy and fulfillment when I help care for animals in need."

85. A father and son are watching a show about the wonders of the Great Lakes. The son asks, "Dad, why are the Great Lakes so awe-inspiring?" The father replies, "Well, son, the Great Lakes are vast bodies of freshwater that support diverse ecosystems, provide drinking water, and serve as a hub for recreational activities. They're a testament to the beauty and significance of our planet's water resources." The son says, "So, when I see the Great

Lakes, is it just a reminder of the importance of water conservation and appreciation?"

86. A son asks his father, "Dad, why do we have to be generous?" The father replies, "Well, son, generosity is the act of giving without expecting anything in return. It's a way to uplift others, create positive change, and make a meaningful impact in the lives of those in need. Through generosity, we foster a spirit of abundance and compassion." The son says, "So, when I practice generosity, is it just my way of sharing the blessings I've received?"

87. A son says to his father, "Dad, when I grow up, I want to be an inventor." The father replies, "That's an innovative choice, son. Remember, inventors need to have a curious mind, problem-solving skills, and a passion for creating new solutions and technologies." The son says, "I've got that, Dad. I always feel a sense of excitement and possibility when I tinker and invent new things."

88. A father and son are watching a show about the wonders of the Amazon rainforest. The son asks, "Dad, why is the Amazon rainforest so vital for our planet?" The father replies, "Well, son, the Amazon rainforest is often referred to as the 'lungs of the Earth' because it produces a significant amount of oxygen and plays a crucial role in regulating the climate and biodiversity. It's a treasure trove of life and a symbol of the intricate web of nature." The

son says, "So, when I see the Amazon rainforest, is it just a reminder of the need to protect and preserve our natural heritage?"

89. A son asks his father, "Dad, why do we need to be resilient?" The father replies, "Well, son, resilience is the ability to bounce back from adversity, setbacks, or challenges. It's through resilience that we find strength within ourselves, develop coping strategies, and emerge stronger and wiser. It's an essential quality that helps us navigate the ups and downs of life." The son says, "So, when I demonstrate resilience, is it just my way of showing the world that I won't be easily defeated?"

90. A son says to his father, "Dad, when I grow up, I want to be a counselor." The father replies, "That's a compassionate choice, son. Remember, counselors need to have empathy, active listening skills, and a desire to support and guide individuals through difficult times. Through their work, they help others find healing and create positive change." The son says, "I've got that, Dad. I always feel a sense of fulfillment when I lend a listening ear and offer guidance to those in need."

91. A father and son are watching a show about the wonders of the Sahara Desert. The son asks, "Dad, why is the Sahara Desert so fascinating?" The father replies, "Well, son, the Sahara Desert is the world's largest hot desert, spanning vast stretches of land with its golden

dunes and harsh beauty. It's a testament to the resilience of life in extreme environments and a reminder of the delicate balance between humans and nature." The son says, "So, when I see the Sahara Desert, is it just a glimpse into the wonders of adaptation and survival?"

92. A son asks his father, "Dad, why do we have to be patient?" The father replies, "Well, son, patience is a virtue that allows us to remain calm in the face of challenges, wait for things to unfold in their own time, and cultivate resilience. It's through patience that we develop inner strength and appreciate the beauty of each moment." The son says, "So, when I practice patience, is it just my way of embracing the art of surrender and acceptance?"

93. A son says to his father, "Dad, when I grow up, I want to be an environmental activist." The father replies, "That's a commendable choice, son. Remember, environmental activists need to have passion, advocacy skills, and a deep commitment to protecting and preserving our planet's natural resources. Through their efforts, they raise awareness and promote sustainable practices." The son says, "I've got that, Dad. I always feel a sense of responsibility and urgency to protect the Earth we call home."

94. A father and son are watching a show about the wonders of the Golden Gate Bridge. The son asks, "Dad, why is the Golden Gate Bridge so iconic?" The father

replies, "Well, son, the Golden Gate Bridge is not only a marvel of engineering but also a symbol of human ingenuity and connection. It stands as a testament to human achievements and the power of bridging gaps, both physical and metaphorical." The son says, "So, when I see the Golden Gate Bridge, is it just a reminder of the potential for unity and collaboration?"

95. A son asks his father, "Dad, why do we have to be kind?" The father replies, "Well, son, kindness is like a gentle breeze that can brighten someone's day, uplift spirits, and create a ripple effect of positivity. It's through acts of kindness that we nourish the human soul and create a harmonious and compassionate world." The son says, "So, when I show kindness, is it just my way of sharing love and spreading light?"

96. A son says to his father, "Dad, when I grow up, I want to be a social entrepreneur." The father replies, "That's an inspiring choice, son. Remember, social entrepreneurs combine business acumen with a deep commitment to addressing social and environmental challenges. Through their innovative solutions, they strive to create positive change and make a lasting impact." The son says, "I've got that, Dad. I always feel a sense of purpose and fulfillment when I imagine using business as a force for good."

97. A father and son are watching a show about the wonders of the Northern Lights. The son asks, "Dad, why are the Northern Lights so enchanting?" The father replies, "Well, son, the Northern Lights, also known as the Aurora Borealis, paint the sky with vibrant colors and dance with ethereal beauty. They remind us of the marvels of our universe and the interconnectedness of nature and cosmic forces." The son says, "So, when I see the Northern Lights, is it just a glimpse into the wonders that lie beyond our earthly existence?"

98. A son asks his father, "Dad, why do we have to be resilient?" The father replies, "Well, son, resilience is the ability to adapt, bounce back, and find strength in the face of adversity. It's through resilience that we overcome challenges, grow as individuals, and find new possibilities in the face of setbacks." The son says, "So, when I demonstrate resilience, is it just my way of embracing life's unpredictable nature and turning obstacles into opportunities?"

99. A son says to his father, "Dad, when I grow up, I want to be a humanitarian." The father replies, "That's a noble choice, son. Remember, humanitarians have a deep empathy for others, a commitment to social justice, and a desire to alleviate suffering and create a more equitable world. Through their actions, they inspire hope and work towards a better future for all." The son says, "I've got that,

Dad. I always feel a calling to support and uplift those in need."

100. A father and son are watching a show about the wonders of the Grand Canyon. The son asks, "Dad, why is the Grand Canyon so awe-inspiring?" The father replies, "Well, son, the Grand Canyon is a magnificent testament to the power of erosion and the passage of time. Its vastness and breathtaking vistas remind us of the incredible forces that shape our planet and leave us in awe of nature's masterpiece." The son says, "So, when I see the Grand Canyon, is it just a glimpse into the immense beauty and grandeur of the Earth?"

101. A son says to his father, "Dad, when I grow up, I want to be an architect." The father replies, "That's a visionary choice, son. Remember, architects need to have a strong sense of design and a love for creating structures." The son says, "I've got that, Dad. I always build the coolest forts with my building blocks."

102. Dad: Son, why did the golfer bring two pairs of pants to the golf course?
Son: I'm not sure, Dad. Why did they bring two pairs?
Dad: In case they got a hole-in-one, they wanted to make sure they had a clean pair for the celebration. It's all about being prepared for that perfect swing!

103. Dad: Son, did you know that the invention of the wheel was a game-changer?
Son: Dad, everyone knows that.
Dad: Well, have you ever thought about it? The wheel took us from "rolling on the ground" to "rolling in style"! It was a revolution in transportation.

104. Dad: Son, why did the music teacher bring a ladder to the orchestra concert?
Son: Dad, that doesn't make sense.
Dad: Well, they wanted to reach new musical heights and help the musicians elevate their performance. It was a symphony of ladders and melodies!

105. Dad: Son, did you hear about the scientist who invented a machine to translate baby talk?
Son: No, Dad, what happened?
Dad: Well, it was quite a breakthrough! The machine could decode all those adorable gurgles and coos into understandable language. It turns out, babies have a lot to say!

106. Dad: Son, why did the book go to therapy?
Son: Dad, books don't have feelings.
Dad: You're right, but that book had some unresolved plot twists and needed a little counseling to find closure. It was a journey of healing through the chapters!

107. Dad: Son, did you know that clouds are the ultimate artists?

Son: Dad, clouds are just water vapor.

Dad: True, but those wispy formations are like living brushstrokes across the sky. Clouds paint breathtaking masterpieces with each passing moment!

108. Dad: Son, why did the tomato turn red and run away from the vegetable garden?

Son: I don't know, Dad. Why did it run away?

Dad: Well, it didn't want to end up in a salad! That tomato wanted to explore the world beyond the garden and embark on a culinary adventure of its own.

109. Dad: Son, did you hear about the scientist who discovered a new species of laughter?

Son: No, Dad, what did they find?

Dad: Well, they named it "gigglius hilarious"! It's a laugh so contagious and joyous that it can brighten even the gloomiest of days.

110. Dad: Son, why did the math book go to the therapist?

Son: Dad, books can't have emotions.

Dad: You're right, but that math book had a lot of unresolved problems and needed a safe space to work through its equations. It was a journey of self-discovery and mathematical healing!

111. Dad: Son, did you know that trees are the true architects of nature?
Son: Dad, trees don't design buildings.
Dad: No, but they create breathtaking structures with their branches and leaves, forming natural canopies and living sculptures. They're nature's architects of beauty!

112. Dad: Son, why did the artist become a barber?
Son: I don't know, Dad. How did that happen?
Dad: Well, they realized that hair could be their canvas, and every haircut was a masterpiece waiting to be created. They combined art and style to give their clients the perfect "cut of creativity"!

113. Dad: Son, did you know that laughter can be the key to success?
Son: Yes, Dad, laughter is important.
Dad: That's right! Laughter unlocks doors, breaks down barriers, and connects people in the most unexpected ways. It's the key that opens the path to a fulfilling and joyful life!

114. Dad: Son, why did the tomato blush when it saw the cucumber?
Son: I don't know, Dad. Why did it blush?
Dad: Well, it had a bit of a crush on the cucumber. It was love at first sight in the vegetable aisle!

115. Dad: Son, did you hear about the scientist who invented a machine to turn dreams into reality?
Son: No, Dad, that sounds amazing!
Dad: It was truly remarkable! With a little imagination and a sprinkle of scientific magic, that machine could bring even the wildest dreams to life.

116. Dad: Son, why did the math teacher bring a ladder to the classroom?
Son: Dad, that doesn't make sense.
Dad: Well, they wanted to climb to new heights of knowledge and help their students reach their full potential. It was a class that aimed for the stars!

117. Dad: Son, did you know that a smile can light up the darkest room?
Son: Dad, that sounds like something you made up.
Dad: Well, it's true! A genuine smile has the power to brighten the gloomiest of moments and spread warmth and happiness wherever it goes. It's a superpower we all possess!

118. A father and son are watching a show about the rainforest. The son asks,
Dad, why is the rainforest so important? The father replies, "Well, son, the rainforest is important because it's home to a wide variety of plants and animals, and it plays a crucial role in maintaining the balance of our planet's

ecosystems." The son says, "So, when I see pictures of the rainforest, is it just nature's treasure trove?"

119. A son asks his father, "Dad, why do we have fingerprints?" The father replies, "Well, son, fingerprints help us with gripping objects and they're unique to each person, making them useful for identification." The son says, "So, when I leave my fingerprints everywhere, is it just my hands leaving their signature?"

120. A son says to his father, "Dad, when I grow up, I want to be a comedian." The father replies, "That's a hilarious choice, son. Remember, comedians need to have a good sense of humor and the ability to make people laugh." The son says, "I've got that, Dad. I always crack jokes that make my friends laugh."

121. A father and son are watching a show about the desert. The son asks, "Dad, why are deserts so dry?" The father replies, "Well, son, deserts are dry because they receive very little rainfall due to their geographic location." The son says, "So, when I see a desert, is it just nature's way of teaching us the value of water?"

122. A son asks his father, "Dad, why do we get goosebumps?" The father replies, "Well, son, goosebumps are a physiological response to cold temperatures or strong emotions like fear or excitement."

The son says, "So, when I get goosebumps, is it just my body saying 'Brrr' or 'Wow'?"

123. A son says to his father, "Dad, when I grow up, I want to be a firefighter." The father replies, "That's a courageous choice, son. Remember, firefighters need to be brave and have a strong desire to help others." The son says, "I've got that, Dad. I always come to the rescue when my friends are in trouble."

124. A father and son are watching a show about the human body. The son asks, "Dad, why do we have a heart?" The father replies, "Well, son, the heart is a vital organ that pumps blood throughout our body, delivering oxygen and nutrients to our cells." The son says, "So, when I feel my heartbeat, is it just my body's rhythm playing a song?"

125. A son asks his father, "Dad, why do we have different time zones?" The father replies, "Well, son, different time zones exist because the Earth rotates on its axis, causing different parts of the world to experience daylight and darkness at different times." The son says, "So, when I travel to a different time zone, is it like stepping into the future or the past?"

126. A son says to his father, "Dad, when I grow up, I want to be a police officer." The father replies, "That's a commendable choice, son. Remember, police officers

need to have integrity and a strong commitment to keeping their communities safe." The son says, "I've got that, Dad. I always make sure everyone follows the rules during our games."

127. A father and son are watching a show about mountains. The son asks, "Dad, why are mountains so tall?" The father replies, "Well, son, mountains are formed by the movement of tectonic plates and the forces of nature, which push the Earth's crust upward." The son says, "So, when I see a mountain, is it just the Earth showing off its grandeur?"

128. A son asks his father, "Dad, why do we have dreams while we sleep?" The father replies, "Well, son, dreams are a reflection of our subconscious thoughts and experiences. They can be like movies playing in our minds." The son says, "So, when I dream, is it like having my own personal cinema?"

129. A son says to his father, "Dad, when I grow up, I want to be a veterinarian." The father replies, "That's a compassionate choice, son. Remember, veterinarians need to have a love for animals and a desire to help them stay healthy." The son says, "I've got that, Dad. I always take care of our pets when they're not feeling well."

130. A father and son are watching a show about the universe. The son asks, "Dad, why is the universe so

vast?" The father replies, "Well, son, the universe is vast because it's constantly expanding. There's so much to explore and discover out there." The son says, "So, when I look up at the night sky, is it just a glimpse into the infinite?"

131. A son asks his father, "Dad, why do we celebrate birthdays?" The father replies, "Well, son, birthdays are a way to celebrate the anniversary of someone's birth. It's a special day to honor and appreciate a person's presence in our lives." The son says, "So, when I blow out the candles, is it just my way of making a wish for the year ahead?"

132. A son says to his father, "Dad, when I grow up, I want to be a teacher." The father replies, "That's an admirable choice, son. Remember, teachers have the power to inspire and shape young minds. They play a vital role in society." The son says, "I've got that, Dad. I always enjoy helping my friends understand new things."

133. A father and son are watching a show about the wonders of the deep sea. The son asks, "Dad, why is the deep sea so mysterious?" The father replies, "Well, son, the deep sea is mysterious because it's largely unexplored. There are so many secrets and unknown creatures lurking in its depths." The son says, "So, when I hear about a new deep-sea discovery, is it like uncovering a hidden treasure?"

134. A son asks his father, "Dad, why do we need to brush our teeth?" The father replies, "Well, son, brushing our teeth helps to remove plaque and bacteria, keeping our teeth and gums healthy." The son says, "So, when I brush my teeth, is it just my way of giving them a fresh start?"

135. A son says to his father, "Dad, when I grow up, I want to be an athlete." The father replies, "That's an active choice, son. Remember, athletes need to have discipline, dedication, and a love for sports." The son says, "I've got that, Dad. I always give my best during our backyard games."

136. A father and son are watching a show about the wonders of the Great Barrier Reef. The son asks, "Dad, why is the Great Barrier Reef so important?" The father replies, "Well, son, the Great Barrier Reef is important because it's the largest coral reef ecosystem in the world, teeming with diverse marine life. It's like a bustling city underwater." The son says, "So, when I see pictures of the Great Barrier Reef, is it just nature's masterpiece?"

137. A son asks his father, "Dad, why do we get curious?" The father replies, "Well, son, curiosity is a natural human trait that drives us to explore, learn, and discover new things. It's what pushes us forward and expands our horizons." The son says, "So, when I feel curious, is it just my mind saying 'Let's go on an adventure'?"

138. A son says to his father, "Dad, when I grow up, I want to be a musician." The father replies, "That's a harmonious choice, son. Remember, musicians need to have a passion for music and a talent for playing an instrument or singing." The son says, "I've got that, Dad. I always create melodies in my mind."

139. A father and son are watching a show about bees. The son asks, "Dad, why do bees make honey?" The father replies, "Well, son, bees make honey as a source of food and to store it for the colony's survival, especially during winter." The son says, "So, when I taste honey, is it just nature's golden delight?"

140. A son asks his father, "Dad, why do we have emotions?" The father replies, "Well, son, emotions are part of being human. They allow us to experience a wide range of feelings and connect with others on a deep level." The son says, "So, when I feel happy, sad, or excited, is it just my heart expressing itself?"

141. A son says to his father, "Dad, when I grow up, I want to be an astronaut." The father replies, "That's an astronomical choice, son. Remember, astronauts need to be physically fit and mentally prepared for the challenges of space exploration." The son says, "I've got that, Dad. I always dream of exploring the galaxies in my rocket ship."

142. A father and son are watching a show about elephants. The son asks, "Dad, why do elephants have such long trunks?" The father replies, "Well, son, elephants use their trunks for various tasks like drinking water, grabbing food, and even communicating with other elephants." The son says, "So, when I see an elephant using its trunk, is it just nature's multi-purpose tool?"

143. A son asks his father, "Dad, why do we celebrate holidays?" The father replies, "Well, son, holidays are special occasions that bring people together to commemorate significant events, traditions, or values. They help us create lasting memories and strengthen our bonds with loved ones." The son says, "So, when I celebrate a holiday, is it just a way of cherishing the moments that matter?"

144. A son says to his father, "Dad, when I grow up, I want to be a scientist." The father replies, "That's an inquisitive choice, son. Remember, scientists need to have a thirst for knowledge and a passion for conducting experiments and making discoveries." The son says, "I've got that, Dad. I always ask 'why' and love exploring the wonders of the world."

145. A father and son are watching a show about dolphins. The son asks, "Dad, why are dolphins so intelligent?" The father replies, "Well, son, dolphins have

highly developed brains and complex social structures, which contribute to their remarkable intelligence and adaptability." The son says, "So, when I see dolphins swimming and playing, is it just nature's display of brilliance?"

146. A son asks his father, "Dad, why do we have to study?" The father replies, "Well, son, studying helps us gain knowledge, develop skills, and prepare for the future. It's an investment in ourselves that opens doors to opportunities." The son says, "So, when I study, is it just my way of building a strong foundation?"

147. A son says to his father, "Dad, when I grow up, I want to be a chef." The father replies, "That's a flavorful choice, son. Remember, chefs need to have a passion for cooking, creativity, and an appreciation for diverse flavors." The son says, "I've got that, Dad. I always experiment with different ingredients to create delicious masterpieces."

148. A father and son are watching a show about the solar system. The son asks, "Dad, why do planets orbit the sun?" The father replies, "Well, son, planets orbit the sun because of the gravitational force between them. It's like a cosmic dance orchestrated by the laws of physics." The son says, "So, when I see the planets in the night sky, is it just the celestial ballet?"

149. A son asks his father, "Dad, why do we need to exercise?" The father replies, "Well, son, exercising keeps our bodies healthy and strong. It boosts our energy, improves our mood, and helps prevent diseases." The son says, "So, when I exercise, is it just my way of telling my body 'I care about you'?"

150. A son says to his father, "Dad, when I grow up, I want to be a lawyer." The father replies, "That's a persuasive choice, son. Remember, lawyers need to have excellent communication skills, critical thinking, and a passion for justice." The son says, "I've got that, Dad. I always defend my case during our friendly debates."

151. A father and son are watching a show about wolves. The son asks, "Dad, why do wolves howl?" The father replies, "Well, son, wolves howl to communicate with their pack, mark their territory, and coordinate hunting. It's like a unique language of the wild." The son says, "So, when I hear a wolf howl, is it just nature's symphony?"

152. A son asks his father, "Dad, why do we have seasons?" The father replies, "Well, son, seasons occur because of the tilt of the Earth's axis as it orbits the sun. It determines the amount of sunlight different regions receive, leading to changes in temperature and weather patterns." The son says, "So, when I experience the seasons, is it just nature's way of keeping things interesting?"

153. Dad: Son, why did the flower go to school?

Son: I don't know, Dad. Why did it go to school?

Dad: Because it wanted to be a "bud-ding" scholar and learn all the secrets of photosynthesis and plant biology. It was a blossoming journey of education!

154. Dad: Son, did you hear about the scientist who invented a machine to turn vegetables into instruments?

Son: No, Dad, that's fascinating!

Dad: It was a "melodi-veg" machine! It could transform carrots into flutes, cucumbers into trumpets, and pumpkins into drums. It was a garden orchestra like no other!

155. Dad: Son, why did the spider go to university?

Son: Dad, spiders don't go to school.

Dad: Well, that spider wanted to learn the art of web design and spin intricate patterns like a master weaver. It was a journey of eight-legged education!

156. Dad: Son, did you know that books can take you on adventures without leaving your seat?

Son: Yes, Dad, books are magical.

Dad: Absolutely! With every turn of the page, you can travel to far-off lands, meet fascinating characters, and experience thrilling escapades. It's the power of the written word!

157. Dad: Son, why did the sandwich go to the gym?

Son: I'm not sure, Dad. Why did it go?

Dad: Well, it wanted to work on its "core" ingredients and get in shape for a beach vacation. It was a sandwich on a mission to achieve sandwich perfection!

158. Dad: Son, did you hear about the scientist who discovered a way to turn frowns upside down?

Son: No, Dad, how did they do it?

Dad: They developed a formula called "smile-etics"! With a sprinkle of laughter and a dash of positivity, they could bring joy to even the most downcast faces.

159. Dad: Son, why did the baker become a musician?

Son: Dad, that doesn't make sense.

Dad: Well, they realized that baking and music are both forms of art that touch people's hearts. They wanted to create melodies that were as delightful to the ears as their pastries were to the taste buds!

160. Dad: Son, did you know that laughter is like a magnet for happiness?

Son: Dad, you always say the most interesting things.

Dad: Well, it's true! Laughter attracts joy, positivity, and good vibes. It's like a magnetic force that pulls happiness into your life!

161. Dad: Son, why did the clock go back four seconds?

Son: I don't know, Dad. Why did it go back?

Dad: Because it wanted to "re-time" itself and make sure it was keeping accurate seconds. Time is precious, and that clock wanted to get it just right!

162. Dad: Son, did you hear about the scientist who invented a machine to turn vegetables into jokes?
Son: No, Dad, that sounds intriguing!
Dad: It was a "pun-derful" invention! With a twist and a sprinkle of veggie humor, that machine could turn even the simplest carrot into a side-splitting joke.

163. Dad: Son, why did the artist always carry a sketchbook?
Son: Dad, I'm not sure. Why did they carry a sketchbook?
Dad: Well, they saw inspiration everywhere and didn't want to miss a single creative moment. They believed that every stroke of the pencil could be a masterpiece in the making!

164. Dad: Son, did you know that clouds are nature's storytellers?
Son: Dad, clouds are just water vapor.
Dad: True, but those fluffy formations in the sky can paint pictures and tell stories if you let your imagination soar. It's like nature's cinema in the heavens!

165. Dad: Son, why did the tomato turn red and run a marathon?

Son: I don't know, Dad. Why did it run?

Dad: Well, it wanted to prove that it wasn't just a juicy fruit but also a champion of endurance. It was a tomato on a mission to show its ripe athleticism!

166. Dad: Son, did you hear about the scientist who invented a machine to translate pet sounds into human language?

Son: No, Dad, that's incredible!

Dad: It was a "bark-lator"! With a few technological tweaks, that machine could turn barks into words and meows into sentences. Our pets had a lot to say!

167. Dad: Son, why did the math book become a stand-up comedian?

Son: I'm not sure, Dad. How did that happen?

Dad: Well, it realized that math could be funny too! It started cracking hilarious equations and telling math-related jokes. It was a "calculus of comedy"!

168. A son says to his father, "Dad, when I grow up, I want to be an explorer." The father replies, "That's an adventurous choice, son. Remember, explorers need to have a spirit of curiosity and a love for discovering new places, cultures, and ideas." The son says, "I've got that, Dad. I always embark on exciting journeys in my imagination."

169. A father and son are watching a show about the wonders of the Amazon rainforest. The son asks, "Dad, why is the Amazon rainforest called the 'lungs of the Earth'?" The father replies, "Well, son, the Amazon rainforest produces a significant amount of oxygen and plays a crucial role in maintaining the planet's oxygen balance." The son says, "So, when I see pictures of the Amazon, is it just nature's life-giving masterpiece?"

170. A son asks his father, "Dad, why do we make wishes?" The father replies, "Well, son, making wishes is a way to express our desires, dreams, and hopes. It gives us a sense of possibility and a chance to envision a brighter future." The son says, "So, when I make a wish, is it just my way of believing in the power of imagination?"

171. A son says to his father, "Dad, when I grow up, I want to be a scientist." The father replies, "That's an inquisitive choice, son. Remember, scientists need to have a curious mind, the ability to think critically, and a passion for unraveling the mysteries of the world." The son says, "I've got that, Dad. I always conduct my own little experiments in the kitchen."

172. A father and son are watching a show about the human brain. The son asks, "Dad, why is the brain so complex?" The father replies, "Well, son, the brain is the control center of our body, responsible for thoughts, emotions, memories, and countless intricate processes. Its

complexity is what makes us who we are." The son says, "So, when I learn something new, is it just my brain expanding its horizons?"

173. A son asks his father, "Dad, why do we feel love?" The father replies, "Well, son, love is a powerful emotion that connects us to others in deep and meaningful ways. It brings joy, compassion, and a sense of belonging." The son says, "So, when I feel love, is it just my heart opening its doors?"

174. A son says to his father, "Dad, when I grow up, I want to be an engineer." The father replies, "That's an ingenious choice, son. Remember, engineers need to have problem-solving skills, creativity, and a love for designing and building things." The son says, "I've got that, Dad. I always find clever solutions to our household challenges."

175. A father and son are watching a show about the wonders of the universe. The son asks, "Dad, why are stars so mesmerizing?" The father replies, "Well, son, stars have captivated humans for ages. Their beauty and vastness remind us of the vastness of the universe and the wonders it holds." The son says, "So, when I look up at the stars, is it just my soul reaching for the infinite?"

176. A son asks his father, "Dad, why do we feel gratitude?" The father replies, "Well, son, gratitude is a

way to acknowledge and appreciate the good things in our lives. It fosters happiness, strengthens relationships, and cultivates a positive outlook." The son says, "So, when I feel grateful, is it just my heart saying 'Thank you'?"

177. A son says to his father, "Dad, when I grow up, I want to be a photographer." The father replies, "That's a picturesque choice, son. Remember, photographers need to have a keen eye for capturing moments, a love for storytelling through images, and a passion for preserving memories." The son says, "I've got that, Dad. I always find beauty in the world through the lens of my camera."

178. A father and son are watching a show about the wonders of the coral reefs. The son asks, "Dad, why are coral reefs so vibrant?" The father replies, "Well, son, coral reefs are teeming with life and a kaleidoscope of colors due to the presence of diverse marine species and the symbiotic relationship between corals and algae." The son says, "So, when I see a coral reef, is it just nature's masterpiece of biodiversity?"

179. A son asks his father, "Dad, why do we have imagination?" The father replies, "Well, son, imagination is a powerful tool of the mind that allows us to create, innovate, and explore limitless possibilities. It's the gateway to creativity and innovation." The son says, "So, when I let my imagination soar, is it just my way of unlocking the doors of my mind?"

180. A son says to his father, "Dad, when I grow up, I want to be a dancer." The father replies, "That's a graceful choice, son. Remember, dancers need to have a passion for movement, rhythm, and expression." The son says, "I've got that, Dad. I always find joy in dancing to the rhythm of my favorite tunes."

181. A father and son are watching a show about the wonders of the Northern Lights. The son asks, "Dad, why are the Northern Lights so breathtaking?" The father replies, "Well, son, the Northern Lights, or Aurora Borealis, are a natural phenomenon caused by charged particles colliding with atoms in the Earth's atmosphere, creating beautiful displays of colorful lights." The son says, "So, when I see the Northern Lights, is it just nature's enchanting light show?"

182. A son asks his father, "Dad, why do we have friends?" The father replies, "Well, son, friends are companions who share our joys, support us during difficult times, and make life more meaningful. They are the family we choose." The son says, "So, when I spend time with my friends, is it just my heart feeling the warmth of connection?"

183. A son says to his father, "Dad, when I grow up, I want to be a scientist." The father replies, "That's a curious choice, son. Remember, scientists need to have a thirst

for knowledge, a love for experimentation, and a dedication to unraveling the mysteries of the universe." The son says, "I've got that, Dad. I always ask questions and seek answers to satisfy my curiosity."

184. A father and son are watching a show about the wonders of the Grand Canyon. The son asks, "Dad, why is the Grand Canyon so awe-inspiring?" The father replies, "Well, son, the Grand Canyon's vastness and majestic beauty are the result of millions of years of geological processes, revealing layers of Earth's history." The son says, "So, when I see the Grand Canyon, is it just nature's masterpiece carved by time?"

185. A son asks his father, "Dad, why do we have to learn from our mistakes?" The father replies, "Well, son, learning from our mistakes helps us grow, develop resilience, and make better choices in the future. It's how we evolve and progress." The son says, "So, when I make a mistake, is it just a lesson in disguise?"

186. A son says to his father, "Dad, when I grow up, I want to be a writer." The father replies, "That's a creative choice, son. Remember, writers need to have a way with words, a vivid imagination, and a love for storytelling." The son says, "I've got that, Dad. I always find joy in crafting tales with my pen."

187. A father and son are watching a show about the wonders of the Serengeti. The son asks, "Dad, why is the Serengeti so remarkable?" The father replies, "Well, son, the Serengeti is home to a vast array of wildlife and showcases the beauty of nature's intricate balance. It's a living testament to the wonders of the animal kingdom." The son says, "So, when I see the Serengeti, is it just nature's epic stage?"

188. A son asks his father, "Dad, why do we need sleep?" The father replies, "Well, son, sleep is essential for our bodies and minds to rest, rejuvenate, and recharge. It allows us to wake up refreshed and ready for the day ahead." The son says, "So, when I sleep, is it just my body saying 'Time to recharge'?"

189. A son says to his father, "Dad, when I grow up, I want to be a psychologist." The father replies, "That's a perceptive choice, son. Remember, psychologists need to have empathy, listening skills, and a deep understanding of human behavior." The son says, "I've got that, Dad. I always lend an ear and offer support to my friends."

190. A father and son are watching a show about the wonders of the Great Wall of China. The son asks, "Dad, why is the Great Wall of China so iconic?" The father replies, "Well, son, the Great Wall of China represents centuries of history, ingenuity, and the human desire to protect and preserve. It's a testament to the power of

human perseverance." The son says, "So, when I see the Great Wall, is it just a reminder of the strength of human spirit?"

191. A son asks his father, "Dad, why do we feel nostalgia?" The father replies, "Well, son, nostalgia is a sentimental longing for the past, a bittersweet mix of joy and longing that reminds us of cherished memories and experiences." The son says, "So, when I feel nostalgic, is it just my heart revisiting beautiful moments?"

192. A son says to his father, "Dad, when I grow up, I want to be an artist." The father replies, "That's a creative choice, son. Remember, artists need to have a unique perspective, a passion for self-expression, and the ability to evoke emotions through their work." The son says, "I've got that, Dad. I always find joy in painting and creating art."

193. A father and son are watching a show about the wonders of the Great Pyramid of Giza. The son asks, "Dad, why are the pyramids so awe-inspiring?" The father replies, "Well, son, the pyramids are a testament to the architectural genius of ancient civilizations. They stand as magnificent structures that have withstood the test of time." The son says, "So, when I see the pyramids, is it just a glimpse into the legacy of human ingenuity?"

194. A son asks his father, "Dad, why do we have courage?" The father replies, "Well, son, courage is the ability to face fear, adversity, or challenges with strength and determination. It's what pushes us beyond our limits and helps us grow." The son says, "So, when I feel courageous, is it just my heart saying 'I won't give up'?"

195. A son says to his father, "Dad, when I grow up, I want to be an environmentalist." The father replies, "That's a noble choice, son. Remember, environmentalists need to have a deep love for nature, a commitment to conservation, and a desire to protect our planet for future generations." The son says, "I've got that, Dad. I always strive to reduce, reuse, and recycle."

196. A father and son are watching a show about the wonders of the Great Barrier Reef. The son asks, "Dad, why is the Great Barrier Reef so important?" The father replies, "Well, son, the Great Barrier Reef is not only a natural wonder but also a vital ecosystem that supports countless marine species and contributes to the overall health of our oceans." The son says, "So, when I see the Great Barrier Reef, is it just nature's call to protect and preserve?"

197. A son asks his father, "Dad, why do stars twinkle?" The father replies, "Well, son, stars twinkle because their light has to pass through Earth's atmosphere, which causes the light to bend and shift." The son says, "So,

when I see a star twinkle, is it just playing a light show for us?"

198. A son says to his father, "Dad, when I grow up, I want to be a sailor." The father replies, "That's a buoyant choice, son. Remember, sailors need to have good sea legs and a love for the ocean." The son says, "I've got that, Dad. I always navigate the bathtub seas with my toy boats."

199. A father and son are watching a show about dinosaurs. The son asks, "Dad, why did dinosaurs go extinct?" The father replies, "Well, son, scientists believe a large asteroid impact and other factors caused the dinosaurs to go extinct." The son says, "So, when I see a dinosaur fossil, is it just a reminder of a time long past?"

200. A son asks his father, "Dad, why do we hiccup?" The father replies, "Well, son, hiccups are involuntary contractions of the diaphragm, the muscle that helps us breathe. They can be caused by eating too quickly or swallowing air." The son says, "So, when I hiccup, is it just my body saying 'Slow down'?"

201. A son says to his father, "Dad, when I grow up, I want to be an astronaut." The father replies, "That's a stellar choice, son. Remember, astronauts need to have a strong knowledge of science and a love for exploration." The son

says, "I've got that, Dad. I always explore the farthest corners of the backyard."

202. A father and son are watching a show about rivers. The son asks, "Dad, why does a river flow?" The father replies, "Well, son, rivers flow because of gravity. They're always trying to find the lowest point." The son says, "So, when I see a river, is it just on a continuous journey?"

203. A son asks his father, "Dad, why do we blush?" The father replies, "Well, son, blushing is a natural response when we feel embarrassed or excited. It's a way our bodies communicate our feelings." The son says, "So, when I blush, is it just my body saying 'I can't hide how I feel'?"

204. A son says to his father, "Dad, when I grow up, I want to be a gardener." The father replies, "That's a blooming choice, son. Remember, gardeners need to have a green thumb and a love for plants." The son says, "I've got that, Dad. I always grow the best bean plants in science class."

205. A father and son are watching a show about volcanoes. The son asks, "Dad, why do volcanoes erupt?" The father replies, "Well, son, volcanoes erupt when magma from beneath the Earth's crust forces its way to the surface." The son says, "So, when a volcano erupts, is it just the Earth saying 'I need to let off some steam'?"

206. A son asks his father, "Dad, why do we yawn?" The father replies, "Well, son, yawning is a natural response when we are tired or bored." The son says, "So, when I yawn, is it just my body saying 'I need a change of pace'?"

207. A son says to his father, "Dad, when I grow up, I want to be a detective." The father replies, "That's a sharp choice, son. Remember, detectives need to have a keen eye for details and a knack for solving puzzles." The son says, "I've got that, Dad. I always find the last piece of the jigsaw puzzle."

208. A father and son are watching a show about animals. The son asks, "Dad, why do dogs wag their tails?" The father replies, "Well, son, dogs wag their tails as a way to communicate their emotions." The son says, "So, when our dog wags his tail, is it just him saying 'I'm happy to see you'?"

209. A son asks his father, "Dad, why do we grow old?" The father replies, "Well, son, aging is a natural process that happens to all living things." The son says, "So, when I see grandpa, is it just a reminder that life is a journey?"

210. A son says to his father, "Dad, when I grow up, I want to be a scientist." The father replies, "That's a smart choice, son. Remember, scientists need to have a curious mind and a love for learning." The son says, "I've got that, Dad. I always love discovering new things."

211. A father and son are watching a show about trees. The son asks, "Dad, why do trees lose their leaves in the fall?" The father replies, "Well, son, trees lose their leaves to conserve water and survive the winter." The son says, "So, when I see a bare tree, is it just preparing for a long winter nap?"

212. A son asks his father, "Dad, why do we get scared?" The father replies, "Well, son, fear is a natural response to potential danger. It's a way our bodies protect us." The son says, "So, when I get scared, is it just my body saying 'Be careful!'?"

213. A son says to his father, "Dad, when I grow up, I want to be a writer." The father replies, "That's a creative choice, son. Remember, writers need to have a good imagination and a love for words." The son says, "I've got that, Dad. I always come up with the best stories."

214. A father and son are watching a show about the ocean. The son asks, "Dad, why is the ocean salty?" The father replies, "Well, son, the ocean is salty because it contains minerals and salts that are washed into it from the land." The son says, "So, when I taste the ocean water, is it just a flavor of the Earth?"

215. A son asks his father, "Dad, why do we have to sleep?" The father replies, "Well, son, sleep is essential for

our bodies to recover and for our brains to process the day's experiences." The son says, "So, when I go to sleep, is it just my body's way of recharging?"

216. A son says to his father, "Dad, when I grow up, I want to be a chef." The father replies, "That's a tasty choice, son. Remember, chefs need to have a good palate and a love for food." The son says, "I've got that, Dad. I always make the best mud pies."

217. A father and son are watching a show about the solar system. The son asks, "Dad, why does the Earth spin?" The father replies, "Well, son, the Earth spins because of the way it was formed. It's been spinning ever since." The son says, "So, when I spin, am I just copying the Earth?"

218. A son asks his father, "Dad, why do we laugh?" The father replies, "Well, son, laughter is a natural response to something funny or joyful. It's a way we express happiness." The son says, "So, when I laugh, is it just my way of saying 'That's hilarious!'?"

219. A son says to his father, "Dad, when I grow up, I want to be an artist." The father replies, "That's a colorful choice, son. Remember, artists need to have a good eye for beauty and a love for creating." The son says, "I've got that, Dad. I always make the most beautiful drawings."

220. A father and son are watching a show about birds. The son asks, "Dad, why do birds sing?" The father replies, "Well, son, birds sing to communicate with each other. They use songs to attract mates and defend territories." The son says, "So, when I hear a bird singing, is it just saying 'This is my home'?"

221. A son asks his father, "Dad, why do we cry?" The father replies, "Well, son, crying is a natural response to strong emotions. It can be a way to release feelings." The son says, "So, when I cry, is it just my body saying 'This is too much'?"

222. A son says to his father, "Dad, when I grow up, I want to be an engineer." The father replies, "That's a solid choice, son. Remember, engineers need to have a good understanding of math and science and a love for solving problems." The son says, "I've got that, Dad. I always build the strongest Lego towers."

223. A father and son are watching a show about the moon. The son asks, "Dad, why does the moon change shape?" The father replies, "Well, son, the moon doesn't really change shape. We see different parts of it illuminated as it orbits the Earth." The son says, "So, when I see a full moon, is it just the moon saying 'Here I am!'?"

224. A son asks his father, "Dad, why do we feel pain?" The father replies, "Well, son, pain is a way our bodies tell

us something might be wrong. It's a protection mechanism." The son says, "So, when I get a cut, is it just my body saying 'Careful next time'?"

225. A son says to his father, "Dad, when I grow up, I want to be a musician." The father replies, "That's a harmonious choice, son. Remember, musicians need to have a good ear for music and a love for playing an instrument or singing." The son says, "I've got that, Dad. I always make the best rhythms with my toy drums."

226. A father and son are watching a show about the weather. The son asks, "Dad, why does it rain?" The father replies, "Well, son, rain happens when the water vapor in the air condenses and falls to the ground." The son says, "So, when it rains, is it just the clouds saying 'Time for a bath'?"

227. A son asks his father, "Dad, why do we dream?" The father replies, "Well, son, dreams are a part of sleep and seem to be a way for our brains to process experiences and emotions." The son says, "So, when I dream, is it just my brain saying 'Let's go on an adventure'?"

228. A son says to his father, "Dad, when I grow up, I want to be a pilot." The father replies, "That's a lofty choice, son. Remember, pilots need to have good spatial awareness and a love for flying." The son says, "I've got that, Dad. I always fly the highest with my toy planes."

229. A father and son are watching a show about butterflies. The son asks, "Dad, why do butterflies have colorful wings?" The father replies, "Well, son, butterflies have colorful wings for various reasons. Some use them for camouflage, some to attract mates, and others to warn off predators." The son says, "So, when I see a butterfly, is it just showing off its outfit?"

230. A son asks his father, "Dad, why do we hiccup?" The father replies, "Well, son, hiccups are caused by a sudden contraction of the diaphragm." The son says, "So, when I hiccup, is it just my body having a dance party?"

231. A son says to his father, "Dad, when I grow up, I want to be an archaeologist." The father replies, "That's a digging choice, son. Remember, archaeologists need to be patient and love history." The son says, "I've got that, Dad. I always take my time when building my sand castles."

232. A father and son are watching a show about deserts. The son asks, "Dad, why are deserts so hot?" The father replies, "Well, son, deserts are hot because they get more sunlight than other areas and have little water to absorb the heat." The son says, "So, when I feel the heat of the sun, is it just a taste of the desert?"

233. A son asks his father, "Dad, why do we have dreams?" The father replies, "Well, son, dreams are a way for our brains to process experiences and emotions." The son says, "So, when I dream of dragons, is it just my brain going on a fantasy adventure?"

234. A son says to his father, "Dad, when I grow up, I want to be a pilot." The father replies, "That's a soaring choice, son. Remember, pilots need to have good spatial awareness and quick reflexes." The son says, "I've got that, Dad. I never crash my toy airplanes."

235. A father and son are watching a show about volcanoes. The son asks, "Dad, why do volcanoes erupt?" The father replies, "Well, son, volcanoes erupt because of the movement of tectonic plates beneath the Earth's surface." The son says, "So, when a volcano erupts, is it just the Earth showing off its fireworks?"

236. A son asks his father, "Dad, why do we fall asleep?" The father replies, "Well, son, sleep is a way for our bodies to rest and recharge." The son says, "So, when I fall asleep, is it just my body saying 'Time for a pit stop'?"

237. A son says to his father, "Dad, when I grow up, I want to be a sailor." The father replies, "That's a seafaring choice, son. Remember, sailors need to understand

navigation and have a love for the sea." The son says, "I've got that, Dad. I never get seasick on our boat trips."

238. A father and son are watching a show about rainbows. The son asks, "Dad, why are rainbows colorful?" The father replies, "Well, son, rainbows appear colorful because of the refraction and dispersion of light in water droplets." The son says, "So, when I see a rainbow, is it just the sky showing off its art skills?"

239. A son asks his father, "Dad, why do we get goosebumps?" The father replies, "Well, son, goosebumps are a reaction to cold or strong emotions, like fear or excitement." The son says, "So, when I get goosebumps during a scary movie, is it just my skin saying 'I'm scared too!'?"

240. A son says to his father, "Dad, when I grow up, I want to be a meteorologist." The father replies, "That's a breezy choice, son. Remember, meteorologists need to be good at understanding patterns and love studying the weather." The son says, "I've got that, Dad. I always know when it's going to rain."

241. A father and son are watching a show about stars. The son asks, "Dad, why do stars twinkle?" The father replies, "Well, son, stars twinkle because their light is refracted as it passes through the Earth's atmosphere."

The son says, "So, when I see stars twinkling, is it just them winking at me?"

242. A son asks his father, "Dad, why do we blush?" The father replies, "Well, son, blushing is a natural response to embarrassment or excitement." The son says, "So, when I blush, is it just my face saying 'I'm feeling a lot right now'?"

243. A son says to his father, "Dad, when I grow up, I want to be a doctor." The father replies, "That's a caring choice, son. Remember, doctors need to be good at science and have a love for helping people." The son says, "I've got that, Dad. I always help my friends when they get hurt."

244. A father and son are watching a show about glaciers. The son asks, "Dad, why are glaciers so slow?" The father replies, "Well, son, glaciers move slowly because they're huge masses of ice being moved by gravity." The son says, "So, when I see a glacier moving, is it just the ice saying 'Slow and steady wins the race'?"

245. A son asks his father, "Dad, why do we sneeze?" The father replies, "Well, son, sneezing is a way for our bodies to get rid of irritants in our nose or throat." The son says, "So, when I sneeze, is it just my body saying 'Get out of here' to dust?"

246. A son says to his father, "Dad, when I grow up, I want to be an astronomer." The father replies, "That's a stellar

choice, son. Remember, astronomers need to be curious and have a love for space." The son says, "I've got that, Dad. I always ask questions about the stars."

247. A father and son are watching a show about dinosaurs. The son asks, "Dad, why did dinosaurs go extinct?" The father replies, "Well, son, it's believed that a large asteroid hit the Earth, leading to their extinction." The son says, "So, when I see a shooting star, is it just a reminder of the dinosaurs?"

248. A son asks his father, "Dad, why do we have memories?" The father replies, "Well, son, memories are a way for us to remember past experiences and learn from them." The son says, "So, when I remember a fun day at the park, is it just my brain saying 'Let's do that again'?"

249. A son says to his father, "Dad, when I grow up, I want to be a firefighter." The father replies, "That's a blazing choice, son. Remember, firefighters need to be brave and have a love for helping others." The son says, "I've got that, Dad. I'm always the first one to help when someone needs it."

250. A father and son are watching a show about bees. The son asks, "Dad, why do bees make honey?" The father replies, "Well, son, bees make honey as a food source for the colony, especially for the winter." The son

says, "So, when I taste honey, is it just a sweet gift from the bees?"

251. A son asks his father, "Dad, why do we dream?" The father replies, "Well, son, dreams are a way our brain processes experiences and emotions." The son says, "So, when I dream about flying, is it just my brain going on an adventure?"

252. A son says to his father, "Dad, when I grow up, I want to be an astronaut." The father replies, "That's a stellar choice, son. Remember, astronauts need to be disciplined and have a strong understanding of math and science." The son says, "I've got that, Dad. I'm the best at following rules and I always finish my homework."

253. A father and son are watching a show about the human brain. The son asks, "Dad, why is the brain so wrinkly?" The father replies, "Well, son, the wrinkles in our brain, called gyri and sulci, increase its surface area and allow for more brain cells." The son says, "So, when I think really hard, are my brain wrinkles flexing?"

254. A son asks his father, "Dad, why do we blink?" The father replies, "Well, son, blinking helps to keep our eyes clean and moist." The son says, "So, when I blink, is it just my eyes taking a mini shower?"

255. A son says to his father, "Dad, when I grow up, I want to be a doctor." The father replies, "That's a healing choice, son. Remember, doctors need to be patient and have a strong knowledge of biology and medicine." The son says, "I've got that, Dad. I always take care of my stuffed animals when they're 'sick.'"

256. A father and son are watching a show about lions. The son asks, "Dad, why do lions roar?" The father replies, "Well, son, lions roar to communicate with each other and to declare their territory." The son says, "So, when I yell out in the playground, am I roaring like a lion?"

257. A son asks his father, "Dad, why do we sneeze?" The father replies, "Well, son, sneezing is a way for our body to get rid of irritants in our nose or throat." The son says, "So, when I sneeze, is it just my nose saying 'Get out!' to dust and other stuff?"

258. A son says to his father, "Dad, when I grow up, I want to be a farmer." The father replies, "That's a cultivating choice, son. Remember, farmers need to be hardworking and have a good understanding of plants and animals." The son says, "I've got that, Dad. I help mom with the garden and I love our pet dog."

259. A father and son are watching a show about stars. The son asks, "Dad, why do stars twinkle?" The father replies, "Well, son, stars twinkle because their light has to

pass through Earth's atmosphere, which is in constant motion." The son says, "So, when I see stars twinkling, is it like they're winking at me?"

260. A son asks his father, "Dad, why do we have shadows?" The father replies, "Well, son, shadows are created when an object blocks light." The son says, "So, when I make shadow puppets, is it just my hands stealing the spotlight?"

261. A son says to his father, "Dad, when I grow up, I want to be a carpenter." The father replies, "That's a crafting choice, son. Remember, carpenters need to be skilled with their hands and have a good eye for detail." The son says, "I've got that, Dad. I build the best block towers in preschool."

262. Dad: Son, did you know that laughter is like a universal language?
Son: Yes, Dad, I've heard that before.
Dad: Well, it's worth repeating! Laughter transcends barriers of language, culture, and age. It's a powerful force that brings people together and creates bonds of joy!

263. Dad: Son, why did the pencil go to art school?
Son: Dad, I think pencils are already good at drawing.

Dad: You're right, but that pencil wanted to sharpen its skills and explore new artistic techniques. It was a graphite journey of self-expression!

264. Dad: Son, did you hear about the scientist who invented a machine to turn dreams into reality?
Son: No, Dad, what happened?
Dad: It was an incredible breakthrough! With a sprinkle of imagination and a touch of science, that machine could transform even the wildest dreams into tangible experiences. It was like living in a world of pure imagination!

265. A father and son are watching a show about the ocean. The son asks, "Dad, why is the ocean salty?" The father replies, "Well, son, the ocean is salty because it contains many dissolved salts, the most common of which is sodium chloride, also known as table salt." The son says, "So, when I taste the salt in the ocean, is it just the sea seasoning itself?"

266. A son asks his father, "Dad, why do we have fingerprints?" The father replies, "Well, son, fingerprints improve our grip and also are unique to each person, which can be useful for identification." The son says, "So, when I leave fingerprints everywhere, is it just my hands leaving their autograph?"

267. A son says to his father, "Dad, when I grow up, I want to be a race car driver." The father replies, "That's a speedy choice, son. Remember, race car drivers need to have quick reflexes and great focus." The son says, "I've got that, Dad. I'm the fastest runner in my class and I always pay attention."

268. A father and son are watching a show about plants. The son asks, "Dad, why do plants need sunlight?" The father replies, "Well, son, plants need sunlight for photosynthesis, a process in which they convert sunlight, water, and carbon dioxide into food." The son says, "So, when I see plants reaching toward the sun, is it just them making breakfast?"

269. A son asks his father, "Dad, why do we yawn?" The father replies, "Well, son, yawning is a natural response to being tired or bored, though it's not fully understood why we do it." The son says, "So, when I yawn during a long car ride, is it just me saying I need a break?"

270. A son says to his father, "Dad, when I grow up, I want to be a detective." The father replies, "That's an investigative choice, son. Remember, detectives need to be observant and good at solving puzzles." The son says, "I've got that, Dad. I always find the missing piece in my jigsaw puzzles."

271. A father and son are watching a show about birds. The son asks, "Dad, why do birds sing?" The father replies, "Well, son, birds sing to communicate with each other, particularly for attracting mates and defending territory." The son says, "So, when I hear birds singing, is it just them saying 'Hey, this is my tree!'?"

272. A son asks his father, "Dad, why do we have birthdays?" The father replies, "Well, son, birthdays are a way of marking another year in our lives, and it's a chance for our loved ones to celebrate us." The son says, "So, when I have a birthday party, is it just everyone saying 'Good job on growing older'?"

273. A son says to his father, "Dad, when I grow up, I want to be a musician." The father replies, "That's a harmonious choice, son. Remember, musicians need to have a good ear for music and a lot of practice." The son says, "I've got that, Dad. I can play 'Twinkle, Twinkle, Little Star' on the piano without mistakes."

274. A father and son are watching a show about the moon. The son asks, "Dad, why does the moon change shape?" The father replies, "Well, son, the moon doesn't actually change shape. What we see from Earth changes based on the moon's position in relation to the Earth and the sun." The son says, "So, when I see the moon changing, is it just playing peek-a-boo with the sun?"

275. A son asks his father, "Dad, why do we laugh?" The father replies, "Well, son, laughing is a way of expressing happiness or amusement, and it's also a way for us to connect with others." The son says, "So, when I laugh at a funny joke, is it just my body saying 'That's a good one!'?"

276. A son says to his father, "Dad, when I grow up, I want to be a chef." The father replies, "That's a flavorful choice, son. Remember, chefs need to have a good palate and a love for food." The son says, "I've got that, Dad. I always help mom with cooking and I love trying new foods."

277. A father and son are watching a show about clouds. The son asks, "Dad, why do clouds move?" The father replies, "Well, son, clouds move because of the wind. Even when it seems like a calm day on the ground, there can be wind higher up in the sky moving the clouds along." The son says, "So, when I see clouds moving, is it just them taking a stroll in the sky?"

278. A son asks his father, "Dad, why do we cry?" The father replies, "Well, son, crying is a way of expressing strong emotions, such as sadness, frustration, or even happiness." The son says, "So, when I cry, is it just my eyes speaking their mind?"

279. A son says to his father, "Dad, when I grow up, I want to be an engineer." The father replies, "That's a constructive choice, son. Remember, engineers need to

be good at math and problem-solving." The son says, "I've got that, Dad. I always find the best solution for my toy train tracks."

280. A father and son are watching a show about snow. The son asks, "Dad, why is snow white?" The father replies, "Well, son, snow appears white because it reflects all colors of light equally." The son says, "So, when I see a field of fresh snow, is it just the world's most natural white canvas?"

281. A son asks his father, "Dad, why do we feel pain?" The father replies, "Well, son, pain is our body's way of telling us something is wrong." The son says, "So, when I scrape my knee, is it just my body saying 'Be careful!'?"

282. A son says to his father, "Dad, when I grow up, I want to be a botanist." The father replies, "That's a blooming choice, son. Remember, botanists need to be curious and have a love for plants and nature." The son says, "I've got that, Dad. I always ask questions and I love exploring our backyard."

283. A father and son are watching a show about space. The son asks, "Dad, why is space black?" The father replies, "Well, son, space appears black to us because there's no atmosphere to scatter the sunlight." The son says, "So, when I look at the night sky, is it just space saying 'Goodnight, Earth!'?"

284. A father and son are watching a show about rainbows. The son asks, "Dad, why are rainbows so colorful?" The father replies, "Well, son, it's because of the way sunlight is refracted, or bent, by raindrops." The son says, "So, when I color with all my crayons, am I creating a mini rainbow?"

285. A son asks his father, "Dad, why do we get hiccups?" The father replies, "Well, son, hiccups are caused by an involuntary contraction of the diaphragm, a muscle in your chest." The son says, "So, when I get hiccups, is it just my diaphragm playing a prank on me?"

286. A son says to his father, "Dad, when I grow up, I want to be a firefighter." The father replies, "That's a heroic choice, son. Remember, firefighters need to be brave and physically fit." The son says, "I've got that, Dad. I'm always the first one up the tree and the last one down."

287. A father and son are watching a show about meteors. The son asks, "Dad, why do meteors burn up when they enter the atmosphere?" The father replies, "Well, son, it's because of the friction between the meteor and the air molecules." The son says, "So, when my toy car heats up after I've been playing with it a lot, is it experiencing friction like a meteor?"

288. A son asks his father, "Dad, why do we get goosebumps?" The father replies, "Well, son, goosebumps are a reaction to cold or strong emotions and are part of our 'fight or flight' response." The son says, "So, when I get goosebumps watching a scary movie, is it just my body saying it's spooked?"

289. A son says to his father, "Dad, when I grow up, I want to be an author." The father replies, "That's a creative choice, son. Remember, authors need to be imaginative and good at telling stories." The son says, "I've got that, Dad. I make up bedtime stories for my teddy bears."

290. A father and son are watching a show about thunderstorms. The son asks, "Dad, why does thunder boom?" The father replies, "Well, son, thunder is the sound that lightning makes when it heats up the air." The son says, "So, when I clap my hands really loud, am I creating mini thunder?"

291. A son asks his father, "Dad, why do we sweat?" The father replies, "Well, son, sweating is our body's way of cooling itself down." The son says, "So, when I sweat after playing tag, is it just my body's air conditioning turning on?"

292. A son says to his father, "Dad, when I grow up, I want to be a police officer." The father replies, "That's a noble choice, son. Remember, police officers need to be

courageous and good at problem-solving." The son says, "I've got that, Dad. I'm always the one to solve the mystery in our games."

293. A father and son are watching a show about earthquakes. The son asks, "Dad, why do earthquakes happen?" The father replies, "Well, son, earthquakes are caused by the movement of tectonic plates in the Earth's crust." The son says, "So, when I shake my snow globe, am I creating a mini earthquake?"

294. A son asks his father, "Dad, why do we have teeth?" The father replies, "Well, son, teeth help us chew our food, and they're important for speaking clearly." The son says, "So, when I lose a baby tooth, is it just making way for a better kitchen tool?"

295. A son says to his father, "Dad, when I grow up, I want to be a scientist." The father replies, "That's an analytical choice, son. Remember, scientists need to be curious and have a strong understanding of math and science." The son says, "I've got that, Dad. I conduct experiments with my toys all the time."

296. A father and son are watching a show about the Sahara Desert. The son asks, "Dad, why is the Sahara Desert so hot?" The father replies, "Well, son, it's because it's located near the equator and gets a lot of direct

sunlight." The son says, "So, when I play in the sandbox on a sunny day, am I creating a mini Sahara Desert?"

297. A son asks his father, "Dad, why do we have hair?" The father replies, "Well, son, hair helps protect our skin, keep us warm, and it also plays a role in sensory activities." The son says, "So, when I style my hair, am I just personalizing my helmet?"

298. A son says to his father, "Dad, when I grow up, I want to be a professional athlete." The father replies, "That's a competitive choice, son. Remember, athletes need to be physically fit and mentally strong." The son says, "I've got that, Dad. I race my friends at the park and never give up."

299. A father and son are watching a documentary about the ocean. The son asks, "Dad, why is the ocean salty?" The father replies, "Well, son, it's because of minerals that wash into the ocean from the land and undersea volcanic activity." The son says, "So, when I add salt to my fish tank, am I making it more like an ocean?"

300. A son asks his father, "Dad, why do we get tired?" The father replies, "Well, son, feeling tired is our body's way of telling us that it needs rest to function properly." The son says, "So, when I feel sleepy after playing all day, is it just my body asking for a time-out?"

301. A son says to his father, "Dad, when I grow up, I want to be a musician." The father replies, "That's a harmonious choice, son. Remember, musicians need to have a good ear and practice their instrument regularly." The son says, "I've got that, Dad. I play my toy guitar and sing songs all the time."

302. A father and son are watching a show about Mount Everest. The son asks, "Dad, why is Mount Everest so tall?" The father replies, "Well, son, it's because of the movement of tectonic plates in the Earth's crust." The son says, "So, when I stack my blocks as high as I can, am I creating a mini Mount Everest?"

303. A son asks his father, "Dad, why do we feel pain?" The father replies, "Well, son, pain is our body's way of letting us know that something is wrong." The son says, "So, when I get a splinter and it hurts, is it just my body saying 'ouch' for me?"

304. A son says to his father, "Dad, when I grow up, I want to be an engineer." The father replies, "That's a constructive choice, son. Remember, engineers need to be good at problem-solving and have a strong understanding of math and science." The son says, "I've got that, Dad. I build bridges with my blocks all the time."

305. A father and son are watching a documentary about the Arctic. The son asks, "Dad, why is the Arctic so cold?"

The father replies, "Well, son, it's because it's located at the North Pole and receives less direct sunlight." The son says, "So, when I play in the snow in winter, am I exploring a mini Arctic?"

306. A son asks his father, "Dad, why do we have a heartbeat?" The father replies, "Well, son, our heartbeat is the sound of our heart pumping blood around our body." The son says, "So, when I can hear my heartbeat after running, is it just my heart telling me it's working hard?"

307. A son says to his father, "Dad, when I grow up, I want to be a chef." The father replies, "That's a tasty choice, son. Remember, chefs need to be creative and have a good palate." The son says, "I've got that, Dad. I make the best mud pies in the neighborhood."

308. Dad: Son, why did the baker become a gardener?
Son: Dad, I'm not sure. How did that happen?
Dad: Well, they realized that both baking and gardening involve creating something beautiful from scratch. They wanted to bring their passion for cultivating delicious flavors from the kitchen to the garden!

309. Dad: Son, did you know that music has the power to heal?
Son: Yes, Dad, I've heard that music can be therapeutic.

Dad: Absolutely! Music has the ability to soothe the soul, uplift spirits, and bring comfort in times of need. It's a universal language of healing!

310. Dad: Son, why did the sandwich go to the gym?
Son: I don't know, Dad. Why did it go?
Dad: Well, it wanted to get fit and "sand-which"! It aimed to shed some excess condiments and be a lean, mean, sandwich-making machine.

311. Dad: Son, did you hear about the scientist who invented a machine to turn vegetables into instruments?
Son: No, Dad, that's fascinating!
Dad: It was a "melodi-veg" machine! It could transform carrots into flutes, bell peppers into saxophones, and zucchinis into guitars. It was a garden symphony like no other!

312. Dad: Son, why did the spider become a web designer?
Son: Dad, spiders don't design websites.
Dad: You're right, but that spider had a knack for creating intricate and visually stunning webs. It realized it could use its skills to build beautiful virtual designs on the world wide web!

313. Dad: Son, did you know that books are like windows to different worlds?
Son: Yes, Dad, books can transport us to new places.

Dad: Absolutely! Each book holds a unique universe waiting to be explored. They allow us to escape reality and embark on extraordinary adventures from the comfort of our own imagination.

314. Dad: Son, why did the sandwich get a promotion at work?
Son: I'm not sure, Dad. How did it get promoted?
Dad: Well, it had all the right ingredients for success! Its layers of flavors and perfect balance made it the talk of the office lunchroom. It was a sandwich on the rise!

315. Dad: Son, did you hear about the scientist who discovered a way to turn frowns into smiles?
Son: No, Dad, how did they do it?
Dad: They developed a formula called "grinetics"! With a combination of laughter, positivity, and a dash of kindness, they could turn even the gloomiest frowns into radiant smiles.

316. Dad: Son, why did the baker become a magician?
Son: Dad, I'm not sure. How did that happen?
Dad: Well, they realized that both baking and magic are all about creating something delightful out of thin air. They wanted to sprinkle their baked goods with a touch of enchantment!

317. Dad: Son, did you know that laughter is like a natural energy booster?
Son: Dad, you always say the most interesting things.
Dad: It's true! A good laugh releases endorphins and revitalizes the body and mind. It's like a natural caffeine kick that leaves you energized and ready to take on the day!

318. Dad: Son, why did the tree go to the dentist?
Son: Dad, trees don't have teeth.
Dad: You're right, but that tree needed some tree-mendous dental care! It had a branch-ache and needed a little tree-tment to ensure its dental health.

319. Dad: Son, did you hear about the scientist who invented a machine to turn vegetables into jokes?
Son: No, Dad, that sounds intriguing!
Dad: It was a "pun-derizer"! With a spin and a sprinkle of veggie humor, that machine could transform even the simplest carrot or broccoli into a rib-tickling joke.

320. Dad: Son, why did the artist always carry a sketchbook?
Son: Dad, I think artists carry sketchbooks to draw.
Dad: True, but that sketchbook was their creative companion. They believed that inspiration could strike at any moment, and they wanted to capture every artistic thought that crossed their mind.

321. Dad: Son, did you know that clouds have a secret language?
Son: Dad, clouds are just water vapor.
Dad: Well, if you watch closely, clouds can tell stories through their formations. They whisper tales of adventure, love, and mystery across the sky. It's a language that only dreamers can understand!

322. Dad: Son, why did the tomato turn red and run a marathon?
Son: I don't know, Dad. Why did it run?
Dad: It was tired of being underestimated as just a salad ingredient. It wanted to prove that it had the strength and determination to run the extra mile. That tomato was ripe for the challenge!

323. Dad: Son, did you hear about the scientist who invented a machine to translate pet sounds into human language?
Son: No, Dad, that's incredible!
Dad: It was a "meow-matic" and "woof-o-tron" device! With a few technological marvels, it could decode the language of cats and dogs, allowing us to understand their thoughts and feelings.

324. Dad: Son, why did the math book go to the therapist?
Son: Dad, books can't have emotions.
Dad: You're right, but that math book needed some mathematical counseling. It had some unresolved

equations that were causing it unnecessary stress. It was a journey of mental arithmetic!

325. A father and son are watching a show about the Great Wall of China. The son asks, "Dad, why is the Great Wall of China so long?" The father replies, "Well, son, it was built to protect China from invaders." The son says, "So, when I build a fort with my blocks, am I creating a mini Great Wall?"

326. A son asks his father, "Dad, why do we laugh?" The father replies, "Well, son, laughter is a way for us to express joy and amusement." The son says, "So, when I laugh at your jokes, is it just my way of saying 'Good one, Dad'?"

327. A son says to his father, "Dad, when I grow up, I want to be a pilot." The father replies, "That's a high-flying choice, son. Remember, pilots need to be calm under pressure and have good hand-eye coordination." The son says, "I've got that, Dad. I fly my toy airplane around the house without crashing."

328. A father and son are watching a show about the pyramids. The son asks, "Dad, why are the pyramids so big?" The father replies, "Well, son, the pyramids were built as tombs for the pharaohs, and their size was meant to reflect their power." The son says, "So, when I build a

huge sandcastle at the beach, am I making a mini pyramid?"

329. A son asks his father, "Dad, why do we cry?" The father replies, "Well, son, crying is a way for us to express strong emotions like sadness, joy, or frustration." The son says, "So, when I cry because I'm happy, is it just my tears throwing a party?"

330. A son says to his father, "Dad, when I grow up, I want to be a zookeeper." The father replies, "That's a wild choice, son. Remember, zookeepers need to be patient and have a love for animals." The son says, "I've got that, Dad. I take care of my stuffed animals like they're real."

331. A father and son are watching a show about pyramids. The son asks, "Dad, why were pyramids built?" The father replies, "Well, son, they were built as tombs for the pharaohs in ancient Egypt." The son says, "So, when I stack my toys into a pyramid, am I building a tomb for my action figures?"

332. A son asks his father, "Dad, why do we blink?" The father replies, "Well, son, blinking helps to keep our eyes moist and clear of dust." The son says, "So, when I blink during a staring contest, is it just my eyes asking for a rain shower?"

333. A son says to his father, "Dad, when I grow up, I want to be a pilot." The father replies, "That's a soaring choice, son. Remember, pilots need to have sharp reflexes and great vision." The son says, "I've got that, Dad. I fly my toy planes with precision and never lose sight of them."

334. A father and son are watching a show about the Northern Lights. The son asks, "Dad, why do the Northern Lights happen?" The father replies, "Well, son, they're caused by solar particles colliding with gases in Earth's atmosphere." The son says, "So, when I mix different colors of paint, am I creating my own Northern Lights?"

335. A son asks his father, "Dad, why do we have eyebrows?" The father replies, "Well, son, eyebrows help keep sweat out of our eyes and they also help with facial expression." The son says, "So, when I raise my eyebrows, am I just keeping my forehead sweat away from my eyes?"

336. A son says to his father, "Dad, when I grow up, I want to be a race car driver." The father replies, "That's a speedy choice, son. Remember, race car drivers need to have quick reflexes and courage." The son says, "I've got that, Dad. I race my toy cars down the hallway at top speed."

337. A father and son are watching a documentary about black holes. The son asks, "Dad, why do black holes

exist?" The father replies, "Well, son, they're a result of a massive star collapsing under its own gravity." The son says, "So, when I pull the plug and watch the water swirl down the drain, am I creating a mini black hole?"

338. A son asks his father, "Dad, why do we hiccup?" The father replies, "Well, son, hiccups are caused by involuntary contractions of your diaphragm." The son says, "So, when I get the hiccups, is it just my body's way of doing jumping jacks?"

339. A son says to his father, "Dad, when I grow up, I want to be a zookeeper." The father replies, "That's a wild choice, son. Remember, zookeepers need to have a love for animals and be patient." The son says, "I've got that, Dad. I take care of my stuffed animals and even let them eat dinner with us."

340. A father and son are watching a show about glaciers. The son asks, "Dad, why do glaciers move?" The father replies, "Well, son, it's because the weight and pressure cause the ice to slowly flow." The son says, "So, when I slide on my belly on the slippery kitchen floor, am I being a glacier?"

341. A son asks his father, "Dad, why do we snore?" The father replies, "Well, son, snoring happens when air can't move freely through your throat while you're sleeping." The son says, "So, when I snore, is it just my throat's way

of playing the trumpet?"

342. A son says to his father, "Dad, when I grow up, I want to be an archaeologist." The father replies, "That's a historic choice, son. Remember, archaeologists need to be patient and meticulous." The son says, "I've got that, Dad. I excavate lost toys from under my bed all the time."

343. A father and son are watching a documentary about rainforests. The son asks, "Dad, why is the rainforest so important?" The father replies, "Well, son, they are home to many species and play a crucial role in our planet's climate." The son says, "So, when I build a fort out of plants in the garden, am I making a mini rainforest?"

344. A son asks his father, "Dad, why do we get goosebumps?" The father replies, "Well, son, goosebumps happen when our body reacts to cold or strong emotions." The son says, "So, when I get goosebumps while watching a scary movie, is it just my skin getting excited?"

345. A son says to his father, "Dad, when I grow up, I want to be a teacher." The father replies, "That's an admirable choice, son. Remember, teachers need to be

understanding and patient." The son says, "I've got that, Dad. I teach my stuffed animals the alphabet."

346. A father and son are watching a show about the Grand Canyon. The son asks, "Dad, how was the Grand Canyon formed?" The father replies, "Well, son, it was formed by the Colorado River eroding the rock over millions of years." The son says, "So, when I dig in the sandbox, am I making a mini Grand Canyon?"

347. A son asks his father, "Dad, why do we have freckles?" The father replies, "Well, son, freckles are small, harmless spots on your skin from exposure to the sun." The son says, "So, when I get freckles, is it just my skin's way of creating constellations?"

348. A son says to his father, "Dad, when I grow up, I want to be a firefighter." The father replies, "That's a brave choice, son. Remember, firefighters need to be strong and have the ability to stay calm under pressure." The son says, "I've got that, Dad. I put out fires in my video games all the time."

349. A father and son are watching a documentary about the solar system. The son asks, "Dad, why does the Earth rotate?" The father replies, "Well, son, it's because of the way the Earth was formed and the momentum from that process." The son says, "So, when I spin in circles, am I being like Earth?"

350. A son asks his father, "Dad, why do we sweat?" The father replies, "Well, son, sweating helps our body cool down when it's hot or when we're exercising." The son says, "So, when I sweat while playing video games, is it just my body cooling down from all the action?"

351. A son says to his father, "Dad, when I grow up, I want to be a doctor." The father replies, "That's a caring choice, son. Remember, doctors need to have a strong stomach and a desire to help others." The son says, "I've got that, Dad. I take care of my sick teddy bear all the time."

352. A father and son are watching a show about volcanoes. The son asks, "Dad, why do volcanoes erupt?" The father replies, "Well, son, it's because of the buildup of magma under the Earth's surface." The son says, "So, when my soda overflows after I drop a mentos in it, am I creating a mini volcano?"

353. A son asks his father, "Dad, why do we dream?" The father replies, "Well, son, dreams are a natural part of sleep, but we're not entirely sure why we dream." The son says, "So, when I dream about being a superhero, is it just my brain's way of telling bedtime stories?"

354. A son says to his father, "Dad, when I grow up, I want to be a magician." The father replies, "That's a magical choice, son. Remember, magicians need to be good at

misdirection and practice their tricks often." The son says, "I've got that, Dad. I make my vegetables disappear at dinner all the time."

355. A father and son are watching a show about the Amazon River. The son asks, "Dad, why is the Amazon River so big?" The father replies, "Well, son, it's because of the large amount of rain that falls in the Amazon basin." The son says, "So, when I turn on the hose in the backyard, am I creating a mini Amazon River?"

356. A son asks his father, "Dad, why do we have fingernails?" The father replies, "Well, son, they protect the sensitive tips of our fingers and help us pick up small objects." The son says, "So, when I clip my nails, am I just doing finger armor maintenance?"

357. A son says to his father, "Dad, when I grow up, I want to be an astronaut." The father replies, "That's a stellar choice, son. Remember, astronauts need to be good at problem-solving and have a strong understanding of science." The son says, "I've got that, Dad. I solve puzzles all the time, and I watch lots of science shows."

358. A father and son are watching a show about lions. The son asks, "Dad, why do lions roar?" The father replies, "Well, son, lions roar to communicate with each other and to establish territory." The son says, "So, when I

shout while playing video games, am I just roaring like a lion?"

359. A son asks his father, "Dad, why do birds fly in a V formation?" The father replies, "Well, son, it's to conserve energy and take advantage of the air currents." The son says, "So, when we line up to get ice cream, should we stand in a V formation to get it faster?"

360. A son says to his father, "Dad, when I grow up, I want to be a musician." The father replies, "That's a harmonious choice, son. Remember, musicians need to practice a lot and have a love for music." The son says, "I've been practicing, Dad. I play the best air guitar solos in the living room."

361. A father and son are watching a documentary about bees. The son asks, "Dad, why do bees make honey?" The father replies, "Well, son, it's their food. They collect nectar from flowers and turn it into honey." The son says, "So, when I turn my apple juice into an apple juice mustache, am I being a bee?"

362. A son asks his father, "Dad, why do we have to brush our teeth?" The father replies, "Well, son, it's to keep our teeth clean and healthy, and to prevent cavities." The son says, "So, when I brush my teeth, am I like a superhero fighting the cavity villains?"

363. A son says to his father, "Dad, when I grow up, I want to be an architect." The father replies, "That's a solid choice, son. Remember, architects need to be good at math and have a creative vision." The son says, "I've got that covered, Dad. I create the most amazing pillow forts, and I count all the pillows before and after."

364. A father and son are watching a solar eclipse. The son asks, "Dad, why do solar eclipses happen?" The father replies, "Well, son, it happens when the moon passes between the sun and the Earth." The son says, "So, when I pass between you and the TV, am I causing a 'son' eclipse?"

365. A son asks his father, "Dad, why do dogs wag their tails?" The father replies, "Well, son, it's a way for dogs to communicate their emotions." The son says, "So, when I dance around when I'm happy, am I wagging my tail?"

366. A son says to his father, "Dad, when I grow up, I want to be a detective." The father replies, "That's an investigative choice, son. Remember, detectives need to be observant and logical." The son says, "I've been practicing, Dad. I always find out who ate the last cookie. It's usually me."

367. A father and son are watching a documentary about rainforests. The son asks, "Dad, why is the rainforest so important?" The father replies, "Well, son, it's home to

many species and it helps regulate the Earth's climate." The son says, "So, when I water the plants in our garden, am I creating a mini rainforest?"

368. A son asks his father, "Dad, why do we get wrinkles as we get older?" The father replies, "Well, son, as we age, our skin loses its elasticity." The son says, "So, when my balloon gets wrinkly after a few days, is it just getting old?"

369. A son says to his father, "Dad, when I grow up, I want to be a magician." The father replies, "That's a magical choice, son. Remember, magicians need to be skilled in illusion and deception." The son says, "I'm already on it, Dad. I make my vegetables disappear at dinner every night."

370. A father and son are watching a lunar eclipse. The son asks, "Dad, why does the moon turn red during a lunar eclipse?" The father replies, "Well, son, it's because of the way the Earth's atmosphere bends the light." The son says, "So, when I look through my red juice at you, am I causing a 'Dad' eclipse?"

371. A son asks his father, "Dad, why do we sneeze?" The father replies, "Well, son, it's your body's way of getting rid of irritants in your nose or throat." The son says, "So, when I sneeze during our cleaning days, is my body just saying it prefers messiness?"

372. A son says to his father, "Dad, when I grow up, I want to be an astronaut." The father replies, "That's an out-of-this-world choice, son. Remember, astronauts need to be brave and disciplined." The son says, "I've got the 'brave' part covered, Dad. I explore the dark abyss of the attic all the time."

373. A father and son are watching a show about volcanoes. The son asks, "Dad, why do volcanoes erupt?" The father replies, "Well, son, it's because of the pressure from the molten rock beneath the Earth's surface." The son says, "So, when I shake up my soda bottle and it fizzes over, am I creating a mini volcano?"

374. A son asks his father, "Dad, why do we dream?" The father replies, "Well, son, it's not fully understood, but dreams might help our brains process our experiences." The son says, "So, when I dream about eating giant marshmallows, is my brain processing my love for s'mores?"

375. A son says to his father, "Dad, when I grow up, I want to be a scientist." The father replies, "That's an intelligent choice, son. Remember, scientists need to be curious and determined." The son says, "I've been practicing, Dad. I conduct experiments all the time, like how many pancakes I can eat in one go."

376. A father and son are watching a documentary about penguins. The son asks, "Dad, why do penguins waddle?" The father replies, "Well, son, it's because of their body structure and it helps them maintain balance on ice." The son says, "So, when I waddle in my giant snow boots, am I being a penguin?"

377. A son asks his father, "Dad, why do we laugh?" The father replies, "Well, son, laughter is a social response and it releases feel-good hormones." The son says, "So, when I laugh at my own jokes, am I just making myself feel good?"

378. A son says to his father, "Dad, when I grow up, I want to be a movie star." The father replies, "That's a shining choice, son. Remember, movie stars need to have talent and be able to handle fame." The son says, "I'm ready for that, Dad. I'm the star of our home movies, and I handle being famous among my stuffed animals pretty well."

379. A father and son are watching a documentary about the desert. The son asks, "Dad, why is the desert so hot?" The father replies, "Well, son, it's because of the lack of moisture and the intense sunlight." The son says, "So, when I'm in the sandbox on a hot day, am I in a mini desert?"

380. A son asks his father, "Dad, why do we get hiccups?" The father replies, "Well, son, hiccups are caused by a

sudden contraction of your diaphragm." The son says, "So, when I get hiccups, is my diaphragm just practicing for a dance-off?"

381. A son says to his father, "Dad, when I grow up, I want to be a writer." The father replies, "That's a creative choice, son. Remember, writers need to be imaginative and persistent." The son says, "I've been practicing, Dad. I write the best stories for my action figures."

382. A father and son are watching a show about the deep sea. The son asks, "Dad, why are some fish able to live in the deep sea?" The father replies, "Well, son, they've evolved to survive the extreme conditions there." The son says, "So, when I swim to the deep end of the pool, am I a deep-sea diver?"

383. A son asks his father, "Dad, why do we have seasons?" The father replies, "Well, son, it's because the Earth's axis is tilted as it orbits the sun." The son says, "So, when I tilt my head while eating my ice cream, am I causing a 'season' in my mouth?"

384. A son says to his father, "Dad, when I grow up, I want to be an artist." The father replies, "That's a colorful choice, son. Remember, artists need to be expressive and original." The son says, "I've got that, Dad. I express myself with crayons on the living room wall all the time."

385. A father and son are watching a snowstorm. The son asks, "Dad, why is snow white?" The father replies, "Well, son, it's because of how light reflects and scatters off the snowflakes." The son says, "So, when I sprinkle powdered sugar on my pancakes, am I making a 'snowstorm'?"

386. A son asks his father, "Dad, why do we grow hair?" The father replies, "Well, son, hair helps protect our skin and regulate body temperature." The son says, "So, when I put on my furry hat in winter, am I just growing extra hair?"

387. A son says to his father, "Dad, when I grow up, I want to be a comedian." The father replies, "That's a funny choice, son. Remember, comedians need to have a good sense of humor and be able to handle rejection." The son says, "I've got that, Dad. I tell jokes to my teddy bears. They never laugh, but they never leave the show either."

388. A father and son are watching a wildlife documentary. The son asks, "Dad, why do kangaroos hop?" The father replies, "Well, son, hopping is an efficient way for kangaroos to travel long distances." The son says, "So, when I hop around the living room, am I being a kangaroo?"

389. A son asks his father, "Dad, why do we yawn?" The father replies, "Well, son, yawning is a natural response when our bodies need more oxygen." The son says, "So,

when I yawn during your long stories, is it just because I need more oxygen?"

390. A son says to his father, "Dad, when I grow up, I want to be a chef." The father replies, "That's a tasty choice, son. Remember, chefs need to have a passion for food and a knack for creativity." The son says, "I've got that, Dad. I create the most interesting cereal and ketchup combinations."

391. A father and son are watching a race on TV. The son asks, "Dad, why do runners lean forward at the finish line?" The father replies, "Well, son, it's to get their chest across the line a fraction of a second faster." The son says, "So, when I lean forward to grab the last cookie, am I just trying to beat my siblings to the finish line?"

392. A son asks his father, "Dad, why do trees lose their leaves in the fall?" The father replies, "Well, son, it's a way for the trees to conserve water during the winter." The son says, "So, when I don't drink my water at dinner, am I just preparing for winter?"

393. A son says to his father, "Dad, when I grow up, I want to be a teacher." The father replies, "That's a noble choice, son. Remember, teachers need to be patient and understanding." The son says, "I think I have what it takes, Dad. I taught my pet hamster how to use his new wheel."

394. A father and son are watching a magician perform on TV. The son asks, "Dad, how do magicians do their tricks?" The father replies, "Well, son, it's all about illusion and quick hand movements." The son says, "So, when I grab the last slice of pizza without anyone noticing, am I a magician?"

395. A son asks his father, "Dad, why do stars twinkle?" The father replies, "Well, son, it's because of the way their light passes through the Earth's atmosphere." The son says, "So, when I see twinkles in your eyes, is it because your love for me is as infinite as the universe?"

396. Dad: Son, why did the computer go to art school?
Son: Dad, that doesn't make sense.
Dad: Well, it wanted to express its creative side through pixel-perfect designs and digital art. It realized that technology and art can go hand in hand!

397. Dad: Son, did you know that laughter is the best accessory you can wear?
Son: Dad, that's an interesting perspective.
Dad: Absolutely! A genuine smile and a hearty laugh can enhance any outfit and make you shine from within. It's the accessory that never goes out of style!

398. Dad: Son, why did the tomato blush when it saw the cucumber?

Son: Dad, that sounds silly. Why did it blush?
Dad: Well, it was love at first sight in the vegetable garden. That tomato couldn't help but turn red with embarrassment and excitement!

399. Dad: Son, did you know that trees are nature's guardians?
Son: Dad, trees are just part of the environment.
Dad: True, but trees stand tall, sheltering us from the scorching sun and providing a home to countless creatures. They're the silent protectors of the natural world!

400. Dad: Son, why did the book go to therapy?
Son: Dad, books can't have feelings.
Dad: You're right, but that book had some unresolved plot twists and complex characters. It needed a little therapy to untangle its literary emotions!

401. Dad: Son, did you know that the journey of a thousand miles begins with a single laugh?
Son: Dad, I think you got that saying a bit mixed up.
Dad: Well, in my version, laughter is the fuel that propels you forward and makes the journey more enjoyable. It's the catalyst for adventure and discovery!

402. Dad: Son, why did the traffic light turn green?
Son: Dad, that's what it's supposed to do.

Dad: Well, that traffic light was feeling "en-light-ened"! It wanted to illuminate the roads and guide vehicles on their way. Green means go, after all!

403. Dad: Son, did you hear about the scientist who discovered a way to turn frowns into smiles?
Son: No, Dad, how did they do it?
Dad: They developed a revolutionary formula called "smile-ology"! With a touch of humor and a sprinkle of positivity, they could turn even the grumpiest frowns upside down.

404. Dad: Son, why did the baker get a promotion at the bakery?
Son: I don't know, Dad. Why did they get promoted?
Dad: Because their pastries were the yeast of their worries! Their delicious creations and dedication to perfection made them rise to the top.

405. Dad: Son, did you know that clouds can be great comedians?
Son: Dad, I didn't know clouds had a sense of humor.
Dad: Well, they're experts at delivering "thunder-ous" punchlines and putting on a show with lightning-fast wit. They know how to brighten up the sky with laughter!

406. Dad: Son, why did the grape roll down the hill?
Son: Dad, that sounds silly. Why did it roll?

Dad: It heard through the grapevine that there was a juicy secret waiting for it at the bottom. It couldn't resist the temptation to find out what all the fuss was about!

407. Dad: Son, did you know that librarians are the ultimate bookworms?
Son: Dad, that's not very nice.
Dad: No, it's a term of endearment! Librarians are passionate about books and dedicated to spreading the joy of reading. They're the guardians of knowledge and the keepers of literary treasures!

408. Dad: Son, why did the scientist become a magician?
Son: I don't know, Dad. How did that happen?
Dad: Well, they realized that both science and magic are about unraveling mysteries and captivating the imagination. They combined their love for experimentation and illusion to create an extraordinary show!

409. Dad: Son, did you know that smiles are contagious?
Son: Yes, Dad, I've heard that before.
Dad: It's true! A smile can start a chain reaction, spreading happiness from one person to another. It's like a ripple of joy that brightens the world!

410. A son says to his father, "Dad, when I grow up, I want to be a chef." The father replies, "That's a tasty choice, son. Remember, chefs need to be creative and have a

passion for food." The son says, "I've been practicing, Dad. I create a gourmet cereal dish every morning."

411. A father and son are watching a nature documentary. The son asks, "Dad, why do bears hibernate?" The father replies, "Well, son, they hibernate to conserve energy when food is scarce in the winter." The son says, "So, when I don't want to get out of bed on a cold morning, am I just hibernating?"

412. A son asks his father, "Dad, why do we get brain freeze?" The father replies, "Well, son, it's your body's reaction to cold food or drink hitting the roof of your mouth." The son says, "So, when I get a brain freeze from eating ice cream, is it my body's way of saying 'slow down'?"

413. A son says to his father, "Dad, when I grow up, I want to be a movie director." The father replies, "That's a glamorous choice, son. Remember, directors need to have a good eye for detail and understand storytelling." The son says, "I've been practicing, Dad. I direct the best puppet shows with my toys."

414. A father and son are watching a basketball game. The son asks, "Dad, why do players dribble the ball?" The father replies, "Well, son, it's a way to move the ball without throwing it." The son says, "So, when I dribble peas off my plate, am I just playing kitchen basketball?"

415. A father and son are watching a documentary about the ocean. The son asks, "Dad, why do waves form?" The father replies, "Well, son, they're caused by wind blowing across the surface of the water." The son says, "So, when I make waves in the bathtub, am I creating a mini storm?"

416. A son asks his father, "Dad, why do we get hiccups?" The father replies, "Well, son, hiccups are caused by a sudden contraction of the diaphragm." The son says, "So, when I hiccup during my piano recital, am I just adding some percussive effects?"

417. A son says to his father, "Dad, when I grow up, I want to be a writer." The father replies, "That's a creative choice, son. Remember, a good writer needs imagination and a way with words." The son says, "I'm working on that, Dad. Just last night, I wrote a thrilling tale about a spoon's journey to the dishwasher."

418. A father and son are watching a lightning storm. The son asks, "Dad, why does lightning strike?" The father replies, "Well, son, it's a release of electricity from the atmosphere." The son says, "So, when I get a static shock from the carpet, am I creating a mini lightning storm?"

419. A son asks his father, "Dad, why do we have to wash our hands?" The father replies, "Well, son, it's to remove dirt and germs that we pick up from our surroundings."

The son says, "So, when I play in the mud and then wash my hands, am I creating and then destroying a germ civilization?"

420. A son says to his father, "Dad, when I grow up, I want to be a builder." The father replies, "That's a strong choice, son. Remember, builders need to be precise and patient." The son says, "I think I have what it takes, Dad. I build and rebuild my Lego tower until it's just right."

421. A father and son are watching a documentary about dinosaurs. The son asks, "Dad, why did dinosaurs go extinct?" The father replies, "Well, son, scientists believe it was due to a massive asteroid hitting the Earth." The son says, "So, when I knock down my domino set, am I like the asteroid?"

422. A son asks his father, "Dad, why do we yawn when we're tired?" The father replies, "Well, son, yawning helps bring more oxygen into the blood and moves more carbon dioxide out." The son says, "So, when I yawn during math homework, am I just trying to oxygenate my brain for better calculations?"

423. A son says to his father, "Dad, when I grow up, I want to be a comedian." The father replies, "That's a fun choice, son. Remember, a good comedian needs to understand

timing and have a sense of humor." The son says, "Well, Dad, I made you laugh when I wore my shirt inside out. That's a good start, right?"

424. A father and son are watching a soccer game. The son asks, "Dad, why do they swap ends at halftime?" The father replies, "Well, son, it's to make sure that neither team has an unfair advantage due to the sun or wind." The son says, "So, when I swap sides of the couch, am I just trying to keep the TV watching fair?"

425. A son asks his father, "Dad, why do birds sing?" The father replies, "Well, son, birds sing to communicate with each other, especially during mating season." The son says, "So, when I sing in the shower, am I just communicating that it's my bathing season?"

426. A son says to his father, "Dad, when I grow up, I want to be a pilot." The father replies, "That's a high-flying goal, son. But remember, pilots need to be disciplined and vigilant." The son says, "Well, I'm disciplined in keeping my toy planes in the air and vigilant in avoiding crashing them into the furniture."

427. A father and son are watching a space documentary. The son asks, "Dad, why does the earth spin?" The father replies, "Well, son, it's due to how our planet was formed billions of years ago." The son says, "So, when I spin my toy top, am I creating a mini earth?"

428. A son asks his father, "Dad, why do we get goosebumps?" The father replies, "Well, son, it's a reaction to cold, fear, or emotional situations. It's part of our 'fight or flight' response." The son says, "So, when I get goosebumps watching cartoons, is it my 'fight or flight' response preparing me to battle animated villains?"

429. A son says to his father, "Dad, when I grow up, I want to be a firefighter." The father replies, "That's a brave choice, son. Remember, firefighters need to be courageous and calm under pressure." The son says, "I've been practicing, Dad. I calmly rescue my teddy bear from under the bed all the time."

430. A son says to his father, "Dad, when I grow up, I want to be a scientist." The father replies, "That's a great ambition, son. Remember, scientists need to be curious and persistent." The son says, "I've got that covered, Dad. I'm curious about what's in the fridge and I'm persistent in asking for ice cream."

431. A father and son are watching a nature documentary. The son asks, "Dad, why do some animals hibernate in the winter?" The father replies, "Well, son, it's a survival strategy. It helps them conserve energy when food is scarce." The son says, "So, when I sleep in on weekends, am I hibernating?"

432. A son asks his father, "Dad, why do some people snore?" The father replies, "Well, son, it usually happens when air doesn't move freely through the throat and nose while sleeping." The son says, "So, is snoring like playing a musical instrument in your sleep?"

433. A son says to his father, "Dad, when I grow up, I want to be an astronaut." The father replies, "That's an out-of-this-world choice, son. But remember, astronauts need to be brave and disciplined." The son says, "I've been practicing by not eating the marshmallows in my cereal. That's discipline, right?"

434. A father and son are watching a football game. The son asks, "Dad, why do they do a huddle before each play?" The father replies, "Well, son, it's a way for the team to communicate their strategy." The son says, "So, when we huddle around the barbecue, is that our strategy to tackle hunger?"

435. A son asks his father, "Dad, why does the sunset look so beautiful?" The father replies, "Well, son, it's because of the way light interacts with the Earth's atmosphere." The son says, "So, if I shine a flashlight through a glass of water, will that make a mini sunset?"

436. Dad: Son, why did the balloon go to school?
Son: Dad, balloons can't go to school.

Dad: Well, that balloon wanted to expand its knowledge and soar to new heights of learning. It was a balloon with big dreams and an insatiable curiosity!

437. Dad: Son, did you hear about the scientist who discovered a way to turn vegetables into laughter?
Son: No, Dad, that sounds amazing!
Dad: It was a "veg-tastic" invention! With a touch of whimsy and a sprinkle of humor, that scientist could turn even the most serious vegetable into a bundle of giggles.

438. Dad: Son, why did the musician bring a ladder to the concert?
Son: Dad, that doesn't make sense.
Dad: Well, they wanted to reach new musical heights and take their performance to the next level! They believed that music could elevate the soul, and a ladder was just the tool to do it.

439. Dad: Son, did you know that laughter is the secret ingredient in every successful recipe?
Son: Dad, I think there are other important ingredients too.
Dad: You're right, but laughter adds flavor to the cooking process and brings people together around the table. It's the spice that makes every dish taste better!

440. Dad: Son, why did the compass go to therapy?
Son: Dad, compasses can't have emotional issues.

Dad: You're correct, but that compass was feeling a bit lost and needed some guidance to find its true direction. It was a journey of self-discovery and inner alignment!

441. Dad: Son, did you hear about the scientist who discovered a way to turn frowns into smiles?
Son: No, Dad, how did they do it?
Dad: They developed a "laughter potion" that could transform even the grumpiest frown into a radiant smile. It was a scientific breakthrough in spreading joy!

442. Dad: Son, why did the chef always carry a spice rack?
Son: Dad, I think chefs need spices for cooking.
Dad: Absolutely! That chef believed that spices were the secret to adding flavor and excitement to every dish. They carried their trusty spice rack to season life with a touch of culinary magic!

443. Dad: Son, did you know that laughter is like a natural wonder drug?
Son: Dad, you always say the most interesting things.
Dad: Well, it's true! A good laugh releases endorphins, reduces stress, and boosts the immune system. It's the ultimate remedy for a happy and healthy life!

444. Dad: Son, why did the kite join a band?
Son: I'm not sure, Dad. Why did it join?

445. Son: Dad, that's a lovely sentiment.

Dad: It's true! Laughter fills the walls with warmth and creates a loving atmosphere that turns a house into a place of joy and togetherness.

446. Dad: Son, why did the bicycle fall over?

Son: Dad, I think it lost its balance.

Dad: Well, that bicycle was tired from all the cycling adventures! It needed a break and decided to take a little rest, but it promised to be back on its wheels soon.

447. Dad: Son, did you hear about the scientist who invented a machine to turn vegetables into musical instruments?

Son: No, Dad, that sounds amazing!

Dad: It was a "veg-o-phone"! With a little scientific magic, that machine could transform carrots into flutes, bell peppers into trumpets, and celery into drums. It was a symphony of healthy eating and music!

448. Dad: Son, why did the artist always carry a sketchbook and a camera?

Son: Dad, I think they wanted to capture moments in different ways.

Dad: Exactly! The sketchbook allowed them to express their artistic vision, while the camera captured the beauty of the world around them. It was a double dose of creative inspiration!

449. Dad: Son, did you know that clouds can dance across the sky?
Son: Dad, clouds are just condensed water vapor.
Dad: True, but if you look closely, you'll see their graceful movements and ever-changing shapes. It's like a mesmerizing ballet performance in the heavens!

450. Dad: Son, why did the tomato turn red and run away from the salad?
Son: I don't know, Dad. Why did it run?
Dad: Well, that tomato wanted to explore the world beyond the salad bowl. It had dreams of becoming a superstar ingredient in a gourmet dish. It was a tomato on a tasty adventure!

451. Dad: Son, did you hear about the scientist who invented a machine to translate animal sounds into human language?
Son: No, Dad, that's incredible!
Dad: It was an "animalogical communicator"! With a few technological marvels, that scientist could understand the barks, meows, and chirps of our furry and feathered friends. It was like having a conversation with the animal kingdom!

452. Dad: Son, why did the math book go to the therapist?
Son: Dad, books can't have feelings.
Dad: You're right, but that math book had some unresolved equations that were causing it distress. It

needed a little mathematical counseling to find the answers it was seeking.

453. Dad: Son, did you know that laughter is like a language that everyone understands?
Son: Yes, Dad, laughter is universal.
Dad: Absolutely! It doesn't matter where you come from or what language you speak—laughter has the power to bring people together, creating connections that transcend any barriers.

454. Dad: Son, why did the sandwich become an actor?
Son: I'm not sure, Dad. How did that happen?
Dad: Well, it realized that it had layers of talent and a flair for performing. It wanted to taste the spotlight and delight audiences with its delicious acting skills. It was a sandwich destined for the silver screen!

455. Dad: Son, did you know that trees are like silent storytellers?
Son: Dad, trees don't tell stories.
Dad: You're right, but if you listen carefully, you'll hear the whispers of their ancient tales carried by the wind. Trees have witnessed countless stories and have stories of their own to share!

456. Dad: Son, why did the sandwich bring a map on its picnic?
Son: I don't know, Dad. Why did it bring a map?

Dad: Because that sandwich was on a culinary adventure! It wanted to explore new flavors and discover the perfect picnic spot. It was a sandwich with an appetite for exploration!

457. A son says to his father, "Dad, when I grow up, I want to be an explorer." The father replies, "That's an adventurous goal, son. Remember, explorers need to be brave and resilient." The son says, "I'm already exploring the deepest, darkest corners of our backyard. I think I'm on the right path."

458. A father and son are watching a meteor shower. The son asks, "Dad, why do meteors glow when they enter the atmosphere?" The father replies, "Well, son, it's because they're moving so fast that they heat up the air around them." The son says, "So, when I slide down the playground slide really fast, am I a meteor?"

459. A son asks his father, "Dad, why do cats always land on their feet?" The father replies, "Well, son, it's because they have a unique skeletal structure that allows them to twist their bodies mid-fall." The son says, "So, if I put my socks on inside out, will I always land on my feet?"

460. A son says to his father, "Dad, when I grow up, I want to be a professional gamer." The father replies, "That's a modern choice, son. But remember, even gamers need

balance in life." The son says, "Of course, Dad. I'll balance my action games with puzzle games."

461. A son asks his father, "Dad, why do leaves change color in the fall?" The father replies, "Well, son, it's because they stop producing chlorophyll, which gives them their green color." The son says, "So, are trees the world's greatest artists?"

462. A son says to his father, "Dad, when I grow up, I want to be a pilot." The father replies, "That's a lofty goal, son. But remember, it takes a lot of training and hard work." The son says, "Well, I've been practicing by flying paper airplanes. I've got the hard work part down!"

463. A father and son are watching a magic trick on TV. The son asks, "Dad, how do magicians pull rabbits out of hats?" The father replies, "Well, son, it's an illusion. There's a lot of skill involved in making it look real." The son says, "So, is doing my homework an illusion when I make it look like it's done?"

464. A son asks his father, "Dad, why do we dream?" The father replies, "Well, son, dreams are a way our brain processes experiences and emotions." The son says, "Does that mean my dream of being an astronaut is my brain processing a future experience?"

465. A son says to his father, "Dad, when I grow up, I want to be a doctor." The father replies, "That's a noble choice, son. Remember, doctors need to be patient and caring." The son says, "I can do that, Dad. I'm patient when waiting for dessert and I care a lot about my video games."

466. A father and son are watching a cooking show. The son asks, "Dad, why do chefs taste the food while they're cooking?" The father replies, "Well, son, that's how they make sure the flavors are just right." The son says, "So, when I eat cookie dough, am I being a responsible chef?"

467. A son asks his father, "Dad, why does the moon change shape?" The father replies, "Well, son, the moon doesn't actually change shape. We just see different parts of it lit by the sun." The son says, "So, does that mean the moon is the world's biggest nightlight?"

468. A son says to his father, "Dad, when I grow up, I want to be a detective." The father replies, "That's an interesting choice, son. Remember, detectives need to be observant and clever." The son says, "I've been practicing by finding all the missing socks in the laundry. I think I'm ready."

469. A father and son are at a music concert. The son asks, "Dad, why do people wave their hands in the air at concerts?" The father replies, "Well, son, it's a way of showing appreciation and excitement." The son says, "So,

when I wave my hand for more dessert, am I appreciating the pie?"

470. A son asks his father, "Dad, why do we have to brush our teeth?" The father replies, "Well, son, it's to keep our teeth healthy and prevent cavities." The son says, "So, does the Tooth Fairy visit more often if you don't brush?"

471. A son asks his father, "Dad, why do people say 'an apple a day keeps the doctor away'?" The father replies, "Well, son, apples are healthy and can help prevent illness." The son says, "So, if I eat an apple, can I skip my dentist appointment?"

472. A son says to his father, "Dad, when I grow up, I want to be a chef." The father replies, "That's great, son. Remember, cooking is about creativity and passion." The son says, "So, when I mix all my food together into a 'super meal', am I being creative?"

473. A father and son are stargazing. The son asks, "Dad, why do stars twinkle?" The father replies, "Actually, son, they're not really twinkling. That's just an effect caused by Earth's atmosphere." The son says, "So, are stars the world's oldest special effects?"

474. A son asks his father, "Dad, why do people get goosebumps when they're scared?" The father replies, "Well, son, it's a natural response of the body to cold or

fear." The son says, "So, when I get goosebumps while watching a horror movie, am I just really scared or is it too cold in here?"

475. A son says to his father, "Dad, when I grow up, I want to be a magician." The father replies, "That's fascinating, son. Remember, magic is all about the art of illusion." The son says, "So, when I hide your car keys and you can't find them, am I performing magic?"

476. A father and son are at a parade. The son asks, "Dad, why do people love parades so much?" The father replies, "Well, son, parades are a celebration. They bring people together." The son says, "So, when we all run to the kitchen for dinner, is that a food parade?"

477. A son asks his father, "Dad, why do birds sing in the morning?" The father replies, "Well, son, that's how birds communicate. It's their way of saying 'Good morning!'" The son says, "So, is my alarm clock a bird?"

478. A son says to his father, "Dad, when I grow up, I want to be a zookeeper." The father replies, "That's a noble profession, son. Remember, taking care of animals is a big responsibility." The son says, "I agree, Dad. That's why I've been practicing by taking care of my pet rock."

479. A father and son are watching a chess tournament. The son asks, "Dad, why do they move the pieces in such

strange patterns?" The father replies, "Well, son, each piece has its own rules of movement." The son says, "So, is it like in our house where Mom's the queen and she makes all the rules?"

480. A son asks his father, "Dad, why do we laugh when something's funny?" The father replies, "Well, son, laughter is a way of expressing joy and amusement." The son says, "So, when you laugh at my drawings, does it mean you find my artistic skills amusing?"

481. A son says to his father, "Dad, when I grow up, I want to be a firefighter." The father replies, "That's a brave choice, son. Remember, firefighters risk their lives to keep us safe." The son says, "Don't worry, Dad. I've been practicing by putting out the flames on my birthday candles."

482. A father and son are at a park, watching a dog catch a Frisbee. The son asks, "Dad, why do dogs love fetching so much?" The father replies, "Well, son, it's in their nature. It's a way of exercising and having fun." The son says, "Does that mean I'm a dog when I run to catch the ice cream truck?"

483. A father and son are watching a basketball game. The son asks, "Dad, why do the players keep bouncing the ball?" The father replies, "Well, son, that's called dribbling. It's how they move the ball without getting

penalized." The son says, "So, is my baby sister dribbling when she drools all over her toys?"

484. A father and son are walking through a museum. The son asks, "Dad, why do people find old stuff so interesting?" The father replies, "Well, son, these artifacts tell us stories about our past." The son says, "So, does the mess under my bed make my room a museum?"

485. A son says to his father, "Dad, when I grow up, I want to be a superhero." The father replies, "That's great, son. But remember, the real heroes are those who help others." The son says, "So, when I save the last slice of pizza for you, am I a hero?"

486. A father and his son are on a road trip. The son, looking at the GPS, says, "Dad, why does the GPS always say 'recalculating' when you make a wrong turn?" The father replies, "Well, son, it's the GPS's way of saying, 'Hold on a second, let me figure out how to fix this mess you've made.'"

487. A son says to his father, "Dad, why do people always say 'it's raining cats and dogs'?" The father, chuckling, replies, "Well, son, it's just a saying. But if it really did, we'd have to start carrying umbrellas made of scratching posts and chew toys."

488. A father and his son are watching a magic show. The son asks, "Dad, do you believe in magic?" The father replies, "In a sense, yes. I see magic every time I see you learn something new." The son, grinning, says, "In that case, is my math homework a magic show?"

489. A son asks his father, "Dad, why is it important to eat vegetables?" The father replies, "Well, son, they're full of nutrients that help your body grow strong and healthy." The son says, "So, if I eat a lot of veggies, can I become strong enough to beat you at arm wrestling?"

490. A son says to his father, "Dad, I want to be a rock star when I grow up." The father replies, "That's great, son. But remember, even rock stars have to practice their scales." The son says, "Okay, I'll start by practicing my air guitar solos."

491. A father and son are watching a football game. The son asks, "Dad, why do they call it football when they use their hands more than their feet?" The father replies, "That's a good question, son. Maybe we should start a campaign to call it 'handball' instead."

492. A son says to his father, "Dad, why do people say 'bless you' when someone sneezes?" The father replies, "Well, son, it's a way of wishing them good health." The son says, "So, if I want to wish someone good luck, should I wait for them to trip?"

493. A father and son are on a hike. The son asks, "Dad, why do we climb mountains?" The father replies, "Because they're there, son. It's a way of challenging ourselves." The son says, "So, if I finish my broccoli, am I a mountain climber?"

494. A son asks his father, "Dad, why does Mom say 'beauty comes from within'?" The father replies, "Because, son, what's inside a person is more important than what's outside." The son says, "So, is that why you eat so much pizza?"

495. A son says to his father, "Dad, when I grow up, I want to be an astronaut." The father replies, "That's a high ambition, son. But remember, the sky's the limit." The son says, "But Dad, if I'm an astronaut, isn't space the limit?"

496. A father and son are on a boat fishing. The son asks, "Dad, why do fish always know when to not take the bait?" The father chuckles and replies, "Well, son, maybe they attended a 'Human Tricks and How to Avoid Them' seminar underwater."

497. A son asks his father, "Dad, why are superheroes always saving the world?" The father replies, "Because, son, they stand up for those who can't defend themselves." The son says, "So, am I a superhero when I protect my sandwich from being eaten by my sister?"

498. A son says to his father, "Dad, I want to be a comedian when I grow up." The father replies, "That's a fun goal, son. But remember, the trick to being a good comedian is timing." The son responds, "Okay, I'll start by timing how long it takes you to laugh at my jokes."

499. A father and son are at a theme park. The son asks, "Dad, why do people love roller coasters so much?" The father replies, "Because, son, they love the thrill and excitement." The son says, "Well, if that's the case, then going shopping with Mom should be an extreme sport."

500. A son asks his father, "Dad, why do we have to learn math?" The father replies, "Well, son, math helps us solve problems and understand the world better." The son says, "So if I learn more math, can I understand why my little brother insists on wearing his underwear on his head?"

501. A son says to his father, "Dad, when I grow up, I want to be a millionaire." The father replies, "That's an ambitious goal, son. But remember, money isn't everything." The son says, "Don't worry, Dad. When I'm a millionaire, I'll buy everything else."

502. A father and son are looking at a rainbow. The son asks, "Dad, why do rainbows appear after it rains?" The father replies, "It's because of the way sunlight refracts, or

bends, in the raindrops." The son says, "So, are raindrops like little artists painting the sky?"

503. A son asks his father, "Dad, why are there so many languages in the world?" The father replies, "Well, son, each language represents a unique culture and way of seeing the world." The son says, "So, if I make up my own language, can I have my own country?"

504. A son says to his father, "Dad, when I grow up, I want to be a filmmaker." The father replies, "That's a great aspiration, son. But remember, every good film starts with a good story." The son says, "Okay, I'll start by making a movie about a boy who never has to do chores again."

505. A father and son are watching a science fiction movie. The son asks, "Dad, do you think aliens exist?" The father replies, "Well, son, the universe is a big place. Who knows what's out there?" The son says, "If I meet an alien, I'll invite him to play video games. Maybe they can help me beat the final boss."

506. A father and son are watching a nature documentary. The son asks, "Dad, why do animals hibernate?" The father replies, "Because, son, they need to save energy during the winter when food is scarce." The son says, "So, when I sleep all day on a weekend, am I hibernating too?"

507. A son says to his father, "Dad, when I grow up, I want to be a detective." The father replies, "That's exciting, son. Just remember, it's all about the details." The son says, "So, when mom asks who ate the last cookie and I find crumbs in my sister's room, am I a detective?"

508. A father and son are at a zoo. The son asks, "Dad, why do peacocks have such colorful feathers?" The father replies, "Well, son, it's to attract a mate." The son says, "So, if I wear bright colors, will I get more friends?"

509. A son asks his father, "Dad, why is the sea salty?" The father replies, "Because, son, rivers carry mineral salts from the land into the sea." The son says, "So, if I cry into a glass of water, will it become a mini sea?"

510. A son says to his father, "Dad, when I grow up, I want to build a spaceship." The father replies, "That sounds ambitious, son. Just remember, it's about the journey, not just the destination." The son says, "So, if I build a spaceship out of cardboard boxes, am I halfway there?"

511. A father and son are at a car show. The son asks, "Dad, why do people like fast cars?" The father replies, "Well, son, some people like the thrill of speed." The son says, "Then why don't they just eat spicy food?"

512. A son says to his father, "Dad, when I grow up, I want to be an inventor." The father replies, "That's a great

aspiration, son. Just remember, innovation comes from solving problems." The son says, "So, if I invent a robot that does my chores, am I innovating?"

513. A father and son are watching a meteor shower. The son asks, "Dad, why do shooting stars look like they're falling?" The father replies, "Actually, son, they're not falling. They're burning up in the Earth's atmosphere." The son says, "So, are they hot-headed because they're burning up?"

514. A son asks his father, "Dad, why do we put candles on birthday cakes?" The father replies, "Well, son, the candles represent the years of your life." The son says, "So, if I blow them out really fast, does that mean I'll live a long life?"

515. A son says to his father, "Dad, when I grow up, I want to be a writer." The father replies, "That's wonderful, son. Remember, writing is about expressing your unique perspective." The son says, "So, if I write a story about an alien pizza delivery guy, am I expressing my unique perspective?"

516. A father and son are watching a sunset. The son asks, "Dad, why does the sun set?" The father replies, "Well, son, it's not really setting. It's just that the Earth is turning away from it." The son says, "So the Earth is giving the sun the cold shoulder every night?"

517. A son says to his father, "Dad, when I grow up, I want to be a movie star." The father replies, "That's great, son. Just remember, it's not about the fame, it's about the art of acting." The son says, "So, when I pretend to clean my room, is that acting?"

518. A father and son are camping. The son asks, "Dad, why do we have to sleep in tents?" The father replies, "Because, son, it's a way to be close to nature." The son says, "I was close to nature when a bee chased me. Can I be close to a comfy bed instead?"

519. A son asks his father, "Dad, why do we celebrate birthdays?" The father replies, "Because, son, it's a way of appreciating the day you came into this world." The son says, "So, can I appreciate it with a new video game?"

520. A son says to his father, "Dad, when I grow up, I want to be a chef." The father replies, "That's a great choice, son. Food brings people together." The son says, "I thought it was video games that brought people together. Have I been doing it wrong?"

521. A father and son are stargazing. The son asks, "Dad, why do stars twinkle?" The father replies, "Well, son, it's because of the Earth's atmosphere." The son says, "So, they're not actually winking at us?"

522. A son says to his father, "Dad, when I grow up, I want to invent a device that makes people happy." The father replies, "Well, son, that's a noble goal. Just remember that real happiness comes from within." The son says, "So, the device should go inside people?"

523. A father and son are watching a magic show. The son asks, "Dad, how do magicians do their tricks?" The father replies, "Well, son, it's all about illusion and distraction." The son says, "Oh, like when you tell me to clean my room and I 'disappear'?"

524. A son asks his father, "Dad, why do we have pets?" The father replies, "Because, son, they bring joy and companionship." The son says, "But my pet fish doesn't do much. Can we get a dog instead?"

525. A son says to his father, "Dad, when I grow up, I want to be just like you." The father replies, "Well, son, I'm flattered. But always remember to be yourself." The son says, "Okay, I want to be just like you, but with more video games."

526. A father and his son are on a fishing trip. The son says, "Dad, I don't understand why we have to get up so early to catch fish." The father replies, "Well, son, it's because the early bird catches the worm." The son,

looking confused, asks, "But Dad, aren't we using bait, not worms?"

527. Dad: Son, why did the computer go to the doctor?
Son: Dad, computers don't get sick.
Dad: Well, that computer had a case of the "byte" bug and needed a tech-savvy doctor to diagnose the issue. It was a digital ailment that required immediate attention!

528. Dad: Son, did you know that laughter is like a magic potion for the soul?
Son: Dad, that's a beautiful way to put it.
Dad: It's true! Laughter has the power to uplift spirits, ease burdens, and sprinkle joy into our lives. It's the elixir that keeps the soul refreshed and vibrant.

529. Dad: Son, why did the tomato blush when it saw the onion?
Son: Dad, that's silly. Why did it blush?
Dad: Well, it realized that it couldn't "ketchup" to the onion's level of spice and flavor. It was a blushing tomato in the presence of culinary greatness!

530. Dad: Son, did you know that trees are nature's guardians?
Son: Dad, trees are just part of the environment.
Dad: True, but trees stand tall, providing shade and protection to all creatures. They're the silent guardians of the natural world, shielding us from the sun's harsh rays.

531. Dad: Son, why did the book go on a journey?
Son: Dad, books can't go anywhere.
Dad: Well, that book embarked on an adventure of the mind! It wanted to transport readers to different worlds, ignite imaginations, and inspire endless possibilities.

532. Dad: Son, did you hear about the scientist who discovered a way to turn sadness into laughter?
Son: No, Dad, how did they do it?
Dad: They developed a formula called "humorolysis"! With a mixture of jokes, silliness, and good vibes, they could transform even the heaviest heart into one filled with laughter and joy.

533. Dad: Son, why did the musician bring a ladder to the concert?
Son: Dad, that doesn't make sense.
Dad: Well, they wanted to climb to new musical heights and reach the crescendo of their performance. It was a ladder of melodies and harmonies!

534. Dad: Son, did you know that laughter is like a musical symphony?
Son: Dad, I've never thought of it that way.
Dad: Imagine each laugh as a note, coming together to create a beautiful composition of happiness and harmony. Laughter is the melody that resonates in our hearts!

535. Dad: Son, why did the cloud become a stand-up comedian?
Son: I don't know, Dad. How did that happen?
Dad: Well, it realized that it had a silver lining of humor and wanted to share its jokes with the world. It was a cloud on a mission to make everyone laugh!

536. Dad: Son, did you hear about the scientist who invented a machine to turn vegetables into instruments?
Son: No, Dad, that's fascinating!
Dad: It was a "veg-strument"! With a sprinkle of innovation, that machine could transform carrots into clarinets, peppers into pianos, and broccoli into drums. It was a veggie orchestra like no other!

537. Dad: Son, why did the spider become a web designer?
Son: Dad, spiders don't design websites.
Dad: True, but that spider realized that it had a knack for spinning intricate patterns. It decided to take its skills to the digital world, weaving beautifully designed websites in its web-making endeavors!

538. Dad: Son, did you know that books hold the key to endless adventures?
Son: Yes, Dad, books can transport us to different worlds.
Dad: Absolutely! Each book is a gateway to explore new realms, meet fascinating characters, and embark on thrilling journeys. It's a passport to the imagination!

539. Dad: Son, why did the sandwich get a promotion at work?
Son: I don't know, Dad. Why did it get promoted?
Dad: Because it had all the right ingredients for success! Its perfect combination of flavors and impeccable presentation made it the talk of the lunchroom. It was a sandwich on the rise!

540. Dad: Son, did you hear about the scientist who discovered a way to turn frowns into smiles?
Son: No, Dad, how did they do it?
Dad: They developed a scientific formula called "cheeriolysis"! With a mixture of positivity, laughter, and a sprinkle of silliness, they could turn even the gloomiest frown into a radiant smile.

541. Dad: Son, why did the chef become a comedian?
Son: I'm not sure, Dad. How did that happen?
Dad: Well, they realized that both cooking and comedy involve creating something delightful and bringing joy to others. They decided to tickle taste buds and funny bones simultaneously!

542. A father and son are at a baseball game. The son asks, "Dad, why do the players keep running in circles?" The father replies, "They're not running in circles, son. They're running bases." The son, looking perplexed, says,

"So they're stealing bases and we're just watching? Isn't that illegal?"

543. A son says to his father, "Dad, why do people say money can't buy happiness? I'm pretty happy when I buy ice cream." The father replies, "That's because, son, ice cream is a moment of happiness. But real happiness comes from things that can't melt away."

544. A son asks his father, "Dad, why do people say that the sky is the limit when there are footprints on the moon?" The father replies, "That's a good point, son. I suppose it's because people haven't set their sights far enough yet."

545. A father and his son are at a restaurant. The son asks, "Dad, why do they give us bread for free but charge us for drinks?" The father replies, "Well, son, it's because bread makes you thirsty and then you'll want to order drinks. It's a bit like how I give you chores to do, and then you appreciate your free time more."

546. A son says to his father, "Dad, I don't understand why people want to be astronauts. It's just floating around in a vacuum." The father replies, "Actually, son, being an astronaut is about exploring the unknown, pushing the limits of human knowledge. But yes, it's also about floating around in a vacuum."

547. A father and his son are watching a science documentary. The son asks, "Dad, if E equals MC squared, what does MC Hammer equal?" The father replies, "Son, in the 90s, MC Hammer equaled U Can't Touch This."

548. A son asks his father, "Dad, why do we have to learn history?" The father replies, "Because, son, those who don't learn history are doomed to repeat it." The son, looking puzzled, asks, "But if we learned it and it was bad, why would we want to repeat it?"

549. A father says to his son, "Son, when you grow up, you should invest in your future." The son replies, "Okay, Dad, I'll buy more video games. They could be worth a lot in the future."

550. A son says to his father, "Dad, when I grow up, I want to invent a time machine." The father replies, "Well, son, make sure to come back and tell me. I could use a few extra hours in the day."

551. A son asks his father, "Dad, why do we celebrate Father's Day?" The father replies, "Well, son, it's to honor and appreciate all the things that fathers do. Also, it's an excellent excuse for dad jokes." The son says, "Oh, so that's why you've been practicing all year."

552. A father and his son are at the beach. The son asks, "Dad, why does the tide go in and out?" The father replies, "Well, son, it's all because of the gravitational pull of the moon." The son says, "Wow, the moon must be really strong. Is it stronger than you, Dad?"

553. A son says to his father, "Dad, I want to be a superhero when I grow up." The father replies, "Well, son, to be a superhero, you need to have a superpower. What's yours?" The son says, "I can eat a whole pizza by myself. Is that a superpower?"

554. A father and his son are playing chess. The son asks, "Dad, why do the pawns go first?" The father replies, "Well, son, in chess as in life, it's often the smallest who are brave enough to make the first move." The son says, "So, the king is a coward because he only moves one square at a time?"

555. A son says to his father, "Dad, when I grow up, I want to be an adventurer." The father replies, "That sounds exciting, son. Just remember, the real adventure is the journey, not the destination." The son says, "So, the journey to the fridge is an adventure? I'm an adventurer every day then!"

556. A father and his son are on a hiking trip. The son asks, "Dad, why do we have to carry all this gear?" The father replies, "Because, son, it's better to have it and not

need it than need it and not have it." The son says, "In that case, I need a helicopter. Can we have that?"

557. A son asks his father, "Dad, why do we have to have rules?" The father replies, "Well, son, rules help us live in harmony with each other." The son says, "But I don't want to live in harmony with my sister. Can we have a rule that she can't come into my room?"

558. A son says to his father, "Dad, when I grow up, I want to be a philosopher." The father replies, "That's interesting, son. Do you know what philosophers do?" The son says, "They think a lot, right? I do that already. Usually about what video game I want to play next."

559. A father and his son are at a museum. The son asks, "Dad, why are old things so valuable?" The father replies, "Because, son, they tell a story of a time we weren't a part of." The son says, "So my dirty socks could be a museum exhibit one day?"

A son asks his father, "Dad, why do I have to share my toys with my sister?" The father replies, "Because, son, sharing is caring." The son says, "Well, I care about my toys. That's why I don't want to share them."

560. A father says to his son, "You know, when Abraham Lincoln was your age, he was studying books by the light

of the fireplace." The son replies, "Yeah, well, when Abraham Lincoln was your age, he was President."

561. A son says to his father, "Dad, what's an alcoholic?" The father replies, "Do you see those four trees? Well, an alcoholic would see eight." The son says, "But Dad, I only see two trees."

562. A father says to his son, "Son, if you keep pulling faces, your face will stay like that." The son replies, "Well, you must have been a real chatterbox then, Dad."

563. A son asks his father, "Dad, how do stars die?" The father looks at his son and replies, "Usually an overdose, son."

564. A son is failing his math class, so his father decides to get him a tutor. After a couple of weeks, the son comes home, "Dad, I think I finally understand math!" The father, thrilled, asks his son to explain. The son says, "Okay, so you know how one plus one equals two, right?" The father nods. "Well," the son continues, "what if I told you that two minus one equals one?" The father says, "That's right! You're getting the hang of it." The son, looking satisfied, says, "I thought so. Now, if only they could make the questions this easy on the test."

565. A father and his son were looking at a photo album. The son asked, "Dad, is that you in the picture with the

fancy clothes and hair?" The father replied, "Yes, son, that was my prom night." The son says, "Wow, so it's true that people used to have fun before the internet."

566. A son asks his father, "Dad, did you ever get shot in the army?" The father replies, "No, son, I was shot in the leggy."

567. A father and his son are on a hunting trip. Suddenly, a gigantic grizzly bear lumbers into their path. The terrified son says, "Dad, what do we do?!" The father replies, "Run, son. You might not be able to outrun the bear, but you only have to outrun me!"

568. A father says to his son, "You were adopted." The son replies, "I knew it! I want to meet my biological parents!" The father says, "No, son, we are your biological parents. Your new ones are coming to pick you up in an hour."

569. A son asks his father, "Dad, why is my sister named Rose?" The father replies, "Because your mother loves roses." The son says, "Thanks, Dad." The father replies, "You're welcome, Son Who Asks Too Many Questions."

570. A father says to his son, "I was just looking at your test scores. You really need to pay more attention in school." The son replies, "I'm trying, but the teacher keeps calling it 'daydreaming.'"

571. A son asks his father, "Dad, why does the food taste different today?" The father replies, "Because your mother cooked it." The son, looking worried, says, "But isn't that dangerous?"

572. A son says to his father, "Dad, I'm going to a party tonight. Can I borrow the car?" The father replies, "Sure, son, as long as you're not planning on driving it."

573. A father says to his son, "Son, you have to stop breaking people's hearts." The son replies, "Don't worry, Dad, I always put them back together before I leave."

574. A son says to his father, "Dad, I think I'm in love." The father, looking surprised, asks, "Really, son? Who is she?" The son replies, "Actually, it's not a she. It's my bed, and we're very happy together."

575. A father and his son are watching a romantic movie. The son asks, "Dad, why does the guy always save the girl?" The father replies, "Because it's his job, son." The son says, "So if the girl saved the guy, would she get his job?"

576. A son asks his father, "Dad, how can I get people to like me?" The father replies, "Son, just be yourself." The son, looking confused, says, "But I want people to like me."

577. A son asks his father, "Dad, what does it feel like to have the greatest son in the world?" The father replies, "I don't know, son, you'll have to ask grandpa."

578. A son asks his father, "Dad, how does it feel to be old?" The father replies, "I don't know, son, I'm not there yet."

579. A father and his son are having a conversation about the son's future. The son says, "Dad, I want to be a musician when I grow up." The father replies, "Son, you can't do both."

580. A son asks his father, "Dad, how does it feel to be a dad?" The father replies, "Well, son, it feels like being broke all the time, but it's totally worth it."

581. A father says to his son, "Son, when I was your age, I was a man." The son replies, "Well, Dad, I hope to be a man one day too."

582. A father says to his son, "Son, when I was your age, we didn't have all these fancy gadgets. We had to use our brains." The son replies, "Wow, Dad, that must have been really hard for you."

583. A son says to his father, "Dad, I'm thinking about becoming a comedian." The father replies, "Well, son, I don't see anything funny about that."

584. A father and his son are looking at the night sky. The son asks, "Dad, how many stars are there?" The father replies, "Only one, son. The rest are just reflections of your mother's eyes."

585. A father says to his son, "Son, if you keep eating candy, your teeth will fall out." The son replies, "Well, then I'll just eat the candy with my gums."

586. A son asks his father, "Dad, why did you marry mom?" The father replies, "Well, son, I couldn't resist her charm. And by charm, I mean the way she threatened to beat me up if I didn't marry her."

587. A son says to his father, "Dad, when I grow up, I want to be a superhero and save the world." The father replies, "Well, son, why wait? You can start by saving your allowance."

588. A father and his son are at the park. The son asks, "Dad, why do the other kids have mothers?" The father replies, "Well, son, it's because their fathers weren't as brave as I am."

589. A father says to his son, "Son, when you grow up, you can be anything you want." The son replies, "In that case, Dad, I want to be retired."

590. A son says to his father, "Dad, what does it feel like to be a grown-up?" The father replies, "Well, son, it's kind of like being a kid, but with more responsibilities and less fun."

591. A father says to his son, "Son, when I was your age, I had to walk 10 miles to school in the snow." The son replies, "Well, Dad, when I'm your age, I'll probably have to fly 10 miles to school on a hoverboard."

592. A son asks his father, "Dad, what does it mean to be a good person?" The father replies, "Well, son, it means not doing things that you wouldn't want others to do to you." The son says, "So, like, not farting in public?"

593. A father says to his son, "Son, you should always respect your elders." The son replies, "But, Dad, you're my elder, and you never listen to me."

594. A father and his son are watching a horror movie. The son asks, "Dad, why are you covering your eyes?" The father replies, "Well, son, it's not the movie that's scary. It's the thought of your mother finding out that I let you watch this movie."

595. A son says to his father, "Dad, I don't want to go to school tomorrow." The father replies, "I know, son, but it's your job to be a student, just like it's my job to go to work." The son says, "Well, then I quit."

596. A son asks his father, "Dad, why is it important to be kind to others?" The father replies, "Well, son, it's because everyone you meet is fighting a battle you know nothing about." The son says, "Like, a battle with zombies?"

597. A father says to his son, "Son, you should always tell the truth." The son replies, "Okay, Dad. In that case, I ate all the cookies."

598. A father and his son are on a camping trip. The son asks, "Dad, why do we have to sleep in a tent?" The father replies, "Well, son, it's because the house wouldn't fit in the car."

599. A son asks his father, "Dad, what does it mean to be a man?" The father replies, "Well, son, being a man isn't about being strong or tough. It's about being kind, respectful, and responsible." The son says, "So, like a superhero?"

600. A father says to his son, "Son, you should always strive to be the best version of yourself." The son replies, "Okay, Dad. I'll start by eating all my vegetables... tomorrow."

601. A son says to his father, "Dad, I want to be just like you when I grow up." The father replies, "Well, son, I hope you can be better."

602. A son asks his father, "Dad, what's the meaning of life?" The father replies, "Well, son, the meaning of life is a deeply philosophical question. It's something you'll have to figure out on your own." The son says, "In that case, can I have some ice cream?"

603. A father and his son are at a football game. The son asks, "Dad, why are they all running after the ball?" The father replies, "Well, son, it's because the one who gets the ball gets to kick it." The son says, "So, it's like a big game of keep away?"

604. A father says to his son, "Son, you need to clean your room." The son replies, "But, Dad, I didn't make the mess." The father says, "Well, son, I didn't make the mess in the world, but it's still my job to help clean it up."

605. A son asks his father, "Dad, why do I have to do chores?" The father replies, "Well, son, it's because we're a family, and in a family, everyone contributes." The son says, "But I didn't agree to be part of this family."

606. A son says to his father, "Dad, I'm scared of the dark." The father replies, "Well, son, the dark is just like the light, but without the light." The son says, "That doesn't help, Dad."

607. A son asks his father, "Dad, why do we have to go to church?" The father replies, "Well, son, it's because we believe in God." The son says, "But I thought we believed in Santa Claus."

608. A father says to his son, "Son, you need to learn how to be patient." The son replies, "Okay, Dad, I'll start being patient... starting now. Is it working yet?"

609. A father and his son are at a zoo. The son asks, "Dad, why is the lion sleeping?" The father replies, "Well, son, it's because he's tired." The son says, "Just like you, Dad."

610. A son says to his father, "Dad, I want to be a writer when I grow up." The father replies, "Well, son, you're going to have to start reading more books." The son says, "Okay, I'll start with comic books."

611. A son asks his father, "Dad, why do I have to go to bed?" The father replies, "Well, son, it's because your body needs rest." The son says, "But my body doesn't feel tired."

612. A father says to his son, "Son, when I was your age, I didn't have a cellphone." The son replies, "Wow, Dad, that must have been so boring."

613. A son says to his father, "Dad, when I grow up, I want to be a millionaire." The father replies, "Well, son, you're going to have to work hard for it." The son says, "In that case, I want to be a billionaire."

614. A son asks his father, "Dad, why do we have to eat vegetables?" The father replies, "Well, son, it's because they're good for your health." The son says, "But they taste like dirt."

615. Dad: Son, did you know that clouds can have a sense of humor?
Son: Dad, clouds are just water vapor.
Dad: True, but if you look up at the sky, you'll see clouds forming funny shapes and designs. They're nature's way of playfully engaging with us!

616. Dad: Son, why did the tomato turn red and run a marathon?
Son: I don't know, Dad. Why did it run?
Dad: Well, that tomato had dreams of becoming a "salsa" superstar! It wanted to show off its vibrant color and tangy taste as it raced towards culinary greatness.

617. Dad: Son, did you hear about the scientist who invented a machine to translate pet sounds into human language?

Son: No, Dad, that's amazing!

Dad: It was an "animaloquium"! With cutting-edge technology, that machine could decode the language of dogs, cats, and other animals, allowing us to understand their thoughts and feelings. It was like having a conversation with our furry friends!

618. Dad: Son, why did the math book go to the therapist?

Son: Dad, books can't have emotions.

Dad: You're right, but that math book was feeling overwhelmed with all those complex equations. It needed a little mathematical counseling to get back on track.

619. Dad: Son, did you know that laughter is a language understood by everyone?

Son: Yes, Dad, laughter brings people together.

Dad: Absolutely! Regardless of where we come from, our laughter unites us. It's a language that needs no translation and bridges any cultural divides.

620. Dad: Son, why did the sandwich audition for a play?

Son: I'm not sure, Dad. Why did it audition?

Dad: Because that sandwich had a taste for the dramatic! It wanted to take center stage and prove that it could deliver a delectable performance.

621. Dad: Son, did you know that trees have their own special way of communicating?
Son: Dad, trees can't talk.
Dad: While they may not speak in words, trees communicate through the rustling of leaves, the swaying of branches, and the exchange of essential nutrients underground. It's a silent language of connection in the forest.

622. Dad: Son, why did the musician become a chef?
Son: Dad, I'm not sure. How did that happen?
Dad: Well, that musician discovered that both music and cooking involve creativity and the art of harmonizing different elements. They decided to compose culinary symphonies with flavors as their notes!

623. Dad: Son, did you know that laughter is like a secret code that unlocks happiness?
Son: Dad, that's a cool way to think about it.
Dad: It's true! When we share laughter, it's like we're part of a joyful conspiracy, spreading happiness wherever we go. It's a code that brightens lives and creates unforgettable moments.

624. Dad: Son, why did the balloon go to school?
Son: Dad, balloons can't go to school.
Dad: Well, that balloon had dreams of floating through the halls of knowledge! It wanted to learn all the science

behind the force of its own buoyancy and share its colorful wisdom.

625. A father and his son are playing catch. The son asks, "Dad, why do you always throw the ball so high?" The father replies, "Well, son, it's because I want you to reach for the stars."

626. A son says to his father, "Dad, when I grow up, I want to travel the world." The father replies, "Well, son, you're going to have to start saving your money." The son says, "Okay, I'll start by not buying any more vegetables."

627. A father says to his son, "Son, when I was your age, I had to work for everything I wanted." The son replies, "Well, Dad, when I'm your age, I'll probably have to work for everything I want, too."

628. A son asks his father, "Dad, why do I have to learn math?" The father replies, "Well, son, it's because math is the language of the universe." The son says, "But I thought English was the language of the universe."

629. A son says to his father, "Dad, when I grow up, I want to be happy." The father replies, "Well, son, that's the best thing you could possibly be." The son says, "Okay, then, I want to be happy... and a billionaire."

630. A father and his son are in the car when they're pulled over by a police officer. The officer says, "I clocked you going 75 miles per hour, sir." The dad turns to his son and says, "Did you hear that? Your old man still has it!"

631. Why do father pirates never play cards? Because they're afraid of walking the plank if they lose!

632. A father says to his son, "I was an ugly kid. When I played in the sandbox, the cat tried to cover me up."

633. Why did the father become a gardener? He believed he could make a budding career out of it.

634. How does a father pepper do his exercises? He gets jalapeno business!

635. Why did the father become an archeologist? Because his career was in ruins.

636. A son asks his father for a car. The father replies, "Sure, but only if you pass your exams, study the Bible and cut your hair." After a few months, the son returns with excellent results and an extensive knowledge of the Bible, but still with long hair. When the father asks why he didn't cut his hair, the son says, "Well, I was reading the Bible and I noticed that Samson had long hair, Moses had long hair, even Jesus had long hair." The father replies, "Yes,

and they all walked everywhere they went."

637. Why did the father become a clockmaker? He wanted to go through the motions.

638. Why do fathers make terrible secret agents? You can hear their dad jokes from a mile away!

639. A father takes his son on a fishing trip. After a few hours in the boat, the boy suddenly becomes curious about the world around him. He asks his father, "How do fish breathe underwater?" The father replies, "I really don't know, son." A little later, the boy looks at his father and asks, "How does our boat float on the water?" Once again, the father replies, "Don't know, son." Puzzled, the boy asks, "Why is the sky blue?" Again, the father replies. "No idea, son." Worried he might be annoying his father, the boy says, "Dad, do you mind me asking so much?" The father heartily replies, "Of course not, son! If you don't ask questions, you'll never learn anything!"

640. A father and son were watching the news when the son asked, "Dad, what's politics?" The dad thought for a bit, then said, "Well, son, let me try to explain it this way: I'm the breadwinner of the family, so let's call me capitalism. Your mother manages the money, so we'll call her the government. We both take care of your needs, so you can be the people. Your nanny, we'll consider her the

working class. And your baby brother, we'll call him the future. Now think about that and see if it makes sense." That night, the boy is woken up by his baby brother's crying. He goes to check on him and finds that the baby has soiled his diaper. He goes to his parent's room and finds his mother sound asleep. Not wanting to wake her, he goes to the nanny's room, but she's out for the night. He goes back to bed and sleeps on it. In the morning, he tells his father his understanding of politics: "Dad, I think I've figured it out. While capitalism is out working, the government is sound asleep, the people are being ignored, the working class is out, and the future is in deep crap."

641. What do you call a dad when he falls through the ice? A "pop"sicle!

642. One day, a son comes up to his father with a puzzled look on his face. "Dad, why do people say that we have itchy feet when we want to travel?" The father chuckles and responds, "Well, son, it's just a saying. We don't really have itchy feet. It means we have a strong urge to travel and explore." The son thinks for a moment before asking, "So why is Mom putting cream on her feet then?"

643. How do you know if a dad is a true artist? Even his dad jokes are sketchy!

644. A boy goes up to his dad and asks, "Dad, why is my sister named Rose?" The dad replies, "Well son, your mother loves roses." The boy then asks, "So why am I named Jack?" The father replies, "That's enough questions, Jack Daniels."

645. Why did the father spider enroll his kids in music school? He wanted them to learn the web-a-nation of sound!

646. A little boy says to his father: "Dad, how big is a million?" His father replies: "Well, to really understand it, you'd need to stack one million pennies." The little boy thinks for a moment and then asks: "Do you think we have enough glue?"

A son asks his father, "Dad, why do we have to be resilient?" The father replies, "Well, son, resilience is the key to overcoming challenges and bouncing back from adversity. It's through resilience that we find the strength to persevere, learn from setbacks, and emerge stronger than before. It's a quality that empowers us to face life's ups and downs with unwavering determination." The son says, "So, when I embody resilience, is it just my way of embracing the warrior spirit within me?"

647. A son says to his father, "Dad, when I grow up, I want to be an explorer." The father replies, "That's an adventurous choice, son. Remember, explorers need to

have curiosity, bravery, and a thirst for discovery. Through their explorations, they expand our knowledge of the world and inspire us to venture into the unknown." The son says, "I've got that, Dad. I always feel a sense of exhilaration when I embark on new journeys and uncover hidden treasures."

648. A father and son are watching a show about the wonders of the Great Wall of China. The son asks, "Dad, why is the Great Wall of China so impressive?" The father replies, "Well, son, the Great Wall of China is a testament to human ingenuity, determination, and the power of unity. It stretches for thousands of miles, standing as a symbol of China's rich history and the collective strength of its people." The son says, "So, when I see the Great Wall, is it just a reminder of the remarkable feats that can be accomplished when we come together?"

649. A son asks his father, "Dad, why do we need to be adaptable?" The father replies, "Well, son, adaptability is the key to thriving in a rapidly changing world. It's through adaptability that we embrace new circumstances, learn new skills, and navigate unexpected challenges. It's a way of staying flexible and resilient in the face of uncertainty." The son says, "So, when I embrace adaptability, is it just my way of riding the waves of change and seizing new opportunities?"

650. A son says to his father, "Dad, when I grow up, I want to be a teacher." The father replies, "That's a noble choice, son. Remember, teachers have the power to shape young minds, inspire a love for learning, and ignite the flame of curiosity. Through their guidance and mentorship, they have the opportunity to make a lasting impact on future generations." The son says, "I've got that, Dad. I always feel a sense of fulfillment when I see the spark of understanding in a student's eyes."

651. A father and son are watching a show about the wonders of the Mayan civilization. The son asks, "Dad, why are the Mayan ruins so fascinating?" The father replies, "Well, son, the Mayan ruins hold the secrets of an ancient civilization that flourished centuries ago. They are a testament to the ingenuity, advanced knowledge, and cultural richness of the Mayan people. They remind us of the enduring legacy of human history." The son says, "So, when I see the Mayan ruins, is it just a glimpse into the achievements and wisdom of our ancestors?"

652. A son asks his father, "Dad, why do we have to be compassionate?" The father replies, "Well, son, compassion is the bridge that connects us to the hearts of others. It's through compassion that we understand and empathize with their joys, sorrows, and struggles. It's a way of showing kindness, support, and love to those around us, fostering a sense of unity and shared humanity." The son says, "So, when I embody

compassion, is it just my way of spreading warmth and healing in a world that sometimes feels cold?"

653. A son says to his father, "Dad, when I grow up, I want to be a chef." The father replies, "That's a flavorful choice, son. Remember, chefs need to have a passion for culinary arts, creativity, and the ability to tantalize taste buds with their delicious creations. Through their culinary skills, they can bring joy and nourishment to people's lives." The son says, "I've got that, Dad. I always feel a sense of fulfillment when I create a delectable dish that brings smiles to people's faces."

654. A father and son are watching a show about the wonders of the Inca civilization. The son asks, "Dad, why are the Inca ruins so awe-inspiring?" The father replies, "Well, son, the Inca ruins hold the stories of a magnificent civilization that thrived in the Andes. They are a testament to the Inca's architectural prowess, cultural richness, and their deep connection with the natural world. They remind us of the power of human creativity and the impermanence of empires." The son says, "So, when I see the Inca ruins, is it just a reminder of the fleeting nature of human achievements and the importance of cherishing our cultural heritage?"

655. A son asks his father, "Dad, why do we have to be patient?" The father replies, "Well, son, patience is the art of waiting gracefully. It's through patience that we cultivate

inner peace, resilience, and understanding. It's a way of recognizing that some things take time to unfold and that the best outcomes often require patience and perseverance." The son says, "So, when I practice patience, is it just my way of surrendering to the rhythm of life and trusting in the process?"

656. A son says to his father, "Dad, when I grow up, I want to be an engineer." The father replies, "That's a brilliant choice, son. Remember, engineers have the power to transform ideas into reality, solve complex problems, and improve the world we live in. Through their innovative thinking and technical expertise, they shape the future and create a better tomorrow." The son says, "I've got that, Dad. I always feel a sense of fulfillment when I see the tangible impact of my engineering designs."

657. A father and son are watching a show about the wonders of the Louvre Museum. The son asks, "Dad, why are the artworks in the Louvre so captivating?" The father replies, "Well, son, the artworks in the Louvre hold the expressions of human creativity, emotions, and stories from different periods of history. They are a testament to the power of artistic expression and the enduring legacy of artists throughout the ages." The son says, "So, when I see the artworks in the Louvre, is it just a glimpse into the kaleidoscope of human imagination and the beauty that can be created with a brushstroke?"

658. A son asks his father, "Dad, why do we need to be courageous?" The father replies, "Well, son, courage is the inner strength that propels us forward in the face of fear or uncertainty. It's through courage that we take risks, pursue our dreams, and stand up for what we believe in. It's a way of embracing life's challenges and discovering the depth of our own capabilities." The son says, "So, when I embrace courage, is it just my way of unlocking the doors to my full potential?"

659. A son says to his father, "Dad, when I grow up, I want to be a writer." The father replies, "That's a captivating choice, son. Remember, writers have the power to weave words into captivating stories, inspire minds, and transport readers to different worlds. Through their narratives, they give a voice to emotions, ideas, and the human experience." The son says, "I've got that, Dad. I always feel a sense of magic and fulfillment when I let my imagination dance on the pages."

660. A father and son are watching a show about the wonders of the Taj Mahal. The son asks, "Dad, why is the Taj Mahal so breathtaking?" The father replies, "Well, son, the Taj Mahal is a marvel of architectural beauty and a symbol of enduring love. It stands as a testament to human craftsmanship, intricate detailing, and the power of immortalizing emotions through art." The son says, "So, when I see the Taj Mahal, is it just a reminder of the beauty that can be born from love and devotion?"

661. A son asks his father, "Dad, why do we have to be grateful?" The father replies, "Well, son, gratitude is the practice of acknowledging and appreciating the blessings in our lives. It's through gratitude that we cultivate a positive mindset, foster happiness, and deepen our connections with others. It's a way of recognizing the abundance that surrounds us and finding joy in the present moment." The son says, "So, when I express gratitude, is it just my way of counting my blessings and cherishing the beauty of each day?"

662. A son says to his father, "Dad, when I grow up, I want to be a psychologist." The father replies, "That's a profound choice, son. Remember, psychologists have the opportunity to understand the complexities of the human mind, offer support, and help people navigate their emotional well-being. Through their expertise, they provide insights and facilitate positive change." The son says, "I've got that, Dad. I always feel a sense of fulfillment when I witness the transformation and healing that comes from understanding ourselves and others."

663. A father and son are watching a show about the wonders of the Eiffel Tower. The son asks, "Dad, why is the Eiffel Tower so iconic?" The father replies, "Well, son, the Eiffel Tower is a symbol of Paris and a testament to human engineering and creativity. It stands tall as a reminder of the power of imagination and the possibilities

that arise when we dare to dream big." The son says, "So, when I see the Eiffel Tower, is it just a spark of inspiration that fuels my own dreams?"

664. A son asks his father, "Dad, why do we have to be resilient?" The father replies, "Well, son, resilience is the strength that emerges when we face adversity head-on, adapt to change, and keep moving forward. It's through resilience that we discover our own inner fortitude, learn from setbacks, and rise above the challenges that come our way." The son says, "So, when I embody resilience, is it just my way of showing the world that I won't let circumstances define me?"

665. A son says to his father, "Dad, when I grow up, I want to be an athlete." The father replies, "That's an inspiring choice, son. Remember, athletes have the discipline, dedication, and perseverance to push their physical limits and excel in their chosen sports. Through their achievements, they inspire others to strive for greatness and demonstrate the power of determination." The son says, "I've got that, Dad. I always feel a sense of exhilaration and personal growth when I challenge my body and push my boundaries."

666. A father and son are watching a show about the wonders of the Colosseum. The son asks, "Dad, why is the Colosseum so fascinating?" The father replies, "Well, son, the Colosseum stands as a testament to the grandeur

of ancient Rome and the prowess of its engineering. It's a reminder of the rich history that shapes our world today and the enduring legacy of human achievements." The son says, "So, when I see the Colosseum, is it just a glimpse into the marvels of our collective human history?"

667. A son asks his father, "Dad, why do we have to be compassionate?" The father replies, "Well, son, compassion is the gentle force that connects us to others' pain and suffering, inspiring us to offer kindness, understanding, and support. It's through compassion that we build bridges of empathy and create a more caring and inclusive world." The son says, "So, when I embody compassion, is it just my way of being a beacon of light in someone's darkness?"

668. A son says to his father, "Dad, when I grow up, I want to be a musician." The father replies, "That's a melodious choice, son. Remember, musicians have the power to stir emotions, convey messages, and uplift spirits through the language of music. Through their melodies, they create harmony and touch the deepest corners of the human soul." The son says, "I've got that, Dad. I always feel a sense of joy and connection when I play an instrument and share my music with others."

669. A father and son are watching a show about the wonders of the Great Barrier Reef. The son asks, "Dad, why is the Great Barrier Reef so captivating?" The father

replies, "Well, son, the Great Barrier Reef is a mesmerizing underwater wonderland, teeming with vibrant coral and marine life. It's a testament to the beauty and fragility of our oceans, reminding us of the importance of environmental stewardship and the interconnectedness of all living things." The son says, "So, when I see the Great Barrier Reef, is it just a reminder of the wonders that lie beneath the surface?"

670. A son asks his father, "Dad, why do we have to be resilient?" The father replies, "Well, son, resilience is the strength that helps us weather the storms of life, bounce back from setbacks, and embrace challenges as opportunities for growth. It's through resilience that we develop inner fortitude, perseverance, and the belief that we can overcome even the toughest obstacles." The son says, "So, when I embody resilience, is it just my way of rising from the ashes and showing the world the power of a resilient spirit?"

671. A son says to his father, "Dad, when I grow up, I want to be a painter." The father replies, "That's a stroke of artistic brilliance, son. Remember, painters have the ability to translate emotions, impressions, and visions onto canvas, creating visual poetry that touches the hearts of others. Through their art, they invite us to see the world through new eyes." The son says, "I've got that, Dad. I always feel a sense of freedom and expression when I hold a paintbrush in my hand."

672. A father and son are watching a show about the wonders of the Amazon River. The son asks, "Dad, why is the Amazon River so extraordinary?" The father replies, "Well, son, the Amazon River is the lifeline of a vast ecosystem, teeming with diverse plant and animal species. It's a symbol of the interconnectedness of nature, providing sustenance, shelter, and a source of wonder for countless creatures." The son says, "So, when I see the Amazon River, is it just a reminder of the intricate tapestry of life and the need to protect our natural resources?"

673. A son asks his father, "Dad, why do we have to be courageous?" The father replies, "Well, son, courage is the fire that burns within us, empowering us to step outside our comfort zones, face our fears, and take bold leaps of faith. It's through courage that we expand our horizons, embrace growth, and unlock new realms of possibility." The son says, "So, when I embrace courage, is it just my way of living life to the fullest and embracing the adventures that await?"

674. A son says to his father, "Dad, when I grow up, I want to be an architect." The father replies, "That's a visionary choice, son. Remember, architects have the power to shape the physical world, create spaces that inspire, and harmonize aesthetics with functionality. Through their designs, they leave a lasting imprint on the landscapes we inhabit." The son says, "I've got that, Dad. I always feel a

sense of pride and accomplishment when I see my architectural visions come to life."

675. A father and son are watching a show about the wonders of the Sahara Desert. The son asks, "Dad, why is the Sahara Desert so captivating?" The father replies, "Well, son, the Sahara Desert is a vast expanse of beauty and mystery. Its golden dunes, shifting landscapes, and serene emptiness remind us of the immense power of nature and the importance of preserving the fragile balance of our planet." The son says, "So, when I see the Sahara Desert, is it just a glimpse into the enigmatic charm of the natural world?"

676. A son asks his father, "Dad, why do we have to be compassionate?" The father replies, "Well, son, compassion is the language of the heart, a way of connecting with others and offering a helping hand. It's through compassion that we create a ripple effect of kindness, understanding, and support, nurturing the seeds of love and humanity in our world." The son says, "So, when I embody compassion, is it just my way of being an instrument of peace and healing?"

677. A son says to his father, "Dad, when I grow up, I want to be a scientist." The father replies, "That's an exploratory choice, son. Remember, scientists have the curious minds, analytical skills, and thirst for knowledge that drive discoveries and push the boundaries of human

understanding. Through their research, they unlock the secrets of the universe and pave the way for progress." The son says, "I've got that, Dad. I always feel a sense of wonder and excitement when I unravel the mysteries of the world through science."

678. A father and son are watching a show about the wonders of the Redwood Forest. The son asks, "Dad, why are the redwood trees so awe-inspiring?" The father replies, "Well, son, the redwood trees stand as giants, reaching for the sky and defying the passage of time. They are a reminder of the resilience and grandeur of nature, showcasing the beauty and harmony that can be found in the embrace of towering trees." The son says, "So, when I see the redwood trees, is it just a glimpse into the magnificence and wisdom of the natural world?"

679. A son asks his father, "Dad, why do we have to be resilient?" The father replies, "Well, son, resilience is the anchor that keeps us steady amidst life's storms, the inner flame that refuses to be extinguished. It's through resilience that we find the strength to face adversity, overcome obstacles, and emerge stronger than before. It's a quality that teaches us the power of perseverance and the art of bouncing back." The son says, "So, when I embody resilience, is it just my way of showing the world that setbacks are not the end, but merely a detour on the path to success?"

680. A son says to his father, "Dad, when I grow up, I want to be a filmmaker." The father replies, "That's a cinematic choice, son. Remember, filmmakers have the power to tell compelling stories, evoke emotions, and transport audiences to different worlds. Through their lens, they capture the essence of humanity, shedding light on diverse perspectives and nurturing empathy." The son says, "I've got that, Dad. I always feel a sense of wonder and magic when I bring my imagination to life on the silver screen."

681. A father and son are watching a show about the wonders of the Galapagos Islands. The son asks, "Dad, why are the Galapagos Islands so extraordinary?" The father replies, "Well, son, the Galapagos Islands are a living laboratory of evolution and biodiversity. They hold a treasure trove of unique species and offer a glimpse into the intricate web of life. They remind us of the delicate balance of nature and the importance of conservation." The son says, "So, when I see the Galapagos Islands, is it just a reminder of the wonders that arise when nature is left undisturbed?"

682. A son asks his father, "Dad, why do we have to be true to ourselves?" The father replies, "Well, son, being true to yourself means embracing your authentic voice, values, and passions. It's through authenticity that we find fulfillment, create genuine connections with others, and make a meaningful contribution to the world. It's a way of

honoring who you are and living a life that aligns with your deepest truth." The son says, "So, when I embody authenticity, is it just my way of shining my unique light and inspiring others to do the same?"

683. A son asks his father, "Dad, why do we have dreams?" The father replies, "Well, son, dreams are a gateway to our subconscious mind. They allow us to explore our deepest desires, fears, and aspirations, and can sometimes offer insights into our own thoughts and emotions." The son says, "So, when I dream, is it just my mind unraveling its hidden mysteries?"

684. A son says to his father, "Dad, when I grow up, I want to be an archaeologist." The father replies, "That's an adventurous choice, son. Remember, archaeologists need to have a passion for history, an eye for detail, and a love for unraveling the secrets of ancient civilizations." The son says, "I've got that, Dad. I always feel like a treasure hunter when I dig in the backyard."

685. A father and son are watching a show about the wonders of the human body. The son asks, "Dad, why do we have fingerprints?" The father replies, "Well, son, fingerprints are unique to each individual. They serve as a form of identification and help us leave our mark on the world, both literally and metaphorically." The son says, "So, when I see my fingerprints, is it just a reminder of my own uniqueness?"

686. A son asks his father, "Dad, why do we have to work?" The father replies, "Well, son, work gives us a sense of purpose, allows us to contribute to society, and provides for our needs and the needs of our loved ones. It's through work that we can grow and achieve our goals." The son says, "So, when I work, is it just my way of making a meaningful impact?"

687. A son says to his father, "Dad, when I grow up, I want to be an astronaut." The father replies, "That's an out-of-this-world choice, son. Remember, astronauts need to have courage, a strong scientific background, and a passion for exploration." The son says, "I've got that, Dad. I always feel like I'm floating among the stars when I gaze up at the night sky."

688. A father and son are watching a show about the wonders of the rainforest. The son asks, "Dad, why is the rainforest so important for the planet?" The father replies, "Well, son, the rainforest is often called the 'lungs of the Earth' because it produces a significant amount of oxygen and plays a crucial role in maintaining the balance of our planet's ecosystems." The son says, "So, when I see pictures of the rainforest, is it just a reminder of the beauty and importance of nature?"

689. A son asks his father, "Dad, why do we have to forgive?" The father replies, "Well, son, forgiveness is a

powerful act of letting go of resentment, anger, or hurt. It allows us to heal, move forward, and nurture healthier relationships with others and ourselves." The son says, "So, when I forgive, is it just my way of finding peace and embracing compassion?"

690. A son says to his father, "Dad, when I grow up, I want to be a chef." The father replies, "That's a delicious choice, son. Remember, chefs need to have creativity, culinary skills, and a passion for bringing joy through food." The son says, "I've got that, Dad. I always feel like a maestro in the kitchen, creating flavors that dance on the palate."

691. A father and son are watching a show about the wonders of the universe. The son asks, "Dad, why is the universe so vast?" The father replies, "Well, son, the universe is vast because it contains billions of galaxies, stars, and planets, all expanding and constantly evolving. It's a reminder of the infinite possibilities and mysteries that await us." The son says, "So, when I gaze at the night sky, is it just a glimpse into the grandeur of the cosmos?"

692. A son asks his father, "Dad, why do we have to be kind?" The father replies, "Well, son, kindness is like a ripple in a pond. It has the power to brighten someone's day, create a sense of belonging, and make the world a better place. It's through acts of kindness that we cultivate compassion and foster harmonious relationships." The son

says, "So, when I show kindness, is it just my way of spreading warmth and positivity?"

693. A son says to his father, "Dad, when I grow up, I want to be a teacher." The father replies, "That's an admirable choice, son. Remember, teachers have the incredible opportunity to inspire and shape young minds, impart knowledge, and ignite a love for learning." The son says, "I've got that, Dad. I always feel a sense of fulfillment when I help others understand and grow."

694. A father and son are watching a show about the wonders of the deep sea. The son asks, "Dad, why is the deep sea so mysterious?" The father replies, "Well, son, the deep sea is vast and largely unexplored. It's home to fascinating creatures and hidden wonders that continue to captivate scientists and explorers." The son says, "So, when I hear about deep-sea discoveries, is it just a reminder of the mysteries that lie beneath the surface?"

695. A son asks his father, "Dad, why do we need to be patient?" The father replies, "Well, son, patience is a virtue that allows us to stay calm in the face of challenges, wait for things to unfold in their own time, and cultivate resilience. It's through patience that we can find inner peace and navigate life's ups and downs." The son says, "So, when I practice patience, is it just my way of trusting in the process?"

696. A son says to his father, "Dad, when I grow up, I want to be an athlete." The father replies, "That's a fantastic choice, son. Remember, athletes need to have discipline, perseverance, and a love for their chosen sport. Through dedication and hard work, they can achieve remarkable feats." The son says, "I've got that, Dad. I always feel alive and free when I'm running and competing."

697. A father and son are watching a show about the wonders of the human brain. The son asks, "Dad, why is the brain so fascinating?" The father replies, "Well, son, the brain is like a complex universe within us. It's the command center that controls our thoughts, emotions, and actions, enabling us to think, feel, and experience the world around us." The son says, "So, when I learn about the brain, is it just a reminder of the marvels of our own minds?"

698. A son asks his father, "Dad, why do we need to take risks?" The father replies, "Well, son, taking risks opens doors to new experiences, growth, and personal development. It's through stepping outside our comfort zones that we discover our true potential and embrace the possibilities that life has to offer." The son says, "So, when I take a risk, is it just my way of writing my own adventure?"

699. A son says to his father, "Dad, when I grow up, I want to be a doctor." The father replies, "That's a noble choice,

son. Remember, doctors need to have compassion, empathy, and a deep desire to heal and care for others. Through their expertise, they can make a significant impact on people's lives." The son says, "I've got that, Dad. I always feel a sense of purpose when I imagine myself serving others in the medical field."

700. A father and son are watching a show about the wonders of the desert. The son asks, "Dad, why is the desert so intriguing?" The father replies, "Well, son, the desert is a place of stark beauty and survival. It's a testament to the resilience of life in harsh conditions and teaches us the value of adaptation and resourcefulness." The son says, "So, when I see pictures of the desert, is it just a reminder of the strength and tenacity of nature?"

701. A son asks his father, "Dad, why do we have to be grateful?" The father replies, "Well, son, gratitude is the practice of acknowledging and appreciating the blessings, big and small, in our lives. It helps us cultivate a positive mindset, enhances our overall well-being, and deepens our connection with others." The son says, "So, when I express gratitude, is it just my way of counting my blessings and cherishing the present moment?"

702. A son says to his father, "Dad, when I grow up, I want to be a musician." The father replies, "That's a melodious choice, son. Remember, musicians need to have a passion for music, dedication to their craft, and the ability

to move hearts with their melodies." The son says, "I've got that, Dad. I always feel a sense of joy and freedom when I play my instrument."

703. A father and son are watching a show about the wonders of the cosmos. The son asks, "Dad, why is space exploration important?" The father replies, "Well, son, space exploration pushes the boundaries of human knowledge, expands our understanding of the universe, and inspires future generations to dream big and reach for the stars." The son says, "So, when I hear about space missions, is it just a reminder of our endless thirst for discovery?"

704. A son asks his father, "Dad, why do we have to be honest?" The father replies, "Well, son, honesty is the foundation of trust, integrity, and healthy relationships. It allows us to be true to ourselves and others, creating an atmosphere of authenticity and respect." The son says, "So, when I choose honesty, is it just my way of honoring the value of truth?"

705. A son says to his father, "Dad, when I grow up, I want to be a firefighter." The father replies, "That's a courageous choice, son. Remember, firefighters need to have bravery, physical strength, and a commitment to protecting and saving lives. Through their selflessness, they become everyday heroes." The son says, "I've got

that, Dad. I always feel a sense of duty and responsibility when I imagine myself in their shoes."

706. A father and son are watching a show about the wonders of the savannah. The son asks, "Dad, why is the savannah so captivating?" The father replies, "Well, son, the savannah is a dynamic ecosystem teeming with diverse wildlife, showcasing the intricate balance between predators and prey. It's a place of raw beauty and the circle of life." The son says, "So, when I see pictures of the savannah, isit just a glimpse into nature's ever-changing tapestry of existence?"

707. A son asks his father, "Dad, why do we have to be resilient?" The father replies, "Well, son, resilience is the ability to bounce back from adversity, setbacks, or challenges. It's through resilience that we grow stronger, learn valuable lessons, and persevere in the face of obstacles." The son says, "So, when I demonstrate resilience, is it just my way of showing the world that I won't be easily defeated?"

708. A son says to his father, "Dad, when I grow up, I want to be an architect." The father replies, "That's a visionary choice, son. Remember, architects need to have creativity, technical skills, and a passion for designing spaces that blend functionality with aesthetics." The son says, "I've got that, Dad. I always find inspiration in the structures that shape our surroundings."

709. A father and son are watching a show about the wonders of the ocean. The son asks, "Dad, why is the ocean so captivating?" The father replies, "Well, son, the ocean covers most of our planet and is home to a staggering array of marine life. It's a place of beauty, mystery, and immense power that continues to intrigue and inspire us." The son says, "So, when I see the ocean, is it just a reminder of the vastness and wonders of the natural world?"

710. A son asks his father, "Dad, why do we need to be open-minded?" The father replies, "Well, son, being open-minded allows us to embrace new ideas, perspectives, and experiences. It fosters growth, understanding, and empathy, and expands our horizons." The son says, "So, when I practice open-mindedness, is it just my way of embracing the rich tapestry of human diversity?"

711. A son says to his father, "Dad, when I grow up, I want to be a social worker." The father replies, "That's a compassionate choice, son. Remember, social workers need to have empathy, strong communication skills, and a dedication to helping individuals and communities overcome challenges." The son says, "I've got that, Dad. I always feel a deep sense of fulfillment when I lend a helping hand to those in need."

712. A father and son are watching a show about the wonders of the Redwood Forest. The son asks, "Dad, why are the Redwood trees so majestic?" The father replies, "Well, son, the Redwood trees are among the tallest and oldest living beings on Earth. They stand as guardians of history, reminding us of the passage of time and the resilience of nature." The son says, "So, when I see the Redwood Forest, is it just a glimpse into the ancient wisdom of the natural world?"

713. A son asks his father, "Dad, why do we have to be adaptable?" The father replies, "Well, son, life is full of changes and uncertainties. Being adaptable allows us to adjust, learn, and thrive in new situations. It's through adaptability that we can navigate the ever-evolving landscape of life." The son says, "So, when I embrace adaptability, is it just my way of dancing gracefully with the rhythm of life?"

714. A son says to his father, "Dad, when I grow up, I want to be a marine biologist." The father replies, "That's a fascinating choice, son. Remember, marine biologists need to have a deep love for the ocean, scientific curiosity, and a commitment to understanding and conserving marine ecosystems." The son says, "I've gotthat, Dad. I always feel a sense of wonder and awe when I explore the mysteries of the underwater world."

715. A father and son are watching a show about the wonders of the Himalayas. The son asks, "Dad, why are the Himalayas so breathtaking?" The father replies, "Well, son, the Himalayas are home to majestic peaks, serene valleys, and a rich cultural heritage. They represent the awe-inspiring beauty and the indomitable spirit of nature and its people." The son says, "So, when I see the Himalayas, is it just a reminder of the majestic power of the Earth?"

716. A son asks his father, "Dad, why do we have to be curious?" The father replies, "Well, son, curiosity is the key that unlocks the doors of knowledge and discovery. It fuels our desire to explore, ask questions, and seek answers, leading to personal growth and the expansion of our understanding." The son says, "So, when I embrace curiosity, is it just my way of embarking on an exciting journey of learning?"

717. A son says to his father, "Dad, when I grow up, I want to be a psychologist." The father replies, "That's an insightful choice, son. Remember, psychologists need to have empathy, active listening skills, and a genuine interest in understanding and supporting others' mental well-being." The son says, "I've got that, Dad. I always find joy in helping others navigate the complexities of the human mind."

718. A father and son are watching a show about the wonders of the Galapagos Islands. The son asks, "Dad, why are the Galapagos Islands so unique?" The father replies, "Well, son, the Galapagos Islands are a living laboratory of evolution, with diverse species found nowhere else on Earth. They remind us of the interconnectedness of all living things and the importance of preserving biodiversity." The son says, "So, when I learn about the Galapagos Islands, is it just a glimpse into the wonders of nature's creativity?"

719. A son asks his father, "Dad, why do we need to be humble?" The father replies, "Well, son, humility is the virtue that keeps us grounded, open to learning from others, and aware of our own limitations. It allows us to appreciate the strengths and contributions of others, fostering meaningful connections and personal growth." The son says, "So, when I embrace humility, is it just my way of acknowledging the vastness of knowledge and the beauty of humility?"

720. A son says to his father, "Dad, when I grow up, I want to be a filmmaker." The father replies, "That's a captivating choice, son. Remember, filmmakers need to have a creative vision, storytelling skills, and the ability to evoke emotions through their visual narratives." The son says, "I've got that, Dad. I always feel a sense of excitement and inspiration when I capture stories through the lens of a camera."

721. A father and son are watching a show about the wonders of the Antarctic. The son asks, "Dad, why is the Antarctic so mesmerizing?" The father replies, "Well, son, the Antarctic is a frozen wilderness of pristine beauty and extraordinary wildlife. It represents the delicate balance of our planet's ecosystems and reminds us of the importance of environmental conservation." The son says, "So, when I see the Antarctic, is it just a reminder of the fragility and resilience of our planet?"

722. A son asks his father, "Dad, why do we have to be compassionate?" The father replies, "Well, son, compassion is the empathy and kindness we extend to others, especially during their times of need. It connects us on a deeper level, encourages acts of kindness, and creates a more compassionate and caring world." The son says, "So, when I show compassion, is it just my way of nurturing the bonds of humanity?"

723. A son says to his father, "Dad, when I grow up, I want to be a scientist." The father replies, "That's an inquisitive choice, son. Remember, scientists need to have a curious mind, critical thinking skills, and a passion for unraveling the mysteries of the universe." The son says, "I've got that, Dad. I always feel a sense of wonder and excitement when I conduct experiments and explore the world of science."

724. A father and son are watching a show about the wonders of the Australian Outback. The son asks, "Dad, why is the Outback so fascinating?" The father replies, "Well, son, the Outback is a vast and rugged landscape that showcases the resilience of nature and the unique adaptations of its inhabitants. It's a symbol of the untamed beauty and the spirit of the wilderness." The son says, "So, when I see the Outback, is it just a reminder of the extraordinary diversity of life on Earth?"

725. A son asks his father, "Dad, why do we have to be authentic?" The father replies, "Well, son, authenticity is the courage to be true to ourselves, to embrace our uniqueness, and to live in alignment with our values and beliefs. It fosters genuine connections and allows us to live a life of purpose and fulfillment." The son says, "So, when I choose authenticity, is it just my way of honoring my true self?"

726. A son says to his father, "Dad, when I grow up, I want to be a veterinarian." The father replies, "That's a compassionate choice, son. Remember, veterinarians need to have a deep love for animals, medical expertise, and a dedication to the well-being of our furry friends." The son says, "I've got that, Dad. I always feel a sense of joy and fulfillment when I help care for animals in need."

727. A father and son are watching a show about the wonders of the Great Lakes. The son asks, "Dad, why are

the Great Lakes so awe-inspiring?" The father replies, "Well, son, the Great Lakes are vast bodies of freshwater that support diverse ecosystems, provide drinking water, and serve as a hub for recreational activities. They're a testament to the beauty and significance of our planet's water resources." The son says, "So, when I see the Great Lakes, is it just a reminder of the importance of water conservation and appreciation?"

728. A son asks his father, "Dad, why do we have to be generous?" The father replies, "Well, son, generosity is the act of giving without expecting anything in return. It's a way to uplift others, create positive change, and make a meaningful impact in the lives of those in need. Through generosity, we foster a spirit of abundance and compassion." The son says, "So, when I practice generosity, is it just my way of sharing the blessings I've received?"

729. A son says to his father, "Dad, when I grow up, I want to be an inventor." The father replies, "That's an innovative choice, son. Remember, inventors need to have a curious mind, problem-solving skills, and a passion for creating new solutions and technologies." The son says, "I've got that, Dad. I always feel a sense of excitement and possibility when I tinker and invent new things."

730. A father and son are watching a show about the wonders of the Amazon rainforest. The son asks, "Dad,

why is the Amazon rainforest so vital for our planet?" The father replies, "Well, son, the Amazon rainforest is often referred to as the 'lungs of the Earth' because it produces a significant amount of oxygen and plays a crucial role in regulating the climate and biodiversity. It's a treasure trove of life and a symbol of the intricate web of nature." The son says, "So, when I see the Amazon rainforest, is it just a reminder of the need to protect and preserve our natural heritage?"

731. A son asks his father, "Dad, why do we need to be resilient?" The father replies, "Well, son, resilience is the ability to bounce back from adversity, setbacks, or challenges. It's through resilience that we find strength within ourselves, develop coping strategies, and emerge stronger and wiser. It's an essential quality that helps us navigate the ups and downs of life." The son says, "So, when I demonstrate resilience, is it just my way of showing the world that I won't be easily defeated?"

732. A son says to his father, "Dad, when I grow up, I want to be a counselor." The father replies, "That's a compassionate choice, son. Remember, counselors need to have empathy, active listening skills, and a desire to support and guide individuals through difficult times. Through their work, they help others find healing and create positive change." The son says, "I've got that, Dad. I always feel a sense of fulfillment when I lend a listening ear and offer guidance to those in need."

733. A father and son are watching a show about the wonders of the Sahara Desert. The son asks, "Dad, why is the Sahara Desert so fascinating?" The father replies, "Well, son, the Sahara Desert is the world's largest hot desert, spanning vast stretches of land with its golden dunes and harsh beauty. It's a testament to the resilience of life in extreme environments and a reminder of the delicate balance between humans and nature." The son says, "So, when I see the Sahara Desert, is it just a glimpse into the wonders of adaptation and survival?"

734. A son asks his father, "Dad, why do we have to be patient?" The father replies, "Well, son, patience is a virtue that allows us to remain calm in the face of challenges, wait for things to unfold in their own time, and cultivate resilience. It's through patience that we develop inner strength and appreciate the beauty of each moment." The son says, "So, when I practice patience, is it just my way of embracing the art of surrender and acceptance?"

735. A son says to his father, "Dad, when I grow up, I want to be an environmental activist." The father replies, "That's a commendable choice, son. Remember, environmental activists need to have passion, advocacy skills, and a deep commitment to protecting and preserving our planet's natural resources. Through their efforts, they raise awareness and promote sustainable practices." The son says, "I've got that, Dad. I always feel a sense of

responsibility and urgency to protect the Earth we call home."

736. A father and son are watching a show about the wonders of the Golden Gate Bridge. The son asks, "Dad, why is the Golden Gate Bridge so iconic?" The father replies, "Well, son, the Golden Gate Bridge is not only a marvel of engineering but also a symbol of human ingenuity and connection. It stands as a testament to human achievements and the power of bridging gaps, both physical and metaphorical." The son says, "So, when I see the Golden Gate Bridge, is it just a reminder of the potential for unity and collaboration?"

737. A son asks his father, "Dad, why do we have to be kind?" The father replies, "Well, son, kindness is like a gentle breeze that can brighten someone's day, uplift spirits, and create a ripple effect of positivity. It's through acts of kindness that we nourish the human soul and create a harmonious and compassionate world." The son says, "So, when I show kindness, is it just my way of sharing love and spreading light?"

738. A son says to his father, "Dad, when I grow up, I want to be a social entrepreneur." The father replies, "That's an inspiring choice, son. Remember, social entrepreneurs combine business acumen with a deep commitment to addressing social and environmental challenges. Through their innovative solutions, they strive to create positive

change and make a lasting impact." The son says, "I've got that, Dad. I always feel a sense of purpose and fulfillment when I imagine using business as a force for good."

739. A father and son are watching a show about the wonders of the Northern Lights. The son asks, "Dad, why are the Northern Lights so enchanting?" The father replies, "Well, son, the Northern Lights, also known as the Aurora Borealis, paint the sky with vibrant colors and dance with ethereal beauty. They remind us of the marvels of our universe and the interconnectedness of nature and cosmic forces." The son says, "So, when I see the Northern Lights, is it just a glimpse into the wonders that lie beyond our earthly existence?"

740. A son asks his father, "Dad, why do we have to be resilient?" The father replies, "Well, son, resilience is the ability to adapt, bounce back, and find strength in the face of adversity. It's through resilience that we overcome challenges, grow as individuals, and find new possibilities in the face of setbacks." The son says, "So, when I demonstrate resilience, is it just my way of embracing life's unpredictable nature and turning obstacles into opportunities?"

741. A son says to his father, "Dad, when I grow up, I want to be a humanitarian." The father replies, "That's a noble choice, son. Remember, humanitarians have a deep

empathy for others, a commitment to social justice, and a desire to alleviate suffering and create a more equitable world. Through their actions, they inspire hope and work towards a better future for all." The son says, "I've got that, Dad. I always feel a calling to support and uplift those in need."

742. A father and son are watching a show about the wonders of the Grand Canyon. The son asks, "Dad, why is the Grand Canyon so awe-inspiring?" The father replies, "Well, son, the Grand Canyon is a magnificent testament to the power of erosion and the passage of time. Its vastness and breathtaking vistas remind us of the incredible forces that shape our planet and leave us in awe of nature's masterpiece." The son says, "So, when I see the Grand Canyon, is it just a glimpse into the immense beauty and grandeur of the Earth?"

743. A son says to his father, "Dad, when I grow up, I want to be an architect." The father replies, "That's a visionary choice, son. Remember, architects need to have a strong sense of design and a love for creating structures." The son says, "I've got that, Dad. I always build the coolest forts with my building blocks."

744. Dad: Son, why did the golfer bring two pairs of pants to the golf course?
Son: I'm not sure, Dad. Why did they bring two pairs?

Dad: In case they got a hole-in-one, they wanted to make sure they had a clean pair for the celebration. It's all about being prepared for that perfect swing!

745. Dad: Son, did you know that the invention of the wheel was a game-changer?
Son: Dad, everyone knows that.
Dad: Well, have you ever thought about it? The wheel took us from "rolling on the ground" to "rolling in style"! It was a revolution in transportation.

746. Dad: Son, why did the music teacher bring a ladder to the orchestra concert?
Son: Dad, that doesn't make sense.
Dad: Well, they wanted to reach new musical heights and help the musicians elevate their performance. It was a symphony of ladders and melodies!

747. Dad: Son, did you hear about the scientist who invented a machine to translate baby talk?
Son: No, Dad, what happened?
Dad: Well, it was quite a breakthrough! The machine could decode all those adorable gurgles and coos into understandable language. It turns out, babies have a lot to say!

748. Dad: Son, why did the book go to therapy?
Son: Dad, books don't have feelings.

Dad: You're right, but that book had some unresolved plot twists and needed a little counseling to find closure. It was a journey of healing through the chapters!

749. Dad: Son, did you know that clouds are the ultimate artists?
Son: Dad, clouds are just water vapor.
Dad: True, but those wispy formations are like living brushstrokes across the sky. Clouds paint breathtaking masterpieces with each passing moment!

750. Dad: Son, why did the tomato turn red and run away from the vegetable garde?
Son: I don't know, Dad. Why did it run away?
Dad: Well, it didn't want to end up in a salad! That tomato wanted to explore the world beyond the garden and embark on a culinary adventure of its own.

751. Dad: Son, did you hear about the scientist who discovered a new species of laughter?
Son: No, Dad, what did they find?
Dad: Well, they named it "gigglius hilarious"! It's a laugh so contagious and joyous that it can brighten even the gloomiest of days.

752. Dad: Son, why did the math book go to the therapist?
Son: Dad, books can't have emotions.
Dad: You're right, but that math book had a lot of unresolved problems and needed a safe space to work

through its equations. It was a journey of self-discovery and mathematical healing!

753. Dad: Son, did you know that trees are the true architects of nature?
Son: Dad, trees don't design buildings.
Dad: No, but they create breathtaking structures with their branches and leaves, forming natural canopies and living sculptures. They're nature's architects of beauty!

754. Dad: Son, why did the artist become a barber?
Son: I don't know, Dad. How did that happen?
Dad: Well, they realized that hair could be their canvas, and every haircut was a masterpiece waiting to be created. They combined art and style to give their clients the perfect "cut of creativity"!

755. Dad: Son, did you know that laughter can be the key to success?
Son: Yes, Dad, laughter is important.
Dad: That's right! Laughter unlocks doors, breaks down barriers, and connects people in the most unexpected ways. It's the key that opens the path to a fulfilling and joyful life!

756. Dad: Son, why did the tomato blush when it saw the cucumber?
Son: I don't know, Dad. Why did it blush?

Dad: Well, it had a bit of a crush on the cucumber. It was love at first sight in the vegetable aisle!

757. Dad: Son, did you hear about the scientist who invented a machine to turn dreams into reality?
Son: No, Dad, that sounds amazing!
Dad: It was truly remarkable! With a little imagination and a sprinkle of scientific magic, that machine could bring even the wildest dreams to life.

758. Dad: Son, why did the math teacher bring a ladder to the classroom?
Son: Dad, that doesn't make sense.
Dad: Well, they wanted to climb to new heights of knowledge and help their students reach their full potential. It was a class that aimed for the stars!

759. Dad: Son, did you know that a smile can light up the darkest room?
Son: Dad, that sounds like something you made up.
Dad: Well, it's true! A genuine smile has the power to brighten the gloomiest of moments and spread warmth and happiness wherever it goes. It's a superpower we all possess!

760. A father and son are watching a show about the rainforest. The son asks, "Dad, why is the rainforest so important?" The father replies, "Well, son, the rainforest is important because it's home to a wide variety of plants and

animals, and it plays a crucial role in maintaining the balance of our planet's ecosystems." The son says, "So, when I see pictures of the rainforest, is it just nature's treasure trove?"

761. A son asks his father, "Dad, why do we have fingerprints?" The father replies, "Well, son, fingerprints help us with gripping objects and they're unique to each person, making them useful for identification." The son says, "So, when I leave my fingerprints everywhere, is it just my hands leaving their signature?"

762. A son says to his father, "Dad, when I grow up, I want to be a comedian." The father replies, "That's a hilarious choice, son. Remember, comedians need to have a good sense of humor and the ability to make people laugh." The son says, "I've got that, Dad. I always crack jokes that make my friends laugh."

763. A father and son are watching a show about the desert. The son asks, "Dad, why are deserts so dry?" The father replies, "Well, son, deserts are dry because they receive very little rainfall due to their geographic location." The son says, "So, when I see a desert, is it just nature's way of teaching us the value of water?"

764. A son asks his father, "Dad, why do we get goosebumps?" The father replies, "Well, son, goosebumps are a physiological response to cold

temperatures or strong emotions like fear or excitement." The son says, "So, when I get goosebumps, is it just my body saying 'Brrr' or 'Wow'?"

765. A son says to his father, "Dad, when I grow up, I want to be a firefighter." The father replies, "That's a courageous choice, son. Remember, firefighters need to be brave and have a strong desire to help others." The son says, "I've got that, Dad. I always come to the rescue when my friends are in trouble."

766. A father and son are watching a show about the human body. The son asks, "Dad, why do we have a heart?" The father replies, "Well, son, the heart is a vital organ that pumps blood throughout our body, delivering oxygen and nutrients to our cells." The son says, "So, when I feel my heartbeat, is it just my body's rhythm playing a song?"

767. A son asks his father, "Dad, why do we have different time zones?" The father replies, "Well, son, different time zones exist because the Earth rotates on its axis, causing different parts of the world to experience daylight and darkness at different times." The son says, "So, when I travel to a different time zone, is it like stepping into the future or the past?"

768. A son says to his father, "Dad, when I grow up, I want to be a police officer." The father replies, "That's a

commendable choice, son. Remember, police officers need to have integrity and a strong commitment to keeping their communities safe." The son says, "I've got that, Dad. I always make sure everyone follows the rules during our games."

769. A father and son are watching a show about mountains. The son asks, "Dad, why are mountains so tall?" The father replies, "Well, son, mountains are formed by the movement of tectonic plates and the forces of nature, which push the Earth's crust upward." The son says, "So, when I see a mountain, is it just the Earth showing off its grandeur?"

770. A son asks his father, "Dad, why do we have dreams while we sleep?" The father replies, "Well, son, dreams are a reflection of our subconscious thoughts and experiences. They can be like movies playing in our minds." The son says, "So, when I dream, is it like having my own personal cinema?"

771. A son says to his father, "Dad, when I grow up, I want to be a veterinarian." The father replies, "That's a compassionate choice, son. Remember, veterinarians need to have a love for animals and a desire to help them stay healthy." The son says, "I've got that, Dad. I always take care of our pets when they're not feeling well."

772. A father and son are watching a show about the universe. The son asks, "Dad, why is the universe so vast?" The father replies, "Well, son, the universe is vast because it's constantly expanding. There's so much to explore and discover out there." The son says, "So, when I look up at the night sky, is it just a glimpse into the infinite?"

773. A son asks his father, "Dad, why do we celebrate birthdays?" The father replies, "Well, son, birthdays are a way to celebrate the anniversary of someone's birth. It's a special day to honor and appreciate a person's presence in our lives." The son says, "So, when I blow out the candles, is it just my way of making a wish for the year ahead?"

774. A son says to his father, "Dad, when I grow up, I want to be a teacher." The father replies, "That's an admirable choice, son. Remember, teachers have the power to inspire and shape young minds. They play a vital role in society." The son says, "I've got that, Dad. I always enjoy helping my friends understand new things."

775. A father and son are watching a show about the wonders of the deep sea. The son asks, "Dad, why is the deep sea so mysterious?" The father replies, "Well, son, the deep sea is mysterious because it's largely unexplored. There are so many secrets and unknown creatures lurking in its depths." The son says, "So, when I

hear about a new deep-sea discovery, is it like uncovering a hidden treasure?"

776. A son asks his father, "Dad, why do we need to brush our teeth?" The father replies, "Well, son, brushing our teeth helps to remove plaque and bacteria, keeping our teeth and gums healthy." The son says, "So, when I brush my teeth, is it just my way of giving them a fresh start?"

777. A son says to his father, "Dad, when I grow up, I want to be an athlete." The father replies, "That's an active choice, son. Remember, athletes need to have discipline, dedication, and a love for sports." The son says, "I've got that, Dad. I always give my best during our backyard games."

778. A father and son are watching a show about the wonders of the Great Barrier Reef. The son asks, "Dad, why is the Great Barrier Reef so important?" The father replies, "Well, son, the Great Barrier Reef is important because it's the largest coral reef ecosystem in the world, teeming with diverse marine life. It's like a bustling city underwater." The son says, "So, when I see pictures of the Great Barrier Reef, is it just nature's masterpiece?"

779. A son asks his father, "Dad, why do we get curious?" The father replies, "Well, son, curiosity is a natural human trait that drives us to explore, learn, and discover new things. It's what pushes us forward and expands our

horizons." The son says, "So, when I feel curious, is it just my mind saying 'Let's go on an adventure'?"

780. A son says to his father, "Dad, when I grow up, I want to be a musician." The father replies, "That's a harmonious choice, son. Remember, musicians need to have a passion for music and a talent for playing an instrument or singing." The son says, "I've got that, Dad. I always create melodies in my mind."

781. A father and son are watching a show about bees. The son asks, "Dad, why do bees make honey?" The father replies, "Well, son, bees make honey as a source of food and to store it for the colony's survival, especially during winter." The son says, "So, when I taste honey, is it just nature's golden delight?"

782. A son asks his father, "Dad, why do we have emotions?" The father replies, "Well, son, emotions are part of being human. They allow us to experience a wide range of feelings and connect with others on a deep level." The son says, "So, when I feel happy, sad, or excited, is it just my heart expressing itself?"

783. A son says to his father, "Dad, when I grow up, I want to be an astronaut." The father replies, "That's an astronomical choice, son. Remember, astronauts need to be physically fit and mentally prepared for the challenges

of space exploration." The son says, "I've got that, Dad. I always dream of exploring the galaxies in my rocket ship."

784. A father and son are watching a show about elephants. The son asks, "Dad, why do elephants have such long trunks?" The father replies, "Well, son, elephants use their trunks for various tasks like drinking water, grabbing food, and even communicating with other elephants." The son says, "So, when I see an elephant using its trunk, is it just nature's multi-purpose tool?"

785. A son asks his father, "Dad, why do we celebrate holidays?" The father replies, "Well, son, holidays are special occasions that bring people together to commemorate significant events, traditions, or values. They help us create lasting memories and strengthen our bonds with loved ones." The son says, "So, when I celebrate a holiday, is it just a way of cherishing the moments that matter?"

786. A son says to his father, "Dad, when I grow up, I want to be a scientist." The father replies, "That's an inquisitive choice, son. Remember, scientists need to have a thirst for knowledge and a passion for conducting experiments and making discoveries." The son says, "I've got that, Dad. I always ask 'why' and love exploring the wonders of the world."

787. A father and son are watching a show about dolphins. The son asks, "Dad, why are dolphins so intelligent?" The father replies, "Well, son, dolphins have highly developed brains and complex social structures, which contribute to their remarkable intelligence and adaptability." The son says, "So, when I see dolphins swimming and playing, is it just nature's display of brilliance?"

788. A son asks his father, "Dad, why do we have to study?" The father replies, "Well, son, studying helps us gain knowledge, develop skills, and prepare for the future. It's an investment in ourselves that opens doors to opportunities." The son says, "So, when I study, is it just my way of building a strong foundation?"

789. A son says to his father, "Dad, when I grow up, I want to be a chef." The father replies, "That's a flavorful choice, son. Remember, chefs need to have a passion for cooking, creativity, and an appreciation for diverse flavors." The son says, "I've got that, Dad. I always experiment with different ingredients to create delicious masterpieces."

790. A father and son are watching a show about the solar system. The son asks, "Dad, why do planets orbit the sun?" The father replies, "Well, son, planets orbit the sun because of the gravitational force between them. It's like a cosmic dance orchestrated by the laws of physics." The

son says, "So, when I see the planets in the night sky, is it just the celestial ballet?"

791. A son asks his father, "Dad, why do we need to exercise?" The father replies, "Well, son, exercising keeps our bodies healthy and strong. It boosts our energy, improves our mood, and helps prevent diseases." The son says, "So, when I exercise, is it just my way of telling my body 'I care about you'?"

792. A son says to his father, "Dad, when I grow up, I want to be a lawyer." The father replies, "That's a persuasive choice, son. Remember, lawyers need to have excellent communication skills, critical thinking, and a passion for justice." The son says, "I've got that, Dad. I always defend my case during our friendly debates."

793. A father and son are watching a show about wolves. The son asks, "Dad, why do wolves howl?" The father replies, "Well, son, wolves howl to communicate with their pack, mark their territory, and coordinate hunting. It's like a unique language of the wild." The son says, "So, when I hear a wolf howl, is it just nature's symphony?"

794. A son asks his father, "Dad, why do we have seasons?" The father replies, "Well, son, seasons occur because of the tilt of the Earth's axis as it orbits the sun. It determines the amount of sunlight different regions receive, leading to changes in temperature and weather

patterns." The son says, "So, when I experience the seasons, is it just nature's way of keeping things interesting?"

795. Dad: Son, why did the flower go to school?
Son: I don't know, Dad. Why did it go to school?
Dad: Because it wanted to be a "bud-ding" scholar and learn all the secrets of photosynthesis and plant biology. It was a blossoming journey of education!

796. Dad: Son, did you hear about the scientist who invented a machine to turn vegetables into instruments?
Son: No, Dad, that's fascinating!
Dad: It was a "melodi-veg" machine! It could transform carrots into flutes, cucumbers into trumpets, and pumpkins into drums. It was a garden orchestra like no other!

797. Dad: Son, why did the spider go to university?
Son: Dad, spiders don't go to school.
Dad: Well, that spider wanted to learn the art of web design and spin intricate patterns like a master weaver. It was a journey of eight-legged education!

798. Dad: Son, did you know that books can take you on adventures without leaving your seat?
Son: Yes, Dad, books are magical.
Dad: Absolutely! With every turn of the page, you can travel to far-off lands, meet fascinating characters, and

experience thrilling escapades. It's the power of the written word!

799. Dad: Son, why did the sandwich go to the gym?
Son: I'm not sure, Dad. Why did it go?
Dad: Well, it wanted to work on its "core" ingredients and get in shape for a beach vacation. It was a sandwich on a mission to achieve sandwich perfection!

800. Dad: Son, did you hear about the scientist who discovered a way to turn frowns upside down?
Son: No, Dad, how did they do it?
Dad: They developed a formula called "smile-etics"! With a sprinkle of laughter and a dash of positivity, they could bring joy to even the most downcast faces.

THANK YOU!

A Big Thank You for joining us on this hilarious journey through our "Dad Jokes Extravaganza"! We hope you thoroughly enjoyed reading this Father's Day book, filled to the brim with over 800 jokes that are sure to bring an explosion of laughter.

It warms our hearts to know that you found this collection of knee-slappers, puns, and good-natured humor to be the perfect Father's Day gift. We crafted this book with the intention of spreading joy and creating moments of shared laughter for the whole family to enjoy.

We sincerely hope that these jokes tickled your funny bone, eliciting groans, giggles, and perhaps even some eyerolls along the way. Laughter truly is the best gift we can give, and we are delighted to have been a part of your Father's Day celebration.

As you continue to embrace the spirit of Father's Day, may the laughter generated by this ultimate joke collection continue to flow, bringing smiles, bonding moments, and unforgettable memories with your loved ones.

Once again, a heartfelt thank you for being a part of our "Dad Jokes Extravaganza" adventure. Wishing you a wonderful Father's Day filled with love, laughter, and moments of pure joy!

DIGIDOG

"Unleash Your Curiosity: Discovering the World - A DigiDog Series of Books in Honour of Chico, Our Beloved Pomeranian"

Welcome to a new series of books, crafted in memory of our dear pet Pomeranian called Chico. For over 15 years, he continued to delight us with his never-ending curiosity, constantly exploring and investigating everything, everywhere he went.

It is in honour of his spirit of exploration that we present this exciting collection of books that we hope will quench your thirst for knowledge and spark your imagination.

In the series, you will embark on a journey of fascinating people with unique life stories, intriguing subjects and the mysteries of the world. Each book provides a number of carefully researched and thoughtfully curated facts that are designed to surprise, enlighten and entertain you.

From the depths of the ocean to the heights of the sky and beyond, our books will transport you to new worlds and reveal the wonders that lie within them. Join us on this adventure and let Chico's legacy inspire you to never stop exploring and learning.

The DigiDog series includes books for both children and adults.

END